Rick Steves'
ROME
2003

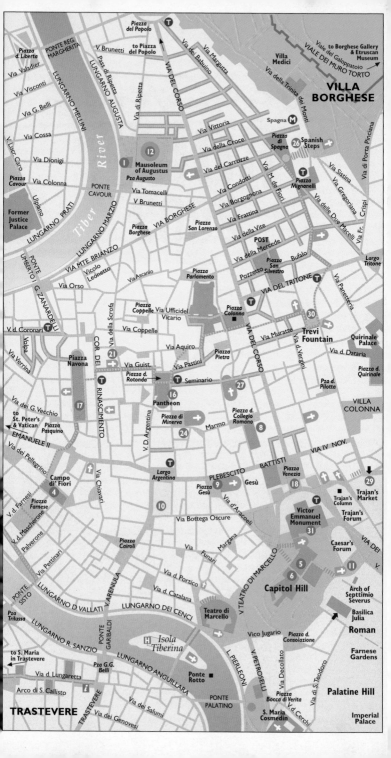

CENTRAL ROME SIGHTS

1. Altar of Peace
2. Arch of Constantine
3. Baths of Diocletian
4. Campo de' Fiori
5. Capitol Hill
6. Capitol Hill Museum
7. Colosseum
8. Galleria Doria Pamphilj
9. Gesu Church
10. Largo Argentina
11. Mammertine Prison
12. Mausoleum of Augustus
13. National Museum
14. Nero's Golden House
15. Palatine Hill
16. Pantheon
17. Piazza Navona
18. Piazza Venezia
19. Roman Forum
20. San Clemente Church
21. San Luigi dei Francesi Church
22. Santa Maria della Vittoria Church
23. Santa Maria Maggiore
24. Santa Maria Sopra Minerva Church
25. Santa Susanna Church
26. Spanish Steps (Piazza di Spagna)
27. St. Ignazio Church
28. St. Peter-in-Chains Church
29. Trajan's Column, Forum, and Market
30. Trevi Fountain
31. Victor Emmanuel Monument
32. Termini Train Station
33. Main Tourist Info

KEY

- Pedestrian Street / Square
- Famous for Shopping
- Stairways
- ■ Landmark; Point of Interest
- □ ➡ Ruins, Entry Points
- ⋯ Recommended Walk
- Ⓜ Ⓣ Metropolitana Stations, Taxi Stands
- ⓘ Tourist Information

0   400 meters

0 miles   1/4 mile

Rick Steves'
ROME
2003

Vatican Museum

Villa Borghese

Spanish Steps

Termini Station

Trevi Fountain

St. Peter's

Pantheon

TIBER

Trajan's Column

Forum

Colosseum

Trastevere

St. John Lateran

DCH

by Rick Steves & Gene Openshaw

AVALON
TRAVEL

Other ATP travel guidebooks by Rick Steves
Rick Steves' Best of Europe
Rick Steves' Europe 101: History and Art for the Traveler (with Gene Openshaw)
Rick Steves' Europe Through the Back Door
Rick Steves' Mona Winks: Self-Guided Tours of Europe's Top Museums
  (with Gene Openshaw)
Rick Steves' Postcards from Europe
Rick Steves' France (with Steve Smith)
Rick Steves' Germany, Austria & Switzerland
Rick Steves' Great Britain
Rick Steves' Ireland (with Pat O'Connor)
Rick Steves' Italy
Rick Steves' Scandinavia
Rick Steves' Spain & Portugal
Rick Steves' Amsterdam, Bruges & Brussels (with Gene Openshaw)
Rick Steves' Florence (with Gene Openshaw)
Rick Steves' London (with Gene Openshaw)
Rick Steves' Paris (with Steve Smith and Gene Openshaw)
Rick Steves' Venice (with Gene Openshaw)
Rick Steves' Phrase Books: French, German, Italian, Portuguese, Spanish,
  and French/Italian/German

Avalon Travel Publishing, 1400 65th Street, Suite 250, Emeryville, CA 94608, USA

Printed in the USA by R.R. Donnelley. Second printing February 2003.
Distributed by Publishers Group West

Portions of this book were originally published in *Rick Steves' Mona Winks* © 2001,
1998, 1996, 1993, 1988 by Rick Steves and Gene Openshaw, and in *Rick Steves' Italy*
© 2002, 2001, 2000, 1999, 1998, 1997, 1996, 1995 by Rick Steves.

ISBN 1-56691-457-4
ISSN 1527-4780

For the latest on Rick's lectures, guidebooks, tours, and public television series,
contact Europe Through the Back Door, Box 2009, Edmonds, WA 98020,
425/771-8303, fax 425/771-0833, www.ricksteves.com, or e-mail: rick@ricksteves.com.

Europe Through the Back Door Editors: Risa Laib, Jill Hodges, Cameron Hewitt
Avalon Travel Publishing Series Manager & Editor: Kate Willis
Research Assistance: Sarah Murdoch, Julie Coen (Roman cuisine)
Copy Editor: Leslie Miller
Production & Typesetting: Kathleen Sparkes, White Hart Design
Cover and Interior Design: Janine Lehmann
Maps and Graphics: David C. Hoerlein, Rhonda Pelikan, Zoey Platt
Photography: p. 61: Dominic Arizona Bonuccelli; p. 120, 122, 123, 124: Risa Laib;
  all others: Rick Steves and Gene Openshaw
Front matter color photos: p. i, the Palatine, Rome © Phyllis Greenberg/Unicorn
  Stock Photos, LLC; p. iv, Spanish Steps, Rome © Photophile/Bachmann
Front cover photo: Colosseum, Rome, Italy; © Blaine Harrington III

CONTENTS

INTRODUCTION 1

ORIENTATION 17

SIGHTS 27

TOURS

Night Walk Across Rome 52

Ancient Rome

Colosseum Tour 58

Roman Forum Tour 64

Palatine Hill Tour 77

Trajan's Column, Forum, and Market 86

Pantheon Tour 90

Baths of Diocletian Tour 100

Museums

National Museum of Rome Tour 106

Capitol Hill Museum Tour 120

Borghese Gallery Tour 127

Vatican Museum Tour 137

Churches

St. Peter's Basilica Tour 164

St. Peter-in-Chains Tour 181

Pilgrim's Rome Tour 185

DAY TRIPS

Ostia Antica 199

Tivoli 207

Naples and Pompeii 209

SLEEPING 228

EATING 244

ROME WITH CHILDREN 261

SHOPPING 264

NIGHTLIFE 267

TRANSPORTATION CONNECTIONS 271

ROMAN HISTORY 275

APPENDIX 280

INDEX 289

INTRODUCTION

Rome is magnificent and brutal at the same time. Your ears will ring; if you're careless, you'll be run down or pickpocketed; you'll be frustrated by the kind of chaos that only an Italian can understand. You may even come to believe Mussolini was a necessary evil.

But Rome is required, and if your hotel provides a comfortable refuge; if you pace yourself; if you accept—and even partake in—the siesta plan; if you're well-organized for sightseeing; and if you protect yourself and your valuables with extra caution and discretion, you'll do fine.

Two thousand years ago, the word Rome meant civilization itself. Everything was either civilized (part of the Roman Empire, Latin- or Greek-speaking) or barbarian. Today, Rome is Italy's political capital, the capital of Catholicism, and a splendid junk pile (OK, that's not quite the right term) of Western civilization. As you peel through its fascinating and jumbled layers, you'll find Rome's buildings, cats, laundry, traffic, and 2.6 million people endlessly entertaining. And then, of course, there are its magnificent sights.

Tour St. Peter's, the greatest church on earth, and scale Michelangelo's 100-meter-tall (328-foot) dome, the world's largest. Learn something about eternity by touring the huge Vatican Museum. You'll find the story of creation—bright as the day it was painted—in the restored Sistine Chapel. Do the "Caesar Shuffle" through ancient Rome's Forum and Colosseum. Savor Europe's most sumptuous building, the Borghese Gallery, and take an early evening "Dolce Vita Stroll" down the Via del Corso with Rome's beautiful people. Enjoy an after-dark walk from Campo de' Fiori to the Spanish Steps, lacing together Rome's Baroque and bubbly nightspots.

This Information Is Accurate and Up-to-Date

This book is updated every year. Most publishers of guidebooks can afford an update only every two or three years (and even then, it's often by letter). Since this book is selective, we can personally update it annually. Even so, things change. But if you're traveling with the current edition of this book, we guarantee you're using the most up-to-date information available (for the very latest, visit www.ricksteves.com/update). This book will help you have an inexpensive, hassle-free trip. Your trip costs about $10 per waking hour. Your time is valuable. This guidebook saves lots of time.

Welcome to Our Rome City Guide

This book is organized this way:

Orientation includes tourist information and public transportation. The "Planning Your Time" section offers a suggested schedule with thoughts on how to best use your limited time.

Sights provides a succinct overview of Rome's most important sights, arranged by neighborhood, with ratings: ▲▲▲—Don't miss; ▲▲—Try hard to see; ▲—Worthwhile if you can make it; No rating—Worth knowing about.

The **Night Walk Across Rome** connects Rome's great monuments and atmospheric squares.

The **Self-Guided Tours** lead you through Ancient Rome, with tours of the Colosseum, Roman Forum, Palatine Hill, Trajan's Column, the Pantheon, and the Baths of Diocletian. You'll tour the pilgrimage churches, including the grandest of all—St. Peter's. And you'll see the great museums: the Vatican Museum, the National Museum of Rome, the Capitol Hill Museum, and the exciting Borghese Gallery.

Day Trips cover nearby sights: Ostia Antica (includes self-guided tour), Tivoli, Naples, and Pompeii.

Sleeping is a guide to my favorite budget hotels, mainly in several convenient (and for Rome, relatively quiet) neighborhoods near the sights.

Eating offers restaurants ranging from inexpensive eateries to splurges, with an emphasis on good value.

Rome with Children, Shopping, and **Nightlife** contain our best suggestions on those topics.

Transportation Connections covers connections by train and by plane (with information on Rome's airports), laying the groundwork for your smooth arrival and departure.

Roman History takes you on a whirlwind tour through the ages, covering three millennia from ancient Rome to the city today.

The **appendix** includes useful Italian phone numbers, a climate chart, and a handy list of Italian survival phrases.

Tips for Tackling Our Self-Guided Tours

Sightseeing can be hard work. Our self-guided tours are designed to help make your visits to Italy's finest museums meaningful, fun, fast, and painless. To make the most of our tours, read the tour the night before your visit, and call ahead to make sure the hours and costs have not changed.

When you arrive at the sight, use the overview map to get the lay of the land and the basic tour route. Expect a few changes—paintings can be on tour, on loan, out sick, or shifted at the whim of the curator. Even museum walls are often moved. To adapt, pick up any available free floor plans as you enter, ask an information person to glance at this book's maps to confirm they're current, or if you can't find a particular painting, just ask any museum worker. Point to the photograph in this book and ask, *"Dove?"* (pronounced doh-vay, meaning "Where?").

We cover the highlights at sights. You might want to supplement with an audioguide (dry-but-useful recorded descriptions in English, $4), or a guided tour (usually $6 or more). Tours in English are most likely to occur during peak season. The quality of a tour depends on the guide's knowledge, fluency, and enthusiasm.

Museums have their rules; if you're aware of them in advance, they're no big deal. Keep in mind that many sights have "last entry" times 30 to 60 minutes before closing. Guards usher people out before the official closing time. Cameras are normally allowed in museums, but no flashes or tripods (without special permission). A handheld camera with ASA-400 film and an F-2 aperture will take a fine picture (or buy slides at the museum bookstore). Video cameras are usually allowed. For security reasons, you're often required to check even small bags. Every museum has a free checkroom at the entrance. They're safe. Prepare to stash anything that you can't bear to part with in a purse or pocket.

At the museum bookshop, thumb through the biggest guidebook (or scan its index) to be sure you haven't overlooked something that is of particular interest to you. If there's an on-site cafeteria, it's usually a good place to rest and have a snack or light meal. Museum WCs are free and generally clean.

Throughout this book, when you see a ✪ in a listing, it means that the sight is covered in much more detail in one of my tours—a page number will tell you just where to look to find more information.

Browse through this book and choose your favorite sights. Then have a great trip! You'll become your own guide with our tours. Traveling like a temporary local, you'll get the absolute most out of every mile, minute, and euro. You won't waste time on mediocre sights because, unlike other guidebooks, this one covers only the best. Since your major financial pitfall is lousy, expensive hotels, we've worked hard to assemble the best accommodations values.

Trip Costs

Six components make up your trip costs: airfare, surface transportation, room and board, sightseeing/entertainment, shopping/miscellany, and gelato.

Airfare: Don't try to sort through the mess. Find and use a good travel agent. A basic, round-trip United States–to–Rome (or even cheaper, Milan) flight should cost $700 to $1,000, depending on where you fly from and when. Always consider saving time and money in Europe by flying "open jaw" (flying into one city and out of another).

Surface Transportation: For a typical one-week visit, allow $60 to $100 for taxis (which can be shared by up to 4 people); if you opt for buses and the Metro, figure about $20 per person. The cost of round-trip transportation to day-trip destinations ranges from minimal ($6–10 for Tivoli, about $6 for Ostia Antica) to affordable ($50 for second-class train tickets for a day trip to Naples and Pompeii). For a one-way trip between Rome's major airport and the city center, allow $8 per person by train or about $35 by taxi (can be shared).

Room and Board: You can thrive in Rome on $80 a day per person for room and board. This allows $10 for lunch, $20 for dinner, and $50 for lodging (based on 2 people splitting the cost of a $100 double room that includes breakfast). If you've got more money, I've listed great ways to spend it. Students and tightwads can enjoy Rome for as little as $40 a day ($20 for a bed, $20 for meals and snacks). But budget sleeping and eating require the skills covered later in this chapter (and in greater detail in *Rick Steves' Europe Through the Back Door*).

Sightseeing and Entertainment: Figure about $7 per major sight (Colosseum, museums), $2 for smaller ones (church treasuries), and $25 for splurge experiences (like concerts). An overall average of $15 per day works for most. Don't skimp here.

After all, this category directly powers most of the experiences all the other expenses are designed to make possible.

Shopping and Miscellany: Figure $1 per postcard, coffee, and soft drink and $2 per gelato. Shopping can vary in cost from nearly nothing to a small fortune. Good budget travelers find that this category has little to do with assembling a trip full of lifelong and wonderful memories.

Exchange Rate
I've priced things throughout this book in euros.

> 1 euro (€) = about $1.

Just like the dollar, one euro is broken down into 100 cents. You'll find coins ranging from 1 cent to 2 euros, and bills from 5 euros to 500 euros.

Prices, Times, and Discounts
The opening hours and telephone numbers listed in this book are accurate as of mid-2002—but once you pin Rome down, it wiggles. Especially in Rome, the opening hours of sights can change from month to month. Always get the latest listing of sights (including hours and entry fees) at a local tourist information office. Any guidebook on Italy starts to yellow even before it's printed, so prices in this book are approximate.

In Rome—and in this book—you'll use the 24-hour clock. It's the same through 12:00 noon, then keep going—13:00, 14:00 ... For anything over 12, subtract 12 and add p.m. (14:00 is 2:00 p.m.)

Discounts for sights are not listed in this book because they are generally limited to European residents and countries that offer reciprocal deals (the United States doesn't).

When to Go
Rome's best travel months (also busiest and most expensive) are May, June, September, and October. Between November and April you can usually expect pleasant weather and generally none of the sweat and stress of the tourist season. The most grueling thing about travel in Rome is the summer heat in July and August. Rome is fine in the winter.

In Rome, temperatures hit the high 80s and 90s in summer and drop to the 40s and 50s in winter. Spring and fall can be chilly, and many hotels do not turn on their heat. Air-conditioning, when available, usually only operates from June through September. Most midrange hotels come with air-conditioning—a worthwhile splurge in the summer. (See climate chart in the appendix.)

Red Tape, Business Hours, and Banking

You need a passport but no visa or shots to travel in Italy.

Business Hours: Traditionally, Italy uses the siesta plan. People work from about 8:00 to 13:00 and from 15:30 to 19:00, Monday through Saturday. Many businesses have adopted the government's recommended 8:00 to 14:00 workday. In tourist areas, shops are open longer. Shoppers interested in pursuing VAT refunds (the tax refunded on large purchases made by non-EU residents) can refer to page 265.

Banking: You'll want to spend local hard cash. The fastest way to get it is by using plastic—your ATM, credit, or debit card— at a cash machine (Bancomat). Bring some traveler's checks only as a backup.

To get a cash advance from a bank machine, you'll need a four-digit PIN (numbers only, no letters, 7-digit PIN won't work) with your bank card. Before you go, verify with your bank that your card will work.

Visa and MasterCard are more commonly accepted than American Express. Bring two cards in case one is demagnetized, eaten by a machine, or rejected by a temperamental cash machine. (If your card is rejected, try again and request a smaller amount; some cash machines won't let you take out more than about €150—don't take it personally). Just like at home, credit or debit cards work easily at larger hotels, restaurants, and shops, but smaller businesses prefer payment in cash.

Regular banks have the best rates for cashing traveler's checks. For a large exchange, it pays to compare rates and fees. Bank of Sicily consistently has good rates. Banking hours are generally 8:30 to 13:30 & 15:30 to 16:30 Monday through Friday, but they can vary wildly. Banks are slow; simple transactions can take 15 to 30 minutes. Post offices and train stations usually change money if you can't get to a bank.

Use a money belt. Thieves target tourists. A money belt (order online at www.ricksteves.com or call 425/771-8303 for our free newsletter/catalog) provides peace of mind and allows you to carry lots of cash safely.

Don't be petty about changing money. The greatest avoidable money-changing expense is wasting time every few days to return to a bank. Change a week's worth of money, get big bills, stuff them in your money belt, and travel!

Travel Smart

Many people travel through Rome thinking it's a chaotic mess. They feel any attempt at efficient travel is futile. This is dead wrong—and expensive. Rome, which seems as orderly as spilled spaghetti, actually functions well. Only those who understand this and travel smart can enjoy Rome on a budget.

Buy a phone card and use it for reservations and double-checking hours of sights. (I've included phone numbers for this purpose.) Enjoy the friendliness of the local people. Ask questions. Most locals are eager to point you in their idea of the right direction. Pack along a pocket-size notebook to organize your thoughts. Those who expect to travel smart, do.

Sundays have the same pros and cons as they do for travelers in the United States: Sightseeing attractions are generally open; shops and banks are closed. City traffic is light. Rowdy evenings are rare on Sundays. Saturdays are virtually weekdays with earlier closing hours.

Hotels are often booked up on Easter weekend (in 2003— Friday, April 18 through Sunday, April 20), April 25, May 1, in August, and on Fridays and Saturdays. Religious holidays and train strikes can catch you by surprise anywhere in Italy.

Really, this book can save you lots of time and money. But to have an "A" trip, you need to be an "A" student. Read it all before your trip; note the days when museums are closed and whether reservations are mandatory. For instance, if you want to see the Borghese Gallery or Nero's Golden House, you must reserve ahead. If you go to the Vatican Museum on a Sunday, you'll run smack into closed doors, or—if it's the last Sunday of the month—huge crowds. You can wait an hour to get into the Colosseum, or buy your ticket at a nearby kiosk at Palatine Hill and walk right in. Day-tripping to Ostia Antica on Monday is bad news. A smart trip is a puzzle—a fun, doable, and worthwhile challenge.

Tourist Information

Rome has a number of tourist information offices (abbreviated TI in this book); for a list, see page 20.

Before your trip, contact the nearest Italian TI in the United States and briefly describe your trip and request information. You'll get the general packet and, if you ask for specifics (city map, calendar of festivals, etc.), an impressive amount of help. If you have a specific problem, they're a good source of sympathy.

Contact the office nearest you...

In **New York:** 630 5th Avenue #1565, New York, NY 10111, brochure hotline 212/245-4822, 212/245-5618, fax 212/586-9249, e-mail: enitny@italiantourism.com.

In **Illinois:** 500 N. Michigan Avenue #2240, Chicago, IL 60611, brochure hotline 312/644-0990, 312/644-0996, fax 312/644-3019, e-mail: enitch@italiantourism.com.

In **California:** 12400 Wilshire Boulevard #550, Los Angeles, CA 90025, brochure hotline 310/820-0098, 310/820-1898, fax 310/820-6357, e-mail: enitla@earthlink.net.

Web sites on Rome: www.romaturismo.com (music, exhibitions, and events, in English), www.wantedinrome.com (job openings and real estate, but also festivals and exhibitions, in English), and www.vatican.va (the pope's Web site, in English).

Web sites on Italy: www.italiantourism.com (Italian Tourist Board in the United States), www.museionline.it (museums in Italy, in English), and www.fs-on-line.com (train info and schedules).

Recommended Guidebooks

For most travelers, this book is all you need. The tall, green Michelin guide to Rome has solid, encyclopedic coverage of sights, customs, and culture, though very little on room and board (also sold in English in Italy).

The well-researched Access and the colorful Eyewitness guides to Rome are very popular with travelers. Eyewitness is fun for its great, easy-to-grasp graphics and photos, and it's just right for people who want only factoids. But the Eyewitness books are relatively skimpy on content and they weigh a ton. You can buy them in Rome (no more expensive than in the United States) or simply borrow them for a minute from other travelers at certain sights to make sure you're aware of that place's highlights. *Let's Go Rome* is youth-oriented, with good coverage of nightlife, hosteling, and cheap transportation deals. If you'll be traveling elsewhere in Italy, consider *Rick Steves' Italy 2003*.

In Rome, the American Bookstore sells all the major guidebooks (Via Torino 136, Metro: Repubblica, tel. 06-474-6877).

Rick Steves' Books and Videos

Rick Steves' Europe Through the Back Door 2003 gives you budget travel skills on minimizing jet lag, packing light, planning your itinerary, traveling by car or train, finding budget beds without reservations, changing money, avoiding rip-offs, outsmarting thieves, hurdling the language barrier, staying healthy, taking great photographs, using your bidet, and much more. The book also includes chapters on 35 of Rick's favorite "Back Doors," six of which are in Italy.

Rick Steves' Country Guides are a series of eight guidebooks that cover: Italy; Great Britain; Ireland; Spain/Portugal; France; Germany/Austria/Switzerland; Scandinavia; and the Best of Europe. These are updated annually; most are available in bookstores in December, the rest in January.

Rick Steves' City Guides include this book, Florence,

Venice, Paris, London, and—new for 2003—*Rick Steves' Amsterdam, Bruges & Brussels*. These handy, easy-to-pack guidebooks offer thorough coverage of Europe's greatest cities, complete with extensive self-guided tours through the greatest museums. They're updated annually and come out in December and January.

Rick Steves' Europe 101: History and Art for the Traveler (with Gene Openshaw, 2000), which gives you the story of Europe's people, history, and art, is heavy on Italy's ancient, Renaissance, and modern histories. Written for smart people who were sleeping in their history and art classes before they knew they were going to Europe, *101* helps resurrect the rubble.

Rick Steves' Mona Winks: Self-Guided Tours of Europe's Top Museums (with Gene Openshaw, 2001) gives you fun, easy-to-follow self-guided tours of Europe's 25 most exhausting, important museums and cultural sites. All of the *Mona Winks* chapters on Rome are included in this guidebook. But if you'd like similar coverage for the great museums in Florence (Uffizi Gallery and Bargello), Venice (St. Mark's Basilica, Doge's Palace, Accademia), Madrid, Paris, London, and Amsterdam, *Mona's* for you.

In Italy, a phrase book is as fun as it is necessary. *Rick Steves' Italian Phrase Book* (1999) will help you meet the people and stretch your budget. It's written by a monoglot who, for 25 years, has fumbled through Italy struggling with all the other phrase books. Use this fun and practical communication aid to make accurate hotel reservations over the telephone, have the man in the deli make you a sandwich, and ask for a free taste of cantaloupe-flavored gelato at the gelateria.

Rick's public-television series, *Rick Steves' Europe*, airs a new season of 14 shows—including five on Italy—in the fall of 2002. Between the new series and the earlier *Travels in Europe* series (more than 80 shows total), Rick has hosted and written 15 half-hour shows on Italy. These air throughout the United States on public television stations. Each episode is also available on an information-packed home video (order online at www.ricksteves .com or call 425/771-8303 for our free newsletter/catalog).

Rick Steves' Postcards from Europe (1999), an autobiographical book, packs 25 years of travel anecdotes and insights into the ultimate 2,000-mile European adventure. Through his guidebooks, Rick shares his favorite European discoveries with you. In *Postcards*, he introduces you to his favorite European friends. Half of the book is set in Italy: Venice, Florence, Rome, and the Cinque Terre.

All of Rick Steves' books are published by Avalon Travel Publishing (www.travelmatters.com).

Maps

The maps in this book, designed and drawn by Dave Hoerlein, are concise and simple. Dave is well-traveled in Rome and Italy and has designed the maps to help you orient quickly and get to where you want to go painlessly. In Rome, your hotel or the tourist office have helpful free maps, but the €3 map sold at kiosks listing all the streets is much better. For a longer Italy trip, consider our new Rick Steves' Italy Planning Map. With sightseeing destinations listed prominently, it's designed for the traveler (go to www.ricksteves.com or call 425/771-8303 for our free newsletter/catalog).

Tours of Rome and Italy

Travel agents will tell you about normal tours of Italy, but they won't tell you about ours. At Europe Through the Back Door, we offer one-week getaways to **Rome** (departures Feb–Dec, 20 people maximum) as well as to **Venice** and **Florence** (spring and fall departures, 20 people maximum).

Our longer Italy tours come with two great guides and a big, roomy bus. The 20-day **Best of Italy** tour features all of the biggies and a few of our favorite "back doors" (April–Oct, 24 people). The 15-day **Village Italy** adventure laces together intimate towns (April, Sept, and Oct, 20 people). For more information, call 425/771-8303 or visit www.ricksteves.com.

Transportation

Transportation concerns within Rome are limited to the Metro, buses, and taxis, all covered in the Orientation chapter. If you have a car, stow it. You don't want to drive in Rome. Transportation to day-trip destinations is covered in the Day Trips chapter. For specifics on transportation throughout Italy by train or car, see *Rick Steves' Italy 2003*.

In Rome, get train tickets and railpass-related reservations and supplements at travel agencies, rather than dealing with the congested train station. The cost is either the same or there's a minimal charge. Your hotel can direct you to the nearest travel agency. Quo Vadis, near the Vatican, is helpful (Via della Conciliazione, 22-24, tel. 06-6880-4941, fax 06-6880-3191, e-mail: qv.viaggi@tiscalinet.it). Or purchase train tickets from the American Express office, near the Spanish Steps (Mon–Fri 9:00–17:30, Sat 9:00–12:30, no train tickets sold on Sat, closed Sun, Piazza di Spagna 38, 00187 Roma, tel. 06-67641).

Telephones, Mail, and E-mail

Smart travelers use the telephone every day to confirm hotel reservations, check opening hours, and phone home.

Phone Cards: There are two kinds of phone cards—official Italian phone cards that you insert into the phone instead of coins, and long-distance scratch-off PIN cards that can be used from virtually any phone (you dial a toll-free number and enter your PIN code).

Insertable Italian phone cards are sold in varying denominations at tobacco shops, post offices, and machines near phone booths (many phone booths indicate where the nearest phone-card sales outlet is located). Rip off the perforated corner to "activate" the card before you insert it into the phone.

PIN cards, sold at small newsstand kiosks and hole-in-the-wall long-distance phone shops, are usually the least expensive way to call back to the United States (about 10 min/$1). Since you don't insert these cards into a phone, you can use them from most phones, including the one in your hotel room (if it's set on pulse, switch it to tone). Because there are so many brand names, just ask for an international telephone card (*carta telefonica prepagate internazionali*, pron. KAR-tah teh-leh-FOHN-ee-kah pray-pah-GAH-tay in-ter-naht-zee-oh-NAH-lee); specify that you want a card for making calls to America or Canada to avoid getting the PIN cards that are only good within particular regions in Italy. After you buy a card, scratch off and reveal your Personal Identification Number, dial the toll-free access number, punch in your PIN, and talk. If the PIN doesn't work on one phone, try another phone. Get a low denomination in case the card is a dud. If you have difficulty using PIN cards to make local calls, use the insertable phone cards, coins, or hotel-room phones for local calls, and save the PIN card for international calls.

The orange SIP public telephones are everywhere and take cards or coins. About a quarter of the phones are broken (which could explain why so many Italians carry cell phones). The rest of the phones work reluctantly. Dial slowly and deliberately, as if the phone doesn't understand numbers very well. Often a recorded message in Italian will break in, brusquely informing you that the phone number does not exist *(non-esistente)*, even if you're dialing your own home phone number. Dial again with an increasing show of confidence, in an attempt to convince the phone of your number's existence. If you fail, try a different phone. Repeat as needed.

When spelling out your name on the phone, you'll find *a* (pronounced "ah" in Italian), *i* (pronounced "ee"), and *e* (pronounced "ay") are confusing to Americans. Say "*a*, Aosta," "*e*, Empoli," and "*i*, Italia" to clear up that problem. If you plan to access your voice mail from Italy, be advised that you can't always dial extensions or secret codes once you connect (you're on vacation—relax).

Dialing within Italy: Italy has a direct-dial phone system (no area codes). To call anywhere within Italy, just dial the number. For example, the number of one of our recommended Rome hotels is 06-482-4696. To call it from the Rome train station, dial 06-482-4696. If you call it from Venice, it's the same: 06-482-4696.

Italian phone numbers vary in length; a hotel can have, say, a 10-digit phone number and an 11-digit fax number.

Italy's toll-free numbers start with 800 (like U.S. 800 numbers, though in Italy you don't dial a "1" first). In Italy, you can dial these 800 numbers—called *freephone* or *numero verde* (green number)—free from any phone without using a phone card or coins.

Dialing International Calls: When calling internationally, dial the international access code (00 if you're calling from Europe, 011 from the U.S. or Canada), the country code of the country you're calling (39 for Italy; see appendix for a list of other countries), and the local number. To call the Rome hotel from the United States, dial 011 (the U.S. international access code), 39 (Italy's country code), then 06-482-4696. To call the ETBD office from Italy, we dial 00 (Europe's international access code), 1 (the U.S. country code), 425 (Edmonds' area code), and 771-8303. European time is six/nine hours ahead of the East/West Coasts of the United States.

Hotel-room phones are reasonable for calls within Italy (the faint beeps stand for €0.10 phone units) but a terrible rip-off for calls to the United States (unless you use a PIN card or your hotel allows toll-free access to your calling card service—see below).

Calling Card Services: While still convenient, these services—AT&T, MCI, and Sprint—are no longer a good value. It's much cheaper to call the United States using a PIN card or Italian phone card, but some people prefer to use their easier, pricier calling cards. Each card company has a toll-free number in each European country (for Italy: AT&T—tel. 172-1011, MCI—tel. 172-1022, Sprint—tel. 172-1877), which puts you in touch with an English-speaking operator. The operator takes your card number and the number you want to call, puts you through, and bills your home phone number for the call. Oddly, you need to use a small-value coin or Italian phone card to dial the toll-free number. MCI, the cheapest of the lot, charges about $2.50 per minute with no surcharges. Sprint and AT&T charge about the same per minute, but tack on hefty surcharges and fees (if you get an answering machine, it'll cost you $7–8 to say, "Hi, sorry I missed you."). For less than 25 cents, call first with a coin or Italian phone card to see if the answering machine is off or if the right person's at home.

It's outrageously expensive to use your calling card to phone from one European country to another (it costs more than calling the U.S.). When you're in Europe—calling internationally to anywhere—it's cheaper to simply dial direct using a phone card you bought in Europe (sold per country at newsstands).

Cell Phones: Affluent travelers like to buy cell phones (about $70 on up) in Europe to use for making local and international calls. The cheaper phones generally work only if you're making calls from the country where you purchased it (e.g., a phone bought in Italy won't work in France). Pricier phones allow you to call from any country, but it'll cost you about $40 per country to outfit the phone with the necessary chip and prepaid phone time. If you're interested, stop by any European shop that sells cell phones (you'll see an array of phones prominently displayed in the store window). Depending on your trip and budget, ask for a phone that works only in that country or one that can be used throughout Europe. And if you're really on a budget, skip cell phones and use PIN cards instead.

Mail: Mail service is miserable throughout Italy. Postcards get last priority. If you must have mail stops, consider a few pre-reserved hotels along your route or use American Express offices. Most American Express offices in Italy will hold mail for one month. This service is free to anyone using an AmEx card (and available for a small fee to others). Allow 14 days for U.S.-to-Italy mail delivery, but don't count on it. Federal Express makes pricey two-day deliveries. Phoning is so easy that we've completely dispensed with mail stops. If possible, mail nothing precious from Italy. But, if you must, use the mail service at the Vatican City (they have 2 post offices, one next to St. Peter's Basilica, the other within the Vatican Museum).

E-mail: E-mail is getting more common among hoteliers. We've listed e-mail addresses where possible. Internet service providers can change with alarming frequency, so if your e-mail message to a hotel bounces back, use an engine such as www.google.com to search for the hotel name to see if it has a new Web site, and if that doesn't work, fax or call the hotel.

The easiest cybercafé in Rome is easyEverything, centrally located on Piazza Barberini (access from €0.50, open 24/7, 350 terminals, www.easyeverything.com). Many small, drab Internet access points abound, such as Thenetgate inside the train station (see page 271) and the Bolle Blu laundrette chain near the train station (see page 229). If the extension dot-com (.com) doesn't work, try .it.

If you're planning to log on from your laptop in your hotel room, you'll need an Internet service provider that has local phone numbers for each country you'll visit. While an American modem

cable plugs into European phone jacks, you may have to tweak
your settings to make your computer recognize a pulse instead
of the U.S. dial tone. Bring a phone jack tester that reverses
line polarity as needed.

Tipping

Tipping in Italy isn't as automatic and generous as it is in the
United States, but for special service, tips are appreciated, if not
expected. As in the United States, the proper amount depends
on your resources, tipping philosophy, and the circumstance,
but some general guidelines apply.

Restaurants: Check the menu to see if the service is included
(*servizio incluso*—generally 15 percent); if not, a tip of 5 to 10 percent is typical (for details, see page 245).

Taxis: To tip the cabbie, round up. For a typical ride, round
up to the next euro on the fare (to pay a €13 fare, give €14); for
a long ride, to the nearest 10 (for a €75 fare, give €80). If the
cabbie hauls your bags and zips you to the airport to help you
catch your flight, you might want to toss in a little more. But
if you feel like you're being driven in circles or otherwise ripped
off, skip the tip.

Special Services: It's thoughtful to tip a couple of euros
to someone who shows you a special sight and who is paid in no
other way (such as the man who shows you an Etruscan tomb in
his backyard). Tour guides at public sites sometimes hold out
their hands for tips after they give their spiel; if I've already paid
for the tour, I don't tip extra, though some tourists do give a euro
or two, particularly for a job well done. I don't tip at hotels, but
if you do, give the porter a euro for carrying bags and leave a
couple of euros in your room at the end of your stay for the maid
if the room was kept clean. In general, if someone in the service
industry does a super job for you, a tip of a couple of euros is
appropriate . . . but not required.

When in doubt, ask. If you're not sure whether (or how
much) to tip for a service, ask your hotelier or the TI; they'll fill
you in on how it's done on their turf.

Culture Shock—Accepting Italy as a Package Deal

We travel all the way to Italy to enjoy differences—to become
temporary locals. You'll experience frustrations. Certain truths
that we find "God-given" or "self-evident," such as cold beer, ice
in drinks, bottomless cups of coffee, hot showers, and bigger being
better, are suddenly not so true. One of the benefits of travel is
the eye-opening realization that there are logical, civil, and even

better alternatives. A willingness to go local ensures that you'll enjoy a full dose of Italian hospitality.

If there is a negative aspect to Italians' image of Americans, it is that we are big, loud, aggressive, impolite, rich, and a bit naive. While Italians, flabbergasted by our Yankee excesses, say in disbelief, "*Mi sono cadute le braccia!*" ("I throw my arms down!"), they nearly always afford us individual travelers all the warmth we deserve.

Send Us a Postcard, Drop Us a Line

If you enjoy a successful trip with the help of this book and would like to share your discoveries, please fill out and send the survey at the end of this book to us at Europe Through the Back Door, Box 2009, Edmonds, WA 98020. We personally read and value all feedback. Thanks in advance—it helps a lot.

For our latest travel information on Italy, tap into our Web site at www.ricksteves.com. To check on any updates for this book, go to www.ricksteves.com/update. Rick's e-mail address is rick@ricksteves.com. Anyone is welcome to request a free issue of our *Back Door* quarterly newsletter.

Judging from all the happy postcards we receive from travelers who have used this book, it's safe to assume you'll enjoy a great, affordable vacation—with the finesse of an independent, experienced traveler. From this point, "we" (your coauthors) will shed our respective egos and become "I".

Thanks, and *buon viaggio!*

BACK DOOR TRAVEL PHILOSOPHY
From *Rick Steves' Europe Through the Back Door*

Travel is intensified living—maximum thrills per minute and one of the last great sources of legal adventure. Travel is freedom. It's recess, and we need it.

Experiencing the real Europe requires catching it by surprise, going casual ... "Through the Back Door."

Affording travel is a matter of priorities. (Make do with the old car.) You can travel—simply, safely, and comfortably—anywhere in Europe for $80 a day plus transportation costs. In many ways, spending more money only builds a thicker wall between you and what you came to see. Europe is a cultural carnival and, time after time, you'll find that its best acts are free and the best seats are the cheap ones.

A tight budget forces you to travel close to the ground, meeting and communicating with the people, not relying on service with a purchased smile. Never sacrifice sleep, nutrition, safety, or cleanliness in the name of budget. Simply enjoy the local-style alternatives to expensive hotels and restaurants.

Extroverts have more fun. If your trip is low on magic moments, kick yourself and make things happen. If you don't enjoy a place, maybe you don't know enough about it. Seek the truth. Recognize tourist traps. Give a culture the benefit of your open mind. See things as different but not better or worse. Any culture has much to share.

Of course, travel, like the world, is a series of hills and valleys. Be fanatically positive and militantly optimistic. If something's not to your liking, change your liking. Travel is addictive. It can make you a happier American, as well as a citizen of the world. Our Earth is home to six billion equally important people. It's humbling to travel and find that people don't envy Americans. They like us, but, with all due respect, they wouldn't trade passports.

Globetrotting destroys ethnocentricity. It helps you understand and appreciate different cultures. Travel changes people. It broadens perspectives and teaches new ways to measure quality of life. Many travelers toss aside their hometown blinders. Their prized souvenirs are the strands of different cultures they decide to knit into their own character. The world is a cultural yarn shop. And Back Door travelers are weaving the ultimate tapestry. Come on, join in!

ORIENTATION

Sprawling Rome actually feels manageable once you get to know it. The old core, with most of the tourist sights, sits in a diamond formed by the train station (in the east), the Vatican (west), the Borghese Gardens (north) and the Colosseum (south). The Tiber River runs through the diamond from north to south. It takes about an hour-plus to walk from the train station to the Vatican.

Consider Rome in these layers:

The ancient city had a million people. The best of the classical sights stand in a line from the Colosseum to the Pantheon. (See Ancient Rome map, page 59.)

Medieval Rome was little more than a hobo camp of 50,000—thieves, mean dogs, and the pope, whose legitimacy required a Roman address. The medieval city, a colorful tangle of lanes, lies between the Pantheon and the river.

Window-shoppers' Rome twinkles with nightlife and ritzy shopping near Rome's main drag, Via del Corso—in the triangle formed by Piazza del Popolo, Piazza Venezia, and the Spanish Steps. (See Dolce Vita Stroll map, page 269.)

Vatican City is a compact world of its own with two great, huge sights: St. Peter's Basilica and the Vatican Museum. (See Vatican City map, page 39.)

Trastevere, the seedy, colorful, wrong-side-of-the-river neighborhood/village, is Rome at its crustiest—and perhaps most "Roman." (See Trastevere map, page 43.)

Baroque Rome is an overleaf that embellishes great squares throughout the town with fountains and church facades.

Since no one is allowed to build taller than St. Peter's dome, the city has no modern skyline. And the Tiber River is ignored. After the last floods (1870), the banks were built up very high and Rome turned its back on its naughty, unnavigable river.

Greater Rome

Planning Your Time

After considering Rome's major tourist sights, I've covered just my favorites. You won't be able to see all of these, so don't try. You'll keep coming back to Rome. After several dozen visits, I still have a healthy list of excuses to return.

Rome in a Day

Some people actually try to "do" Rome in a day. Crazy as that sounds, if all you have is a day, it's a great one. See the Vatican City (2 hrs in the Vatican Museum and Sistine Chapel, 1 hr in St. Peter's), taxi over the river to the Pantheon (picnic on its steps), then hike over Capitol Hill, through the Forum, and to the Colosseum. Have dinner on Campo de' Fiori and dessert on Piazza Navona.

Rome in Two to Three Days

On the first day, do the "Caesar Shuffle" from the Colosseum to the Forum, then over Capitol Hill to the Pantheon. After a siesta,

Daily Reminder

Sunday: These sights are closed: Vatican Museum (except for the last Sunday of the month, when it's free) and the Catacombs of San Sebastian. The Pantheon and E.U.R.'s Museum of Roman Civilization close early in the afternoon. In the morning, the Porta Portese flea market hops, and the old center is delightfully quiet.

Monday: Many sights are closed: National Museum of Rome, Borghese Gallery, Capitol Hill Museum, Octagonal Hall and Museum of the Bath (both at Baths of Diocletian), Etruscan Museum, Castel Sant' Angelo, Trajan's Market, Protestant Cemetery, E.U.R.'s Museum of Roman Civilization, Ostia Antica, and Villa d'Este (at Tivoli). All of the ancient sites and the Vatican Museum, among others, *are* open. The Baths of Caracalla close early in the afternoon.

Tuesday: All sights are open in Rome except for Nero's Golden House. Not a good day to side-trip to Naples (its Archaeological Museum is closed).

Wednesday: All sights are open except for the Catacombs of San Callisto.

Thursday: All sights are open except for the Cappuccin Crypt.

Friday/Saturday: All sights are open in Rome.

join the locals strolling from Piazza del Popolo to the Spanish Steps (see my recommended Dolce Vita Stroll, page tk). Have dinner near your hotel. On the second day, see the Vatican City (St. Peter's, climb the dome, tour the Vatican Museum). Have dinner on the atmospheric Campo de' Fiori, then walk to the Trevi Fountain and Spanish Steps (see my recommended Night Walk Across Rome, page 52). With a third day, add the Borghese Gallery (reservations required) and the National Museum of Rome.

Rome in Seven Days

Rome's a great one-week getaway. Its sights can keep even the most fidgety traveler well-entertained for a week.

Day 1: City orientation tour (walking tour or bus tour), then the National Museum of Rome and the nearby Baths of Diocletian. Afternoon: Dolce Vita Stroll (page 269) and shopping.

Day 2: Do the "Caesar Shuffle" from Nero's Golden House (reservation required) to the Colosseum, Forum, Mammertine Prison, Trajan's Forum, Capitol Hill, and Pantheon.

Day 3: Vatican City: St. Peter's Basilica, climb the dome, Vatican Museum. (The museum is less crowded right before it closes but last admission is early—either 12:20 or 14:20, depending on the day.)
Day 4: Side trip to Ostia Antica (page 199). Take recommended "Night Walk Across Rome" (page 52) from Campo de' Fiori to the Spanish Steps.
Day 5: Borghese Gallery (reservation required) and Pilgrims' Rome (the churches Santa Maria Maggiore, San Clemente, and San Giovanni in Laterano).
Day 6: Side trip to Naples and Pompeii.
Day 7: Personal choice—Hadrian's Villa, Appian Way with Catacombs, E.U.R., Castel Sant' Angelo, Testaccio sights, Baths of Caracalla, Cappuccin Crypt, more shopping, or more time at the Vatican.

Arrival in Rome

For a rundown on Rome's train station and airports, see "Transportation Connections," page 271.

Tourist Information

While Rome has three main tourist information offices, the dozen or so TI kiosks scattered around the town at major tourist centers are handy and just as helpful. If all you need is a map, forget the TI and get one at your hotel.

The main TI, near Piazza della Repubblica's huge fountain, covers the city and the region. It's a five-minute walk out the front of the train station (Mon–Sat 9:00–19:00, next to car dealership, Via Parigi 5, free Internet access to Rome tourism sites, www.romaturismo.com, tel. 06-360-64399). It's air-conditioned, less crowded, and more helpful than the station TI (see below), and it has seats and a study table.

You'll also find TIs at the airport (daily 9:00–19:00, tel. 06-6595-6074) and the train station (daily 8:00–21:00, near track 3, accessible from platforms or lobby, marked "Informazioni Turistiche/Tourist Info," crowded, combined with travel agency, tel. 06-4890-6300).

At any TI, ask for a city map, a listing of sights and hours (in the free *Tesori di Roma* booklet), and *L'Evento*, the free bimonthly entertainment guide for evening events and fun. All hotels list an inflated rate to cover the hefty commission any TI room-finding service charges. Save money by booking direct.

Smaller TIs (daily 9:00–18:00) include kiosks near the Forum (on Piazza del Tempio della Pace), at Via del Corso (on Largo Goldoni), in Trastevere (on Piazza Sonnino), on Via Nazionale (at Palazzo delle Esposizioni), at Castel Sant' Angelo, Santa Maria

Maggiore, and at San Giovanni in Laterano. For more information, call 06-3600-4399 (daily 9:00–19:00).

Roma c'è is a cheap little weekly entertainment guide with a helpful English section (at the back) on musical events and the pope's schedule for the week (new edition every Thu, sold at newsstands for €1, www.romace.it, Web site in Italian).

Dealing with (and Avoiding) Problems

Theft Alert: With sweet-talking con artists meeting you at the station, well-dressed pickpockets on buses, and thieving gangs of children at the ancient sites, Rome is a gauntlet of rip-offs. There's no great physical risk, but green tourists will be scammed. Thieves strike when you're distracted. Don't trust kind strangers. Keep nothing important in your pockets. Assume you're being stalked. (Then relax and have fun.) Be most on guard while boarding and leaving buses and subways. Thieves crowd the door, then stop and turn while others crowd and push from behind. The sneakiest thieves are well-dressed businessmen (generally with something in their hands); lately many are posing as tourists with fanny packs and cameras. Scams abound: Don't give your wallet to self-proclaimed "police" who stop you on the street, warn you about counterfeit (or drug) money, and ask to see your wallet.

If you know what to look out for, the gangs of children picking the pockets and handbags of naive tourists are no threat but an interesting, albeit sad, spectacle. Gangs of city-stained children (sometimes as young as 8–10 years old), too young to be prosecuted but old enough to rip you off, troll through the tourist crowds around the Colosseum, Forum, Piazza Repubblica, and train and Metro stations. Watch them target tourists who are overloaded with bags or distracted with a video camera. The kids look like beggars and hold up newspapers or cardboard signs to confuse their victims. They scram like stray cats if you're onto them. A fast-fingered mother with a baby is often nearby. The terrace above the bus stop near the Colosseum Metro stop is a fine place to watch the action and maybe even pick up a few moves of your own.

Reporting Losses: To report lost or stolen passports and documents or to file an insurance claim, you must file a police report (at the train station with Polizia at track 1 or with Carabinieri at track 20, also at Piazza Venezia). To replace a passport, file the police report, then go to your embassy (see below). To report lost traveler's checks, call your bank (Visa—tel. 800-874-155, Thomas Cook/MasterCard—tel. 800-872-050, American Express—tel. 800-872-000), then file a police report. To report stolen or lost credit cards, call the company (Visa—tel. 800-877-232 or 800-819-014, MasterCard—tel. 800-870-866, American Express tel. 800-874-333), then file a police report. All of these toll-free 800 numbers are Italian (dialed free in Italy), not American.

Embassies: United States (Mon–Fri 8:30–13:00 & 14:00–17:30, Via Vittorio Veneto 119/A, tel. 06-46741, www.usembassy .it) and Canada (Via Zara 30, tel. 06-445-981, www.canada.it).

Emergency Numbers: Police—tel. 113. Ambulance—tel. 118.

Hit and Run: Walk with extreme caution. Scooters don't need to stop at red lights, and even cars exercise what drivers call the "logical option" of not stopping if they see no oncoming traffic. As Vespa scooters become electric, they'll get quieter (hooray) but more dangerous for pedestrians. Follow locals like a shadow when you cross a street (or spend a good part of your visit stranded on curbs).

Staying/Getting Healthy: The siesta is a key to survival in summertime Rome. Lie down and contemplate the extraordinary power of gravity in the eternal city. I drink lots of cold, refreshing water from Rome's many drinking fountains (the Forum has 3). There's a pharmacy (marked by a green cross) in every neighborhood, including a handy one in the train station (daily 7:30–22:00, located downstairs, at west end), and a 24-hour pharmacy on Piazza dei Cinquecento 51 (next to train station on Via Cavour, tel. 06-488-0019). Embassies can recommend English-speaking doctors. Consider MEDline, a 24-hour home medical service (tel. 06-808-0995, doctors speak English). Anyone is entitled to free emergency treatment at public hospitals. The hospital closest to the train station is Policlinico Umberto 1 (entrance for emergency treatment on Via Lancisi, translators available, Metro: Policlinico). The American Hospital is a private hospital on the edge of town accustomed to helping Yankees (tel. 06-225-571).

Getting around Rome

Sightsee on foot, by city bus, or by taxi. I've grouped your sightseeing into walkable neighborhoods.

Public transportation is efficient, cheap, and part of your Roman experience. It starts running around 5:30 and stops around 23:30, sometimes earlier. After midnight, there are a few very crowded night buses, and taxis become more expensive and hard to get. Don't try to hail one—go to a taxi stand.

Buses and subways use the same ticket. You can buy tickets at newsstands, tobacco shops (*tabacchi*, marked by a black-and-white "T" sign), or at major Metro stations or bus stops, but not on board. Since many Metro stations have no human ticket-sellers and the machines are either broken or require exact change (helps to put in smallest coin first), it's easier to buy a few tickets above ground at newsstands or *tabacchi* (€0.80, good for 75 min—Metro ride and unlimited buses) or an all-day bus/Metro pass (€3.25, for

Rome's Metro

more info, visit www.atac.roma.it). Fancy new tickets with bar codes eventually will replace the plain paper tickets. Until then, buses and the Metro have two different validation machines; if you've got a new ticket, use the one with the slot on top.

Buses (especially the touristic #64) and the subway are havens for thieves and pickpockets. Assume any commotion is a thief-created distraction.

By Metro: The Roman subway system (Metropolitana) is simple, with two clean, cheap, fast lines that intersect at Termini train station. While much of Rome is not served by its skimpy subway, these stops are helpful: Termini (train station, National Museum of Rome at Palazzo Massimo, recommended hotels), Repubblica (Baths of Diocletian/Octagonal Hall, main TI, recommended hotels), Barberini (Cappuccin Crypt, Trevi Fountain), Spagna (Spanish Steps, Villa Borghese, classy shopping area), Flaminio (Piazza del Popolo, start of recommended Dolce Vita Stroll down Via del Corso), Ottaviano (St. Peter's and Vatican City), Cipro-Musei Vaticani (Vatican Museum, recommended hotels), Colosseo (Colosseum, Roman Forum, recommended hotels), and E.U.R. (Mussolini's futuristic suburb).

By Bus: Bus routes are clearly listed at the stops. Ask the TI for a bus map. Punch your ticket in the orange stamping machine as you board (even if you've already stamped it for the

Metro)—or you are cheating. Riding without a stamped ticket on the bus, while relatively safe, is stressful. Inspectors fine even innocent-looking tourists €52. If the validation machine won't work, you can write the date, time, and bus number on the ticket. Ideally, buy a bunch of tickets from a tobacco shop or newsstand first thing so you can hop a bus without first having to search for a tobacco shop that's open.

Here are a few buses worth knowing about:

#64: Termini (train station), Piazza della Repubblica (sights), Via Nazionale (recommended hotels), Piazza Venezia (near Forum), Largo Argentina (near Pantheon), St. Peter's Basilica. Ride it for a city overview and to watch pickpockets in action (can get horribly crowded).

#40: This express route is especially helpful—it's the same route as #64, but with fewer stops, crowds, and pickpockets.

#8: This tram connects Largo Argentina with Trastevere (get off at Piazza Mastai).

#H: Express connecting Termini train station and Trastevere, with a few stops on Via Nazionale (for Trastevere, get off at Piazza Belli, just over bridge).

#492: Stazione Tiburtina, Piazza Barberini, Piazza Venezia, Piazza Cavour (Castel Sant' Angelo), Piazza Risorgimento (near Vatican Museum).

#714: Termini, Santa Maria Maggiore, San Giovanni in Laterano, Terme di Caracalla (Baths of Caracalla).

Rome has cute *"elettrico"* minibuses that wind through the narrow streets of old and interesting neighborhoods (daily except Sun). These are handy for sightseeing and fun for simply joyriding:

Elettrico **#116:** Through the medieval core of Rome from Campo de' Fiori to Piazza Barberini via the Pantheon.

Elettrico **#117:** San Giovanni in Laterano, Colosseo, Via dei Serpenti, Trevi Fountain, Piazza di Spagna, Piazza del Popolo.

"J" (for Jubilee) buses are bigger, come with a hostess, and provide more convenient access to some places farther out, such as St. Peter's (Cavalleggeri stop) and the Catacombs. Purchase tickets (€1) on the bus (info: tel. 800-076-287).

By Taxi: I use taxis in Rome more often than in other cities. They're relatively cheap and useful for efficient sightseeing in a big, hot city. Taxis start at about €2.75 (surcharges of €1 on Sun, €2.75 for night hours of 22:00–7:00, €1 surcharge for luggage, €7.25 extra for airport, tip about 10 percent by rounding up to the nearest euro). Sample fares: Train station to Vatican-€9; train station to Colosseum-€6; Colosseum to Trastevere-€7. Three or four companions with more money than time should taxi almost everywhere. It's tough to wave down a taxi in Rome. Find the nearest taxi stand. (Ask a local or in a shop *"Dov'è* [doh-vay] *una fermata dei tassi?"* Some are listed on my maps.) Unmarked, unmetered taxis at train stations and the airport are usually a rip-off. Taxis listing their telephone number on the door have fair meters—use them. To save time and energy, have your hotel call a taxi; the meter starts when the call is received. (To call a cab on your own, dial 06-3570, 06-4994, or 06-88177.)

Tours of Rome

Scala Reale—Tom Rankin (an American architect in love with Rome and his Roman wife) runs Scala Reale, a company committed to sorting out the rich layers of Rome for small groups with a longer-than-average attention span. Their excellent walking tours vary in length from two to four hours and start at €16 per person. Try to book in advance, since their groups are limited to six and fill up fast. Their fascinating "Rome Orientation" walks lace together lesser-known sights from antiquity to the present (tel. 06-474-5673, 888/467-1986 in the U.S., www.scalareale.org, e-mail: info@scalareale.org).

If you're interested in weeklong classes on Rome, look into the Institute for Roman Culture, an innovative, educational organization run by Tom Rankin and his colleague, archaeologist Darius Arya (see www.romanculture.org for prices, details, and booking).
Through Eternity—This company, which gets mixed reviews from readers, offers four walking tours, all led by native English speakers. The tours include St. Peter's and the Vatican Museum (€35, museum entry not included, 5.5 hrs, daily except Sun); the Colosseum and Roman Forum (€20, 2.5 hrs, daily); Rome at Twilight (€20, nightly); and a Wine Sampling Tour (€35, nightly, includes a glass at 4 or 5 wine bars and dinner). Call to get the schedule and to book in advance (max of 25 people, tel. 06-700-9336, cellular 347-336-5298, private tours possible, www.througheternity.com, e-mail: info@througheternity.com).
Rome Walks—Students working for "Rome Walks" give tours in fluent English. Sample tours include Colosseum/Forum Walk (€33, includes admission to Colosseum, 2.5 hrs), Palatine Hill/ Mouth of Truth Walk (€33, includes Palatine admission, 2 hrs), Scandal Tour (€25, 2 hrs to dig up the dirt on Roman emperors, royalty, and popes), Vatican City Walk (€45, includes admission to Vatican Museum, 4.5 hrs), and a Twilight Rome Evening Walk (€25, 2 hrs). See their Web site for the latest (www.rome-walks.com) and book in advance by e-mail (info@romewalks.com) or phone (cellular 347-795-5175, private tours also available). You'll need to give your hotel name and phone number. Your guide will call or e-mail you to let you know the meeting place.

Hop-on, Hop-off Bus Tour—The ATAC city bus tour offers your best budget orientation tour of Rome. In under two hours, you'll have 80 sights pointed out to you (by a live guide in English and maybe one other language). If you've got a little more time and money, you can get out at any of the nine stops and catch a later bus (though stops are poorly marked and the included map is useless). While the guide's spiel is limited to simple identification of the sights, this tour provides an efficient and economical orientation to Rome. The stops are: Piazza Barberini, Via Veneto, Villa Borghese, Piazza Cavour, St. Peter's Square, Corso Vittorio Emanuele (for Piazza Navona), Piazza Venezia, Colosseum, and Via Nazionale. I'd take the nonstop tour for €7.75; the hop-on, hop-off tour is €13. Bus #110 departs every 30 minutes—at the top and bottom of the hour—from in front of the Termini train station (near platform C, buy tickets at info kiosk there—marked "i bus"—or buy on the bus and pay about 10 percent more, runs March–Sept 9:00–20:00, Oct–Feb 10:00–18:00, tel. 06-4695-2252).

Archeobus—This handy hop-on, hop-off bus runs hourly from the west side of Piazza Venezia way out the Appian Way. By far the easiest way to see the sights down this ancient Roman road, it includes a basic, uninspired two-hour (longer if there's traffic) tour in Italian and English in an air-conditioned minibus (buy €7.75 tickets at green kiosk on Piazza Venezia, good from 9:00–17:00, tel. 06-4695-4695).

SIGHTS

I've clustered Rome's sights into walkable neighborhoods, some quite close together. The Colosseum and the Forum are a few minutes' walk from Capitol Hill. Beyond that is the Pantheon, a 10–minute walk. I like to group these sights in one great day, starting at the Colosseum and ending at the Pantheon.

In this chapter, Rome's most important sights have the shortest listings and are marked with a ⭐ (and page number). These sights are covered in much more detail in one of the tours included in this book.

To connect some of the sights by night, try my Night Walk Across Rome (page 52), which includes the Trevi Fountain and Spanish Steps. To join the parade of people strolling down Via del Corso every evening, take my recommended Dolce Vita Stroll (see page 268).

Ancient Rome: The Colosseum and Forum Area

The core of the ancient city, where the grandest monuments were built, is between the Colosseum and Capitol Hill.

Beware of gangs of young thieves, particularly between the Colosseum and the Forum. They're harmless if you know what to look for (see "Theft Alert," page 21).

The following sights are listed in roughly geographical order from the Colosseum area to Capitol Hill. Except for the small St. Peter–in–Chains Church, the sights date from ancient Rome.

▲**St. Peter–in–Chains Church (San Pietro in Vincoli)**— Built in the fifth century to house the chains that held St. Peter, this church is most famous for its Michelangelo statue. Check out the much–venerated chains under the high altar, then focus on Moses (free, Mon–Sat 7:00–12:30 & 15:30–19:00, Sun 7:30–12:30,

Tips on Sightseeing in Rome

Museums: Plan ahead. The marvelous Borghese Gallery and Nero's Golden House both require reservations. For the Borghese Gallery, it's safest to make reservations well in advance of your trip (for specifics, see page 127). You can wait until you're in Rome to call for a reservation time at Nero's Golden House, but it's wise to book ahead (see page 30).

Audioguides are becoming increasingly common at museums. These small, portable devices give you information in English on what you're seeing. After you dial a number that appears next to a particular work of art, you listen to the spiel (cutting it short if you want). Though the information can be dry, it's usually worthwhile (€4, sometimes 2 earphones are available at an extra cost).

A special **combo–ticket,** which costs €20, covers the National Museum of Rome, Colosseum, Palatine Hill, Baths of Caracalla, Crypt Balbi (medieval art), Museum of the Bath (Roman inscriptions), and Palazzo Altemps (so–so sculpture collection). The combo–ticket allows you to see seven sights for the price of three (purchase at participating sites, valid for 5 days). When you buy this, you can upgrade to a "Coupon Servizi" pass for an extra €5, giving you tours or audioguides at each site (normally about €4 each). The big plus of this ticket is that you avoid the long lines at the Colosseum (if you purchase it at a participating site other than the Colosseum).

Get a current listing of **museum hours** from one of Rome's TIs—ask for the booklet *Tesori di Roma* (Treasures of Rome). Some museums may stay open later in summer (usually on Sat). On holidays, expect shorter hours or closures. Hours listed anywhere can vary. You can confirm sightseeing plans each morning with a quick 10–cent telephone call, asking, "Are you open today?"

---

modest dress required, a short walk uphill from the Colosseum, Metro: Colosseo). ⭐ See St. Peter-in-Chains Tour on page 181.
▲**Nero's Golden House (Domus Aurea)**—The barren remains of Emperor Nero's "Golden House" were reopened to the public in 1999. The original entrance to the house was all the way over at the Arch of Titus in the Forum. This massive house once sprawled across the valley (where the Colosseum now stands) and up the hill—the part you tour today. Larger even than Bill Gates' place, it was a pain to vacuum. A colossal, 33–meter–tall (100-foot) bronze statue of Nero towered over everything. The house incorporated

("*Aperto oggi?*"; ah-PER-toh OH-jee) and "What time do you close?" ("*A che ora chiuso?*"; ah kay OH-rah kee-OO-zoh). I've included telephone numbers for this purpose.

Rooms can begin closing about 30 to 60 minutes before the overall closing time. If your heart is set on seeing a particular piece of art, don't save it for the finale.

In museums, art is dated with A.C. (for *Avanti Cristo*, or B.C.) and D.C. (for *Dopo Cristo*, or A.D.). O.K.?

Churches: Churches offer some amazing art (usually free), a cool respite from the heat, and a welcome seat. They generally open early (around 7:00), close for lunch (roughly 12:00–15:00), and close late (around 19:00). Kamikaze tourists maximize their sightseeing hours by visiting churches before 9:00 and seeing the major sights that stay open during the siesta (St. Peter's, Colosseum, Forum, Capitol Hill Museum, National Museum of Rome) while Romans are taking it cool and easy.

Many churches have "modest dress" requirements, which means no bare shoulders, miniskirts, or shorts—for men, women, or children. However, this dress code is only strictly enforced at St. Peter's. Elsewhere, you'll see many tourists in shorts touring many churches.

Carry coins. A coin box near a piece of art in a church often illuminates the art for a coin (and a better photo). Whenever possible, let there be light. Some churches have coin-operated audio-boxes that describe the art and history.

Miscellaneous tips: Carry a plastic water bottle that can be refilled at Rome's many public drinking spouts. Use toilets when you can (Mom always said, "Just try"), because public restrooms are scarce. Don't leave a museum, restaurant, or bar without considering their facilities.

an artificial lake (where the Colosseum was later built) and a forest stocked with game. It was decorated with the best multi-colored marble and the finest frescoes. No expense was too great for Nero—his mistress soaked daily in the milk of 500 wild asses kept for her bathing pleasure.

Nero (ruled A.D. 54–68) was Rome's most notorious emperor. He killed his own mother, kicked his pregnant wife to death, crucified St. Peter, and—most galling to his subjects—was a bad actor. When Rome burned in A.D. 64, Nero was accused of torching it to clear land for an even bigger house. The Romans rebelled and Nero stabbed himself in the neck, crying, "What an artist dies in me!"

While only hints of the splendid, colorful frescoes survive, the towering vaults and the basic immensity of the place are impressive. As you wander through rooms that are now under ground, look up at the holes in the ceiling. Imagine how much of old Rome still hides underground...and why the subway is limited to two lines.

Visits are allowed only with an escort (30 people, about every 30 min) and a reservation (€6.20, Wed–Mon 9:00–19:45, last entry at 18:40, closed Tue, tour lasts 50 min, audioguide–€2, but listen to the intro before entering or you'll be forever behind, Metro: Colosseo, 200 meters, or 650 feet, northeast of Colosseum, through a park gate, up a hill, and on the left). Guided tours in English are offered twice daily (€8.50); to reserve a place, call 06-3996-7700. If you just show up (particularly on a late afternoon on a weekday), you could luck out and get on a tour; if tours aren't booked up, the remaining seats are sold to drop–ins.

▲▲▲**Colosseum**—This 2,000–year–old building is *the* great example of Roman engineering (€8 includes Palatine Hill—valid 24 hrs, covered by €20 combo–ticket—valid 7 days, daily 9:00–19:00, or 1 hour before sunset, Metro: Colosseo, tel. 06-3974-9907). ✪ See Colosseum Tour on page 58.

There are three ways to avoid the long lines here: 1. Buy your ticket at either Palatine Hill entrance (inside Forum entry near Arch of Titus, and on Via di San Gregorio—facing Forum entry, go left). 2. Reserve a ticket in advance by calling 06-3996-7700 (follow the automated prompts in English, pick up ticket at Colosseum ticket office's side window). 3. Get a €20 combo–ticket and walk right in (purchase at either Palatine Hill entrance, National Museum of Rome, Baths of Caracalla, Museum of the Bath, or other participating sites).

▲**Arch of Constantine**—This well–preserved arch, which stands between the Colosseum and the Forum, commemorates a military coup and, more importantly, the acceptance of Christianity in the Roman Empire. When the ambitious Emperor Constantine (who'd had a vision he'd win under the sign of the cross) defeated his rival Maxentius in A.D. 312, Constantine became sole emperor and legalized Christianity. (Free, always open and viewable.) ✪ See Colosseum Tour on page 58.

▲▲▲**Roman Forum (Foro Romano)**—This is ancient Rome's birthplace and civic center, and the common ground between Rome's famous seven hills (free, daily 9:00–19:00 or an hour before dark, Metro: Colosseo, tel. 06-3974-9907). ✪ See Roman Forum Tour on page 64.

▲**Palatine Hill**—The hill overlooking the Forum was the home of the emperors and contains a museum, scant remains of imperial palaces, and a view of the Circus Maximus (€8 includes Colosseum, covered by €20 combo–ticket, audioguide–€4, daily 9:00–19:00 or an hour before dark). The ticket booths—which also sell Colosseum tickets, enabling smart sightseers to avoid the long Colosseum line—are inside the Forum entry and on Via di San Gregorio. ✪ See Palatine Hill Tour on page 77.

▲**Mammertine Prison**—This 2,500–year–old, cistern–like prison, which once held Saints Peter and Paul, is worth a look (donation requested, daily 9:00–12:30 & 14:30–18:00, at the foot of Capitol Hill, near Forum's Arch of Septimius Severus). When you step into the room, you'll hit a modern floor. Ignore that and look up at the hole in the ceiling, from which prisoners were lowered. Then take the stairs down to the level of the actual prison floor. As you descend, you'll walk past a supposedly miraculous image of Peter's face, created when a guard pushed him into the wall. Downstairs, you'll see the column to which Peter was chained. It's said that a miraculous fountain sprang up in this room so Peter could baptize other prisoners. The upside–down cross commemorates Peter's upside–down crucifixion.

Imagine humans, amid fat rats and rotting corpses, awaiting slow deaths. On the walls near the entry are lists of notable prisoners (Christian and non–Christian) and the ways they were executed: *strangolati*, *decapitato*, *morto di fame* (died of hunger)....

▲**Trajan's Column, Forum, and Market**—This is the grandest column and best example of "continuous narration" we have from antiquity (free, always open and viewable, on Piazza Venezia across street from Victor Emmanuel Monument). For a fee, you can go inside Trajan's Market (boring) and part of Trajan's Forum (€6.20, summer Tue–Sun 9:00–18:30, winter 9:00–16:30, closed Mon, entrance is uphill from the column on Via IV Novembre, tel. 06-3600-4399). ✪ See Trajan's Column and Forum Tour on page 86.

Capitol Hill Area

There are several ways to get to the top of Capitol Hill. If you're coming from the north (Piazza Venezia), take the grand stairs located to the right of the big, white Victor Emmanuel Monument (described below). Coming from the south (the Forum), take either the steep staircase or the winding road, which converge near the top of the hill at a great Forum overlook and a refreshing water fountain. Block the spout with your fingers; water spurts up for drinking. Romans, who call this *il nasone* (the nose), joke that a cheap Roman boy takes his date out for a drink at *il nasone*.

▲▲**Capitol Hill (Campidoglio)**—This hill was the religious and

political center of ancient
Rome. It's still the home
of the city's government.
Michelangelo's Renais-
sance square is bordered
by two fine museums and
the mayoral palace. Its
centerpiece is a copy of
the famous equestrian
statue of Marcus Aurelius

(the original is behind glass in the adjacent museum).

Michelangelo intended that people approach the square from
the grand stairway off Piazza Venezia. From the top of the stairway, you see the new Renaissance face of Rome with its back to
the Forum, facing the new city. Notice how Michelangelo gave
the buildings the "giant order"—huge pilasters make the existing
two–story buildings feel one–storied and more harmonious with the
new square. Notice also how the statues atop these buildings welcome you and then draw you in. The terraces just downhill (past
either side of the mayor's palace) offer fine views of the Forum.

▲▲**Capitol Hill Museum**—This museum encompasses two
buildings (Palazzo dei Conservatori and Palazzo Nuovo) connected by an underground passage that leads to the vacant Tabularium and its panoramic overlook of the Forum (€8, Tue–Sun
9:00–20:00, last entry 60 min before closing, closed Mon, Jan 1,
May 1, and Dec 25, audioguide-€4, tel. 06-3996-7800). ✪ See
Capitol Hill Museum Tour on page 120.

From Capitol Hill to Piazza Venezia—Leaving Capitol Hill,
descend the stairs leading to Piazza Venezia. At the bottom of the
stairs, look left several blocks down the street to see a condominium
actually built around surviving ancient pillars and arches of Teatro
Marcello—perhaps the oldest inhabited building in Europe.

Still at the bottom of the stairs, look up the long stairway
to your right (which pilgrims climb on their knees) for a good
example of the earliest style of Christian church. While pilgrims
find it worth the climb, sightseers can skip it. As you walk toward
Piazza Venezia, look down into the ditch on your right and see
how modern Rome is built on the forgotten frescoes and mangled
mosaics of ancient Rome.

Piazza Venezia—This vast square is the focal point of modern
Rome. The Via del Corso, which starts here, is the city's axis,
surrounded by Rome's classiest shopping district. In the 1930s,
Mussolini whipped up Italy's nationalistic fervor here from a
balcony above the square (to your left with your back to Victor
Emmanuel Monument). Fascist masses filled the square screaming,

"Four more years!"—or something like that. Fifteen years later, they hung Mussolini from a meat hook in Milan.

Victor Emmanuel Monument—This oversized monument to an Italian king was part of Italy's rush to overcome the new country's strong regionalism and to create a national identity after unification in 1870. It's now open to the public, offering a new view of the Eternal City (free, long hours, 242 punishing steps to the top).

Romans think of the 60-meter-high (200-foot), 150-meter-wide (500-foot) monument not as an altar of the fatherland, but as "the wedding cake," "the typewriter," or "the dentures." It wouldn't be so bad if it weren't sitting on a priceless acre of ancient Rome and if they had chosen better marble (this is too in–your–face white and picks up the pollution horribly), though one of this book's authors happens to like the monument. Soldiers guard Italy's *Tomb of the Unknown Soldier* as the eternal flame flickers. At this level, stand with your back to the flame and see how Via del Corso bisects Rome.

Pantheon Area

▲▲▲**Pantheon**—For the greatest look at the splendor of Rome, antiquity's best–preserved interior is a must. Built two millennia ago, this influential domed temple served as the model for Michelangelo's dome of St. Peter's and many others (free, Mon–Sat 8:30–19:30, Sun and holidays 9:00–18:00, tel. 06-6830-0230). ✪ See Pantheon Tour on page 90.

▲▲**Churches near the Pantheon**—✪ For more information on the following churches, see page 92. The **Church of San Luigi dei Francesi** has a magnificent chapel painted by Caravaggio (free, Fri–Wed 7:30–12:30 & 15:30–19:00, Thu 7:30–12:30, sightseers should avoid Mass at 7:30 and 19:00). The only Gothic church in Rome is **Santa Maria sopra Minerva**, with a little–known Michelangelo statue, *Christ Bearing the Cross* (the church is on a little square behind the Pantheon, to the east). The **Church of St. Ignazio**, several blocks east of the Pantheon, is a riot of Baroque illusions with a false dome. (Both Sopra Minerva and St. Ignazio churches open early; take a siesta: Sopra Minerva closes at 12:00, St. Ignazio at 12:30; and reopen from around 15:30–19:00). A few blocks away, back across Corso Vittorio Emmanuele, is the rich and Baroque **Gesu Church**, headquarters of the Jesuits in Rome (daily 7:00–12:00 & 15:00–20:00). Modest dress is recommended at all churches.

Heart of Rome

Walk out the Gesu Church and two blocks down Corso
V. Emmanuele to the **Sacred Area** (Largo Argentina), an excavated square facing the boulevard, about four blocks south of the
Pantheon. Walk around this square and look into the excavated
pit at some of the oldest ruins in Rome. Julius Caesar was assassinated near here. Today it's a refuge for cats—some 250 of them
are cared for by volunteers. You'll see them (and their refuge) at
the far (west) side of the square.

▲**Galleria Doria Pamphilj**—This gallery, filling a palace on
Piazza del Collegio Romano, offers a rare chance to wander
through a noble family's lavish rooms with the prince who calls
this downtown mansion home. Well, almost. Through an audioguide, the prince lovingly narrates his family's story, including
how the Doria Pamphilj (pron. pahm-FEEL-yee) family's cozy

relationship with the pope inspired the word nepotism. Highlights include paintings by Caravaggio, Titian, and Raphael, and portraits of Pope Innocent X by Velázquez (on canvas) and Bernini (in marble). The fancy rooms of the palace are interesting, with a mini–Versailles–like hall of mirrors and paintings stacked to the ceiling in the style typical of 18th–century galleries (€8, includes fine audioguide, Fri–Wed 10:00–17:00, closed Thu, from Piazza Venezia walk 2 blocks up Via del Corso and take a left, tel. 06-679-7323, www.doriapamphilj.it).

▲**Trevi Fountain**—This bubbly Baroque fountain of Neptune with his entourage, worth ▲ by day and ▲▲ by night, is a minor sight to art scholars but a major nighttime gathering spot for teens on the make and tourists tossing coins. ✪ See Night Walk Across Rome on page 52

East Rome: Near the Train Station

These sights are within a 10–minute walk of the train station. By Metro, use the Termini stop for the National Museum and the Piazza Repubblica stop for the rest.

▲▲▲**National Museum of Rome in Palazzo Massimo**— This museum houses the greatest collection of ancient Roman art anywhere, including busts of emperors and a Roman copy of the *Greek Discus Thrower* (€6, covered by €20 combo–ticket, Tue–Sun 9:00–19:45, some summer Sat until 23:00, last entry 45 min before closing, closed Mon, audioguide–€4, Metro: Termini, tel. 06-481-4144). The museum is about 100 meters (330 feet) from the Termini train station. As you leave the station, it's the sandstone–brick building on your left. Enter at the far end, at Largo di Villa Peretti. ✪ See National Museum of Rome Tour on page 106.

▲**Baths of Diocletian**—Around A.D. 300, Emperor Diocletian built the largest baths in Rome. This sprawling meeting place, with baths and schmoozing spaces to accommodate 3,000 bathers at a time, was a big deal in ancient times. While much of it is still closed, three sections are open: the **Church of Santa Maria degli Angeli**, once the great central hall of the baths (free, Mon–Sat 7:00–18:30, Sun 8:00–19:30, closed to sightseers during Mass, faces Piazza Repubblica); the **Octagonal Hall**, once a gymnasium, now a gallery showing off fine bronze and marble statues—the kind that decorated the baths of imperial Rome (free, Tue–Sat 9:00–14:00, Sun 9:00–13:00, closed Mon, faces Piazza Repubblica); and the **Museum of the Bath**, which displays ancient Roman inscriptions on tons of tombs, stelae, and tablets, but has nothing on the baths despite its name (€5, covered by €20 combo–ticket, Tue–Sun 9:00–19:45, last entry 45 min before closing, closed Mon,

East Rome

Viale E. de Nicola 79, entrance faces Termini station, tel.
06-4782-6152). ✪ See Baths of Diocletian Tour on page 100.
▲**Santa Maria della Vittoria**—This church houses Bernini's
statue of a swooning *St. Teresa in Ecstasy* (free, daily 7:00–13:00 &
15:00–19:00, on Largo Susanna, about 5 blocks northwest of train
station, Metro: Repubblica). Once inside the church, you'll find
St. Teresa to the left of the altar.

Teresa has just been stabbed with God's arrow of fire. Now,
the angel pulls it out and watches her reaction. Teresa swoons,
her eyes roll up, her hand goes limp, she parts her lips...and
moans. The smiling, cherubic angel understands just how she
feels. Teresa, a 16th–century Spanish nun, later talked of the

"sweetness" of "this intense pain,"
describing her oneness with God
in ecstatic, even erotic, terms.

Bernini, the master of multimedia, pulls out all the stops to
make this mystical vision real. Actual
sunlight pours through the alabaster
windows; bronze sunbeams shine
on a marble angel holding a golden
arrow. Teresa leans back on a cloud
and her robe ripples from within,
charged with her spiritual arousal.
Bernini has created a little stage–
setting of heaven. And watching from the "theater boxes" on either
side are members of the family that commissioned the work.
Santa Susanna—The home of the American Catholic Church
in Rome, Santa Susanna holds Mass in English daily at 18:00
and Sunday at 9:00 and 10:30. Their excellent Web site in
English, www.santasusanna.org, contains tips for travelers
(Via XX Settembre 15, near recommended Via Firenze hotels,
Metro: Repubblica, tel. 06-4201-4554).

North Rome: Villa Borghese and nearby Via Veneto

▲**Villa Borghese**—Rome's scruffy "Central Park" is great for
people–watching (plenty of modern–day Romeos and Juliets).
Take a row on the lake or visit its fine museums.

▲▲▲**Borghese Gallery**—This private museum, filling a cardinal's mansion in the park, was recently restored and offers one of
Europe's most sumptuous art experiences. Observe its slick mandatory reservation system, and you'll enjoy a collection of world–class
Baroque sculpture, including Bernini's *David* and his excited statue
of Apollo chasing Daphne, as well as paintings by Caravaggio,
Raphael, Titian, and Rubens—with manageable crowds.

Cost, Hours, and Reservations: €8, Tue–Sun 9:00–19:30,
may be open until 23:00 on Sat during June–Sept, closed Mon.
No photos are allowed. Reservations are mandatory and easy to
get in English over the Internet (www.ticketeria.it) or by phone:
call 06-32810 (if you get an Italian recording, press 2 for English;
office hours: Mon–Fri 9:00–18:00, Sat 9:00–13:00). Reserve a
minimum of several days in advance for a weekday visit, at least a
week ahead for weekends. ✪ For more on reservations, as well
as a self-guided tour, see Borghese Gallery Tour on page 127.
Etruscan Museum (Villa Giulia Museo Nazionale Etrusco)—
The Etruscan civilization thrived in this part of Italy around 600
B.C., when Rome was an Etruscan town. The Etruscan civilization

is fascinating, but the Villa Giulia Museum is extremely low-tech and in a state of disarray. I don't like it, and Etruscan fans will prefer the Vatican Museum's Etruscan section. Still, the Villa Giulia does have the famous "husband and wife sarcophagus" (a dead couple seeming to enjoy an everlasting banquet from atop their tomb—sixth century B.C. from Cerveteri); the *Apollo from Veio* statue (of textbook fame); and an impressive room filled with gold sheets of Etruscan printing and temple statuary from the Sanctuary of Pyrgi (€4.20, Tue–Sun 8:30–19:30, closed Mon, closes earlier off–season, Piazzale di Villa Giulia 9, tel. 06-322-6571).

▲**Cappuccin Crypt**—If you want bones, this is it. The crypt is below the church of Santa Maria della Immaculata Concezione on Via Veneto, just up from Piazza Barberini. The bones of more than 4,000 monks who died between 1528 and 1870 are in the basement, all artistically arranged for the delight—or disgust— of the always–wide–eyed visitor. The soil in the crypt was brought from Jerusalem 400 years ago, and the monastic message on the wall explains that this is more than just a macabre exercise. Pick up a few of Rome's most interesting postcards (donation, Fri–Wed 9:00–12:00 & 15:00–18:00, closed Thu, Metro: Barberini, tel. 06-487-1185). A painting of St. Francis by Caravaggio is upstairs. Just up the street you'll find the American Embassy, Federal Express, and fancy Via Veneto cafés filled with the poor and envious looking for the rich and famous.

Ara Pacis (Altar of Peace)—This will reopen in 2005 after restoration. In 9 B.C., after victories in Gaul and Spain, Emperor Augustus celebrated the beginning of the Pax Romana by building this altar of peace. Peace is almost worshiped here. The north and south walls show a procession with realistic portraits of the imperial family in Greek Hellenistic style. It's a fine combination of Roman grandeur and Greek elegance. Even during restoration, the altar can sometimes be seen through the windows (a long block west of Via del Corso on Via di Ara Pacis, on east bank of river near Ponte Cavour, nearest Metro: Spagna).

West Rome: Vatican City Neighborhood

Vatican City, a tiny independent country, contains the Vatican Museum (with Michelangelo's Sistine Chapel) and St. Peter's Basilica (with Michelangelo's exquisite *Pietà*). A helpful TI is just to the left of St. Peter's Basilica (Mon–Sat 8:30–18:30,

Vatican City

- ❶ HOTEL ALIMANDI
- ❷ HOTEL SPRING HOUSE
- ❸ HOTEL GERBER
- ❹ HOSTARIA BASTIONI
- ❺ LA RUSTICHELLA
- ❻ ENTRANCE TO VATICAN MUSEUM
- ❼ TOURIST INFO, POST & WC
- ❽ HOTEL SANT' ANNA
- ❾ HOTEL BRAMANTE

closed Sun, tel. 06-6988-1662, Vatican switchboard tel. 06-6982, www.vatican.va). The entrances to St. Peter's and to the Vatican Museum are a 15–minute walk apart (follow the outside of the Vatican wall, which links the 2 sights). The nearest Metro stops still involve a 10–minute walk to either sight: for St. Peter's, the closest stop is Ottaviano; for the Vatican Museum, it's Cipro–Musei Vaticani. For information on Vatican tours, post offices, and the pope's schedule, see page 137.

▲▲▲**St. Peter's Basilica**—There is no doubt: This is the richest and most impressive church on earth. To call it vast is like calling God smart. The church strictly enforces its dress code. Dress modestly—a dress or long pants, shoulders covered (men and women).

Hours: Daily May–Sept 7:00–19:00, Oct–April 7:00–18:00. All are welcome to join the hour–long Mass at the front altar (Mon–Sat 8:30, 10:00, 11:00, 12:00, and 17:00, Sun and holidays 9:00, 10:30, 12:10, 13:00, 16:00, and 17:30). Tours in English are offered daily at 14:15 plus Mon, Wed, and Fri at 15:00 (meet at TI outside the basilica's entrance). The view from the dome is worth the climb (€5 elevator plus 300–step climb, allow an hour to go up and down, May–Sept daily 8:00–18:00, Oct–April daily 8:30–17:00). The best time to visit the church is early or late. ✪ See St. Peter's Basilica Tour on page 164.

▲▲▲**Vatican Museum**—The six kilometers (4 miles) of displays in this immense museum—from ancient statues to Christian frescoes to modern paintings—are topped by the Raphael Rooms and Michelangelo's glorious Sistine Chapel.

Cost and Hours: €10, March–Oct Mon–Fri 8:45–15:45; Sat 8:45–13:45; Nov–Feb Mon–Sat 8:45–13:45, closed Sun except last Sun of the month (when it's free, crowded, and open 8:45–13:45). Last entry is about 90 minutes before the closing time (12:20 when museum closes at 13:45, 14:20 when museum closes at 16:45). Guided two-hour tours in English are offered daily at 11:00 for €16.50 (call 06-6988-4466 to reserve).

The Sistine Chapel may shut down 30 minutes before the museum closes. The museum is closed on many holidays (mainly religious ones), including—for 2003: Jan 1 and 6, Feb 11, March 19, Easter and Easter Monday (April 20 and 21), May 1 and 29, June 19, Aug 14 and 15, Nov 1, and Dec 8 and 25. Modest dress (no short shorts or bare shoulders for men or women) is appropriate and often required. ✪ See Vatican Museum Tour on page 137.

▲**Castel Sant' Angelo**—Built as a tomb for the emperor; used through the Middle Ages as a castle, prison, and place of last refuge for popes under attack; and today, a museum, this giant pile of ancient bricks is packed with history.

Ancient Rome allowed no tombs, not even the emperor's, within its walls. So Hadrian grabbed the most commanding position just outside the walls and across the river and built a towering tomb (circa A.D. 139) well within view of the city. His mausoleum was a huge cylinder (64 meters wide and 21 meters high, or 210 by 70 feet) topped by a cypress grove and crowned by a huge statue of Hadrian himself riding a chariot. For nearly a hundred years, Roman emperors (from Hadrian to Caracalla in A.D. 217) were buried here.

In the year 590, the Archangel Michael appeared above the

mausoleum to Pope Gregory the Great. Sheathing his sword, the angel signaled the end of a plague. The fortress that was Hadrian's mausoleum eventually became a fortified palace, renamed for the "holy angel."

After Dark Age centuries as a fortress and prison, the pope built the elevated corridor connecting Castel Sant' Angelo with the Vatican (1277). Since Rome was repeatedly plundered by invaders, Castel Sant' Angelo was a handy place of last refuge for threatened popes. In anticipation of long sieges, rooms were decorated with papal splendor (you'll see paintings by Crivelli, Signorelli, and Mantegna). In the 16th century, during a sack of Rome by troops of Charles V of Spain, the pope lived inside the castle for months with his entourage of hundreds (an unimaginable ordeal, considering the food service at the top–floor bar).

After you walk around the entire base of the castle, take the small staircase down to the original Roman floor. In the atrium, study the model of the castle in Roman times and imagine the niche in the wall filled with a towering "welcome to my tomb" statue of Hadrian. From here, a ramp leads to the right, spiraling 125 meters (410 feet). While some of the fine brickwork and bits of mosaic survive, the marble veneer is long gone (notice the holes in the wall which held it in place). At the end of the ramp, stairs climb to the room where the ashes of the emperors were kept. These stairs continue to the top, where you'll find the papal apartments. Don't miss the Sala del Tesoro (treasury), where the wealth of the Vatican was locked up in a huge chest. Do miss the 58 rooms of the military museum. The views from the top are great—pick out landmarks as you stroll around—and a restful coffee with a view of St. Peter's is worth the price.

Cost, Hours, Tours: €5, Tue–Sun 9:00–19:00, plus June–Sept Sat 21:00–23:45, closed Mon. You can take an English–language tour with an audioguide (€4) or live guide (€5, Tue–Fri at 15:00, Sat at 12:15 & 16:30, confirm times, tel. 06-3996-7600, Metro: Lepanto or bus #64, near Vatican City).

Ponte Sant' Angelo—The bridge leading to Castel Sant' Angelo was built by Hadrian for quick and regal access from downtown to his tomb. The three middle arches are actually Roman originals and a fine example of the empire's engineering expertise. The angels were designed by Bernini and finished by his students.

Southwest Rome: Trastevere

Trastevere is the colorful neighborhood across *(tras)* the Tiber *(tevere)* River. Trastevere offers the best look at medieval–village Rome. The action marches to the chime of the church bells. Go there and wander. Wonder. Be a poet. This is Rome's Left Bank.

This proud neighborhood was long a working–class area. Now that it's becoming trendy, high rents are driving out the source of so much color. Still, it's a great people scene, especially at night. Wander the backstreets (for restaurant recommendations, see page 244).

To get to Trastevere, taxi or ride the bus (from Vatican area—#23; or from Via Nazionale hotels—take the #40 express to Piazza Belli just over bridge, or catch #64, #70, #115, or #640 to Largo Argentina, then transfer to tram #8 and get off at Piazza Mastai).

Santa Maria in Trastevere: The Church and Square—Start your exploratory stroll at Piazza di Santa Maria in Trastevere. While today's fountain is from the 17th century, there has been a fountain here since Roman times.

Santa Maria in Trastevere, one of Rome's oldest churches, was made a basilica in the fourth century, when Christianity was legalized (free, daily 7:30–13:00 & 15:00–19:00). It was the first church dedicated to the Virgin Mary. The portico (covered area just outside the door) is decorated with fascinating ancient fragments filled with early Christian symbolism. Most of what you see today dates from around the 12th century, but the granite columns come from an ancient Roman temple, and the ancient basilica floor plan (and ambience) survive. The 12th–century mosaics behind the altar are striking and notable for their portrayal of Mary—the first to show her at the throne with Jesus in Heaven. Look below the scenes from the life of Mary to see ahead–of–their–time paintings (by Cavallini, from 1300), predating the Renaissance by 100 years.

Gianicolo Hill Viewpoint—From this park atop a hill, the city views are superb, and the walk to the top holds a treat for architects. Start your walk at Trastevere's Piazza di San Cosimato, and follow Via Luciano Manara to Via Garibaldi, at the base of the hill. Via Garibaldi winds its way up the side of the hill to the church of San Pietro in Montorio. To the right of the church, in a small courtyard, is the Tempietto by Bramante. This tiny church, built to commemorate the spot where St. Peter was martyred, is considered a jewel of Italian Renaissance architecture. Continuing up the hill, Via Garibaldi connects to Passeggiata del Gianicolo. From here, you'll find a pleasant park with panoramic city views. Ponder the many Victorian–era statues, including that of baby–carrying, gun–wielding, horse–riding Anita Garibaldi. She was the Brazilian

Trastevere

❶ HOTEL SANTA MARIA	❺ OSTERIA PONTE SISTO
❷ TAVERNA DEL MORO DA TONY	❻ PANIFICIO ARNESE BAKERY
❸ TRATTORIA DA LUCIA	❼ GELATERIA
❹ TRATTORIA DE OLINDO	

wife of the revolutionary General Giuseppe Garibaldi, who helped forge a united Italy in the late 19th century.

Linking Trastevere with "Night Walk Across Rome"—You can easily walk from Trastevere to Campo de' Fiori to link up with the beginning of the Night Walk Across Rome (page 52): From Trastevere's church square (Piazza di Santa Maria), take Via del Moro to the river and cross at Ponte Sisto, a pedestrian bridge with a good view of St. Peter's dome. Continue straight ahead for one block. Take the first left, which leads down Via di Capo di Ferro through the scary and narrow darkness to Piazza Farnese, with the imposing Palazzo Farnese. Michelangelo contributed to the facade of this palace, now the French Embassy. The fountains on the square feature huge, one-piece granite hot tubs from the ancient Roman Baths of Caracalla. One block from there (opposite the palace) is the atmospheric square of Campo de' Fiori.

South Rome

▲St. Paul's Outside the Walls (Basilica San Paolo Fuori le Mura)—One of the greatest churches in Christendom, St. Paul's was originally built in 324, then destroyed by fire in the 1820s. Today it's mammoth and pristine, rebuilt true to the ancient basilica plan. It feels sterile, but in a good way—like you're already in heaven. Along with St. Peter's Basilica, San Giovanni in Laterano, and Santa Maria Maggiore, this church is part of the Vatican rather than Italy. St. Paul is supposed to be buried under the altar (without his head, which San Giovanni in Laterano got). Alabaster windows light the vast interior, fifth–century mosaics decorate the triumphal arch leading to the altar, and mosaic portraits of all 264 popes, from St. Peter to John Paul II, ring the place—with blank spots ready for future popes. Find John Paul II (to right of the high altar: Jo Paulus II, no date) and John Paul I (to his right, with a reign of one month and three days). Wander the ornate yet peaceful cloister (closed 13:00–15:00). The courtyard leading up to the church is typical of early Christian churches; even the first St. Peter's had this kind of welcoming zone (free, daily 7:00–18:00, modest dress code enforced, Via Ostiense 186, Metro: San Paolo).

▲Montemartini Museum (Musei Capitolini Centrale Montemartini)—This museum houses a dreamy collection of 400 ancient statues, set evocatively in a classic 1932 electric power plant among generators and Metropolis–type cast-iron machinery. While the art is not as famous as the collections you'll see downtown, the effect is fun and memorable—and you'll encounter absolutely no tourists (€4.20, Tue–Sun 9:30–19:00, closed Mon, Via Ostiense 106, a short walk from Metro: Garbatella, tel. 06-574-8042).

Baths of Caracalla (Terme di Caracalla)—Today it's just a shell—a huge shell—with all of its sculptures and most of its mosaics moved to museums. Inaugurated by Emperor Caracalla in A.D. 216, this massive complex could accommodate 1,600 visitors at a time. Today you'll see a two–story, roofless brick building surrounded by a garden, bordered by ruined walls. The two large rooms at either end of the building were used for exercise. In between the exercise rooms was a pool flanked by two small mosaic–floored dressing rooms. Niches in the walls once held statues. In its day, this was a remarkable place to hang out. For ancient Romans, the baths were a social experience.

The Baths of Caracalla functioned until Goths severed the aqueducts in the sixth century. In modern times, operas were performed here from 1938 to 1993. For the same reason concerts no longer take place in the Forum—to keep the ruins from becoming more ruined—the performances were discontinued (€5, covered

South Rome

by €20 combo–ticket, Mon 9:00–17:30, Tue–Sun 9:00–19:30, last entry 1 hour before closing, audioguide-€4, fine €8 guidebook—can read in shaded garden while sitting on a chunk of column, Metro: Circus Maximus, and a 5–min walk south along Via delle Terme di Caracalla, tel. 06-575-8628). Several of the baths' statues are now in Rome's Octagonal Hall; the immense *Toro Farnese* (a marble sculpture of a bull surrounded by people) snorts in Naples' Archaeological Museum.

Testaccio—Four fascinating but lesser sights cluster at the Piramide Metro stop between the Colosseum and E.U.R., in the gritty Testaccio neighborhood. (This is a quick and easy stop as you return from E.U.R. or when changing trains en route to Ostia Antica.)

Working–class since ancient times, Testaccio has recently

Testaccio

gone trendy–bohemian, and visitors will wander through an awkward mix of yuppie and proletarian worlds, not noticing—but perhaps feeling—the "keep Testaccio for the Testaccians" graffiti.

Pyramid of Gaius Cestius:
The Marc Antony/Cleopatra scandal (around the time of Christ) brought exotic Egyptian styles into vogue. A rich Roman magistrate, Gaius Cestius, had a pyramid built as his tomb. Made of brick covered in marble, it was completed in just 330 days (as stated in its Latin inscription) and fell far short of Egyptian pyramid standards. Later incorporated into the Aurelian Wall, it's now next to the Piramide Metro stop.

Porta Ostiense: This formidable gate (also next to Piramide Metro stop) is from the Aurelian Wall, begun in the third century under Emperor Aurelius. The wall, which encircled the city, was 20 kilometers (12 miles) long and eight meters (26 feet) high, with 14 main gates and 380 22–meter–tall (72-foot) towers. Most of what you'll see today is circa A.D. 400. The barbarians reconstructed this gate in the sixth century. (For more on the wall, visit the Museum of the Walls at Porta San Sebastian; see "Ancient Appian Way," below.)

Protestant Cemetery: The *Cimitero Acattolico per gli Stranieri al Testaccio* (cemetery for the burial of non–Catholic foreigners) is a Romantic tomb–filled park, running along the wall just beyond the pyramid. From the Piramide Metro stop, walk between the pyramid and the Roman gate on Via Persichetti, then go left on Caio Cestio to the gate of the cemetery. Ring the bell (donation box, April–Sept Tue–Sun 9:00–18:00, Oct–March 9:00–17:00, closed Mon).

Originally, none of the Protestant epitaphs were allowed to make any mention of heaven. Signs direct visitors to the graves of notable non–Catholics who died in Rome since 1738. Many of the buried were diplomats. And many, such as poets Shelley and Keats, were from the Romantic Age; they came on the Grand Tour and— "captivated by the fatal charms of Rome," as Shelley wrote—never left. Head left toward the pyramid to find Keats' tomb, in the far corner. At the pyramid, look down on Matilde Talli's cat hospice (flier at the gate). Volunteers use donations to care for these "Guardians of the Departed" who "provide loyal companionship to these dead."

Monte Testaccio: Just behind the Protestant Cemetery (as you leave, turn left and continue 2 blocks down Caio Cestio) is a 35–meter–tall (115-foot) ancient trash mountain. It's made of broken *testae*—broken earthenware jars used to haul mostly wine 2,000 years ago, when this was a gritty port warehouse district. After 500 years of sloppy dock work, Rome's lowly eighth hill was built. Because the caves dug into the hill stay cool, trendy bars, clubs, and restaurants compete with gritty car–repair places for a spot. The neighborhood was once known for a huge slaughter- house and a Gypsy camp that squatted inside an old military base. Now it's home to the Villagio Globale, a site for concerts and techno–raves. For a youthful and lively night scene, adventurers might consider a trip out to Monte Testaccio (Metro: Piramide).

Ancient Appian Way (Via Appia Antica)

Since the fourth century B.C., this has been Rome's gateway to the East. The first section was perfectly straight. It was the larg- est, widest, fastest road ever, the wonder of its day, called the "Queen of Roads." Eventually, this most important of Roman roads stretched 700 kilometers (430 miles) to the port of Brindisi— where boats sailed for Greece and Egypt. Twenty–nine such roads fanned out from Rome. Just as Hitler built the autobahn system in anticipation of empire maintenance, the emperors realized the military and political value of a good road system. A central strip accommodated animal–powered vehicles, and elevated sidewalks served pedestrians. As it left Rome, the road was lined with tombs and funerary monuments. Imagine a funeral procession passing under the pines and cypress and past a long line of pyramids, private mini–temples, altars, and tombs.

Hollywood created the famous image of the Appian Way lined with Spartacus and his gang of defeated and crucified slave rebels. This image is only partially accurate. Spartacus was killed in battle.

Tourist's Appian Way: The road starts about three kilometers (less than 2 miles) south of the Colosseum at the massive San Sebastian Gate. The Museum of the Walls, located at the gate, offers an interesting look at Roman defense and a chance to scramble along a stretch of the ramparts (€2.60, Tue–Sun 9:00–19:00, closed Mon, tel. 06-7047-5284). A kilometer (0.6 mile) down the road are the two most historic and popular catacombs, those of San Callisto and San Sebastian (described below). Beyond that, the road becomes pristine and traffic–free, popular for biking and hiking.

To reach the Appian Way, take the Archeobus from Piazza Venezia (see "Tours of Rome," page 25) or take the Metro to the Colli Albani stop, then catch bus #660 to Via Appia Antica—its last stop and the start of an interesting stretch of the ancient road. The segment between the third and 11th milestones is most interesting.

You can rent bikes at the Appian park office on weekends and holidays. To reach the office by bus (Archeobus or city bus), get off at the park entrance—the Sede Parco Appia Antica stop (€2.50/hr, Via Appia Antica 42, tel. 06-512-6314, www.parcoappiaantica.org).

▲▲**Catacombs**—The catacombs are burial places for (mostly) Christians who died in ancient Roman times. By law, no one was allowed to be buried within the walls of Rome. While pagan Romans were into cremation, Christians preferred to be buried. But land was expensive and most Christians were poor. A few wealthy, landowning Christians allowed their land to be used as burial places.

The 40 or so known catacombs circle Rome about five kilometers (3 miles) from its center. From the first through the fifth centuries, Christians dug an estimated 600 kilometers (375 miles) of tomb–lined tunnels, with networks of galleries as many as five layers deep. The tufa—soft and easy to cut, but becoming very hard when exposed to air—was perfect for the job. The Christians burrowed many layers deep for two reasons: to get more mileage out of the donated land and to be near martyrs and saints already buried there. Bodies were wrapped in linen (like Christ's). Since they figured the Second Coming was imminent, there was no interest in embalming the body.

When Emperor Constantine legalized Christianity in 313, Christians had a new, interesting problem. There would be no more persecuted martyrs to bind them and inspire them. Thus the early martyrs and popes assumed more importance, and Christians began making pilgrimages to their burial places in the catacombs.

In the 800s, when barbarian invaders started ransacking the tombs, Christians moved the relics of saints and martyrs to the safety of churches in the city center. For a thousand years, the catacombs were forgotten. Around 1850, they were excavated and became part of the romantic Grand Tour of Europe.

Finding abandoned plates and utensils from ritual meals in the candlelit galleries led 18th– and 19th–century Romantics to guess that persecuted Christians hid out and lived in these catacombs. This Romantic legend grew. But catacombs were not used for hiding out. They are simply early Christian burial grounds. With a million people in Rome, the easiest way for the 10,000 or so early Christians to hide out was not to camp in the catacombs (which everyone, including the government, knew about), but to melt into the city.

The underground tunnels, while empty of bones, are rich in early Christian symbolism, which functioned as a secret language. The dove symbolized the soul. You'll see it quenching its thirst (worshiping), with an olive branch (at rest), or happily perched (in paradise). Peacocks, known for their "incorruptible flesh,"

symbolized immortality. The shepherd with a lamb on his shoulders was the "good shepherd," the first portrayal of Christ as a kindly leader of his flock. The fish was used because the first letters of these words—"Jesus Christ, Son of God, Savior"—

spelled "fish" in Greek. And the anchor is a cross in disguise. A second–century bishop had written on his tomb: "All who understand these things, pray for me." You'll see pictures of people praying with their hands raised up—the custom at the time.

Catacomb tours are essentially the same. Which one you take is not important. The **Catacombs of San Callisto** (a.k.a. Callixtus), the official cemetery for the Christians of Rome and burial place of third–century popes, is the most historic. Sixteen bishops (early popes) were buried here. Buy your €5 ticket and wait for your language to be called. They move lots of people quickly. If one group seems ridiculously large (over 50 people), wait for the next tour in English (Thu–Tue 8:30–12:00 & 14:30–17:30, closed Wed and Feb, closes at 17:00 in winter, Via Appia Antica 110, tel. 06-5130-1580). Dig this: The catacombs have a

Web site—www.catacombe.roma.it—focusing mainly on San Callisto, featuring photos, site info, and a history.

The **Catacombs of San Sebastian** (Sebastiano) are 300 meters (984 feet) farther down the road (€5, Mon–Sat 8:30–12:00 & 14:30–17:30, closed Sun and Nov, closes at 17:00 in winter, Via Appia Antica 136, tel. 06-5130-1580).

E.U.R.

In the late 1930s, Italy's dictator, Benito Mussolini, planned an international exhibition to show off the wonders of his fascist society. But these wonders brought us World War II, and Il Duce's celebration never happened. The unfinished mega–project was completed in the 1950s and now houses government offices and big, obscure museums.

If Hitler and Mussolini won the war, our world might look like E.U.R. (pronounced "ay-oor"). Hike down E.U.R.'s wide, pedestrian–mean boulevards. Patriotic murals, aren't–you–proud–to–be–an–extreme–right–winger pillars, and stern squares decorate the soulless, planned grid and stark office blocks. Boulevards named for Astronomy, Electronics, Social Security, and Beethoven are more exhausting than inspirational. Today E.U.R. is worth a trip for its Museum of Roman Civilization (described below).

The Metro skirts E.U.R. with three stops (10 min from the Colosseum). Use E.U.R. Magliana for the "Square Colosseum" and E.U.R. Fermi for the Museum of Roman Civilization (both described below). Consider walking 30 minutes from the palace to the museum through the center of E.U.R.

From the Magliana subway stop, stairs lead uphill to the **Palace of the Civilization of Labor (Palazzo del Civilta del Lavoro)**, the essence of fascist architecture. With its giant, no–questions–asked, patriotic statues and its black–and–white simplicity, this is E.U.R.'s tallest building and landmark. It's understandably nick-named the "Square Colosseum." Around the corner, Café Palombini is still decorated in a 1930s style and is now quite trendy with young Romans (daily 7:00–24:00, good gelato, pastries, and snacks, Piazzale Adenauer 12, tel. 06-591-1700).

▲**Museum of Roman Civilization (Museo della Civilta Romana)**—With 59 rooms filled with plaster casts and models

E.U.R.

illustrating the greatness of classical Rome, this vast and heavy museum gives a strangely lifeless, close–up look at Rome. Each room has a theme, from military tricks to musical instruments. One long hall is filled with casts of the reliefs of Trajan's Column. The highlight is the 1:250–scale model of Constantine's Rome—circa A.D. 300 (€4.20, Tue–Sat 9:00–18:45, Sun 9:00–13:30, closed Mon, Piazza G. Agnelli, from Metro: E.U.R. Fermi, walk 10 min up Via dell' Arte, you'll see its colonnade on the right, tel. 06-592-6041).

NIGHT WALK ACROSS ROME

Rome can be grueling. But a fine way to enjoy this historian's rite of passage is an evening walk lacing together Rome's floodlit night spots and fine urban spaces with real-life theater vignettes.

Sitting so close to a Bernini fountain that traffic noises evaporate; jostling with local teenagers to see all the gelato flavors; enjoying lovers straddling more than the bench; jaywalking past flak-proof-vested *polizia*; and marveling at the ramshackle elegance that softens this brutal city for those who were born here and can imagine living nowhere else—these are the flavors of Rome best tasted after dark.

Campo de' Fiori

Start at the Campo de' Fiori (Field of Flowers), my favorite outdoor dining room after dark (see the Eating chapter, page 244). The statue of Giordano Bruno, a heretic who was burned in 1600 for believing the world was round and not the center of the universe, marks the center of this great and colorful square. Bruno overlooks a busy produce market in the morning and strollers after sundown. This neighborhood is still known for its free spirit and occasional demonstrations. When the statue of Bruno was erected in 1889, local riots overcame Vatican protests against honoring a heretic. Bruno faces his executioner, the Vatican Chancellory (the big white building in the corner a bit to his right), while his pedestal reads: "And the flames rose up."

At the east end of the square (behind Bruno), the ramshackle apartments are built right into the old outer wall of ancient Rome's mammoth Theater of Pompey. This entertainment complex covered several city blocks, stretching from here to Largo Argentina. Julius Caesar was assassinated in the Theater of Pompey, where the Senate was renting space.

Night Walk Across Rome

The square is lined with and surrounded by fun eateries. Bruno faces La Carbonara, the only real restaurant on the square. The Forno, next door, is a popular place for hot and tasty take-out *pizza bianco* (plain but spicy pizza bread).

• *If Bruno did a hop, step, and jump forward, then turned right on Via dei Baullari and marched 200 meters (650 feet), he'd cross the busy Corso Vittorio Emanuele and find . . .*

Piazza Navona

Rome's most interesting
night scene features street
music, artists, fire-eaters,
local Casanovas, ice cream,
fountains by Bernini, and
outdoor cafés (worthy of a
splurge if you've got time to
sit and enjoy the human
river of Italy).

This oblong square retains the shape of the original racetrack
that was built by the emperor Domitian. (You can still see the
ruins of the original entrance. Exit the square at the north end,
take an immediate left, and look down to the left 7 meters, or
23 feet, below the current street level.) Since ancient times, the
square has been a center of Roman life. In the 1800s, the city
would flood the square to cool off the neighborhood.

The **Four Rivers fountain** in the center is the most famous
fountain by the man who remade Rome in Baroque style, Gian

Lorenzo Bernini. Four burly
river gods (representing the
four continents that existed
in 1650) support an obelisk,
while the water of the world
gushes everywhere. The
Nile has his head covered
(since the headwaters were
unknown then). The Ganges
holds an oar. The Danube
turns to admire the obelisk, which originally stood here in
Domitian's stadium. And the Rio de la Plata from Uruguay
tumbles backward in shock, wondering how he ever made the top
four. Bernini enlivens the fountain with horses plunging through
the rocks and exotic flora and fauna from these newly discovered
lands. Homesick Texans may want to find the armadillo. (It's the
big, weird armor-plated creature behind the Plata river statue.)

The Plata river god is gazing upward at the church of Saint
Agnes, worked on by Bernini's former student turned rival,
Borromini. Borromini's concave facade helps reveal the dome
and epitomizes the curved symmetry of Baroque. Tour guides
say that Bernini designed his river god to look horrified at Borromini's work. Or he may be shielding his eyes from St. Agnes'
nakedness, as she was stripped before being martyred. But the
fountain was completed two years before Borromini even started
work on the church.

At the **Tre Scalini** café (near the fountain), sample some *tartufo* "death-by-chocolate" ice cream, world-famous among connoisseurs of ice cream and chocolate alike (€3.50 to go, €7 at a table, closed Wed). Seriously

admire a painting by a struggling artist. Request "Country Roads" from an Italian guitar player, and don't be surprised when he knows it. Listen to the white noise of gushing water and exuberant humans.

• *Leave Piazza Navona directly across from Tre Scalini café, go east past rose peddlers and palm readers, jog left around the guarded building, and follow the brown sign to the Pantheon. The Pantheon is straight down Via del Salvatore (cheap pizza place on left just before the Pantheon, WC at McDonald's).*

The Pantheon

Sit for a while under the floodlit and moonlit Pantheon's portico.

The 12-meter (39-foot) single-piece granite columns of the Pantheon's entrance show the scale the ancient Romans built on. The columns support a triangular, Greek-style roof with an inscription that says that "M. Agrippa" built it. In fact, it was

built (*"fecit"*) by Emperor Hadrian (A.D. 120), who gave credit to the builder of an earlier structure. This impressive entranceway gives no clue that the greatest wonder of the building is inside—a domed

room that inspired later domes, including Michelangelo's St. Peter's and Brunelleschi's Duomo (in Florence). Notice how the pavement slants down from McDonald's to the Pantheon, showing how high modern Rome has built on ancient rubble.

✪ For more information, see Pantheon Tour on page 90.
• *With your back to the Pantheon, veer to the right down Via Olfeni.*

From the Pantheon to Piazza Colonna

After passing Bar Pantheon, you'll see **Tazza d'Oro Casa del Caffè**, one of Rome's top coffee shops, dating back to the days

when this area was licensed to roast coffee beans. Look back at
the fine view of the Pantheon from here. Via Olfeni leads to
Piazza Capranica.

   Piazza Capranica is home to the big, plain, Florentine
Renaissance–style Palazzo Capranica. Big shots, like the Capranica
family, built stubby towers on their palaces—not for any military
use, but just to show off. Leave the piazza to the right of the palace,
between the palace and the church. Via in Aquiro leads to a sixth-
century B.C. **Egyptian obelisk** (taken as a trophy by Augustus
after his victory in Egypt over Mark Antony and Cleopatra).
Walk into the guarded square past the obelisk and face the huge
parliament building.

   A short detour to the left (past Albergo National) brings you
to Rome's most famous gelateria. **Gelateria Caffè Pasticceria
Giolitti** is cheap to go or elegant and splurge-worthy for a sit
among classy locals (open daily until very late, Via Uffici del
Vicario 40); get your gelato in a cone (*cono*) or cup (*bicchierini*).
You'll find better gelato at the nearby **Gelateria della Palma**
(2 blocks in front of Pantheon, Via della Maddalena 20/23).
Or head directly from the parliament building into the next,
even grander square.

   Piazza Colonna features a huge second-century column
honoring Marcus Aurelius. The big, important-looking palace
is the prime minister's residence.

• *Cross Via del Corso, Rome's noisy main drag, jog right (around the
Y-shaped shopping gallery from 1928), and head down Via dei Sabini
to the roar of the water, light, and people of the Trevi Fountain.*

The Trevi Fountain

The Trevi Fountain shows how Rome took full advantage of the
abundance of water brought into the city by its great aqueducts. This
watery Baroque avalanche was built in 1762 by Nicola Salvi, hired by

a pope celebrating his reopening of
the ancient aqueduct that powers
it. Salvi used the palace behind the
fountain as a theatrical backdrop
for Neptune's "entrance" into the
square. Neptune surfs through his
watery kingdom while Triton blows
his conch shell. (The water, after
tickling Neptune's toes, goes underground, then bubbles up again at
Bernini's Four Rivers Fountain in
Piazza Navona.)

   The square is always lively,

with lucky Romeos clutching dates while unlucky ones clutch beers. Romantics toss a coin over their shoulder, thinking it will give them a wish and assure their return to Rome. That may sound silly, but every year I go through this touristic ritual... and it actually seems to work.

Take some time to people-watch (whisper a few breathy *bellos* or *bellas*) before leaving.

• *Face the fountain, then go past it on the right down Via delle Stamperia to Via del Triton. Cross the busy street and continue to the Spanish Steps (ask, "Dov'è Piazza di Spagna?"—Spagna rhymes with "lasagna,") a few blocks and thousands of dollars of shopping opportunities away.*

Spanish Steps *(Piazza di Spagna)*

The Piazza di Spagna, with the very popular Spanish Steps, got its name 300 years ago when this was the site of the Spanish Embassy. It's been the hangout of many Romantics over the years (Keats, Wagner, Openshaw, Goethe, and others). The

British poet John Keats pondered his mortality, then died in the pink building on the right side of the steps. Fellow Romantic Lord Byron lived across the square at #66.

The Sinking Boat Fountain at the foot of the steps, which was done by Bernini or his father, Pietro, is powered by an aqueduct. All of Rome's fountains are aqueduct-powered; their spurts are determined by the water pressure provided by the various aqueducts. This one, for instance, is much weaker than Trevi's gush.

The piazza is a thriving night scene. Window-shop along Via Condotti, which stretches away from the steps. This is where Gucci and other big names cater to the trendsetting jet set. Facing the Spanish Steps, you can walk right about a block to tour one of the world's biggest and most lavish McDonald's (salad bar, clean WC). There's a taxi stand in the courtyard outside McDonald's; or, if you'd prefer, the Spagna Metro stop (usually open until 23:30) is just to the left of the Spanish Steps, ready to zip you home.

COLOSSEUM
TOUR

Rome has many layers—modern, Baroque, Renaissance, Christian. But let's face it, "Rome" is Caesars, gladiators, chariots, centurions, *"Et tu, Brute,"* trumpet fanfares, and thumbs up or thumbs down. That's the Rome we'll look at. Our "Caesar Shuffle" begins with the downtown core of ancient Rome, the Colosseum. A logical next stop is the Forum, just next door (and the next chapter), past the Arch of Constantine.

Orientation

Cost: €8 (exact change preferred), includes Palatine Hill visit within 24 hours; also covered by €20 combo-ticket.

Hours: Daily 9:00–19:00, or an hour before sunset.

Avoid Long Lines: Instead of waiting in line (sometimes an hour long) at the Colosseum to purchase a ticket, you have three good alternatives:

1. Buy your ticket at either of the two rarely crowded Palatine Hill entrances near the Colosseum—there's one inside the Forum and another on Via di San Gregorio (facing Forum entry, with Colosseum at your back, go left on street). This €8 ticket includes entry to both the Colosseum and Palatine (valid for 24 hours).

2. Consider buying a €20 combo-ticket at a less-crowded sight. The combo-ticket—covering the Colosseum, Palatine Hill (see tour, page 77), National Museum of Rome (see tour, page 106), Museum of the Bath (see page 104), Baths of Caracalla, and more—allows you to walk right past the Colosseum ticket line,

Ancient Rome

through the turnstile, and into the Colosseum. Buy it at any of the included sights.

3. You can reserve your ticket in advance for an additional €1.50 fee by calling 06-3996-7700 (automated info in English, pay for ticket at side window of Colosseum's ticket office).

Getting There: The Metro stop, Colosseo, lets you out just across the street from the monument. Look out for young street thieves (see page 21).

Information: Outside the entrance of the Colosseum, vendors sell handy little *Rome, Past and Present* books with plastic overlays to un-ruin the ruins (marked €11, offer €8). For a fee, the modern-day gladiators snuff out their cigarettes and pose for photos. A WC is behind the Colosseum (facing ticket entrance, go right; WC is under stairway). Tel. 06-3974-9907.

Tour: An audioguide is available at the ticket office (€4 for 2 hours of use). Guided tours in English depart several times per day and last about one hour (€3.50).

Length of Our Tour: Allow 45 minutes.

Cuisine Art: For a quick lunch, climb the steps above the WC and cross the busy street to the cafés (with expansive views of the Colosseum). However, for a better value (but no views at all), see my listings on page 244.

Exterior of Colosseum

• *View the Colosseum from the Forum fence, across the street from the "Colosseo" subway station.*

Built when the Roman Empire was at its peak (A.D. 80), the Colosseum represents Rome at its grandest. The Flavian Amphitheater (its real name) was an arena for gladiator contests and public spectacles. When killing became a spectator sport, the Romans wanted to share the fun with as many people as possible. They did this by outbuilding the Greeks. The Greeks built their theaters into hillsides. The Romans, in essence, stuck two Greek theaters together to create a freestanding amphitheater. The outside (where slender cypress trees stand today) was decorated with a 33-meter-tall (100-foot) bronze statue of Nero that gleamed in the sunlight. The final structure was colossal—a "coloss-eum," the wonder of its age. It could accommodate 50,000 roaring fans (100,000 thumbs).

The Romans pioneered the use of the rounded arch and concrete, enabling them to build on this colossal scale. The exterior is a skeleton of 3.5 million cubic feet of travertine stone. (Each of the pillars flanking the ground-level arches weighs 5 tons.) It took 200 ox-drawn wagons shuttling back and forth every day for four years just to bring the stone here. Iron pegs held the larger stones together—notice the small holes that pockmark the sides. When it was done, the whole thing was faced with shining marble (still visible on the top level).

The exterior says a lot about the Romans. They were great engineers, not artists. While the essential structure is Roman, the facade is Greek, decorated with the three types of Greek columns—Doric (bottom), Ionic (middle), and Corinthian (top). Originally, copies of Greek statues stood in the arches of the upper two stories. The Colosseum was more functional than beautiful. If ancient Romans visited the United States today as tourists, they'd send home postcards of our greatest works of "art"—freeways.

Only a third of the original Colosseum remains. Earthquakes destroyed some of it, but most was carted off as easy pre-cut stones for other buildings during the Middle Ages and Renaissance.

• *Enter by the south entrance—to your right, past the Arch of Constantine. Buy your ticket—or if you've already purchased a ticket elsewhere, bypass the line and go inside. Move up to a railing overlooking the arena.*

Interior of Colosseum

You're at the "50-yard line" on arena level. What you see now are the underground passages beneath the playing surface. The oval-shaped arena (86 by 50 meters, or 282 by 165 feet) was originally covered with boards, then sprinkled with sand (*arena* in Latin).

Like modern stadiums, the spectators ringed the playing area in bleacher seats that slant up from the arena floor. To build these bleachers, they made a shell of brick, then filled it in with concrete. The brick masses around you supported the first small tier of seats, and you can see two larger, slanted supports higher up. A few marble seats survive (at the right end). The whole thing was topped with an enormous canvas awning that could be hoisted across by armies of sailors to provide shade for the spectators—the first domed stadium.

"Hail, Caesar! *(Ave, Cesare!)* We who are about to die salute you!" The gladiators would enter the arena from the left end, parade around to the sound of trumpets, stop at the emperor's box (where you're standing), raise their weapons, shout this salute—and the fights would begin. The fights pitted men against men, men against beasts, and beasts against beasts.

• *If a walkway stretches across the arena—and if it's open—you can contemplate the games from a gladiator-eye view, right in the center of the action. Picture 50,000 screaming people around you (did gladiators get stage fright?), and imagine that they hate you and want to see you die.*

The games began with a few warm-up acts—watching dogs bloody themselves attacking porcupines, female gladiators fighting each other, or a dwarf battling a one-legged man. Then came the main event—the gladiators.

Some wielded swords, protected only with a shield and a heavy helmet. Others represented fighting fishermen, with a net to snare opponents and a trident to spear them. The gladiators were usually slaves, criminals, or poor people who got their chance for freedom, wealth, and fame in the ring. They learned to fight in training schools, then battled their way up the ranks. The best

were rewarded like our modern sports stars with fan clubs, great wealth, and, yes, product endorsements.

The animals came from all over the world: lions, tigers, and bears (oh my!), crocodiles, elephants, and hippos (not to mention exotic human "animals" from the "barbarian" lands). They were kept in cages beneath the arena floor, then lifted up in elevators. Released at floor level, the animals would pop out from behind blinds into the arena—the gladiator didn't know where, when, or by what he'd be attacked. (This brought howls of laughter from the hardened fans in the cheap seats who had a better view of the action.) Nets ringed the arena to protect the crowd. The stadium was inaugurated with a 100-day festival in which 2,000 men and 9,000 animals were killed. Colosseum employees squirted perfumes around the stadium to mask the stench of blood.

If a gladiator fell helpless to the ground, his opponent would approach the emperor's box and ask: Should he live or die? Sometimes the emperor left the decision to the crowd, who would judge based on how valiantly the man had fought. They would make their decision—thumbs up or thumbs down. When a brave gladiator died, they'd drain his blood and sell it as a tonic.

Did they throw Christians to the lions like in the movies? Christians were definitely thrown to the lions, made to fight gladiators, crucified, and burned alive...but probably not here in this particular stadium. Maybe, but probably not.

Rome was a nation of warriors that built an empire by conquest. The battles fought against Germans, Egyptians, barbarians, and strange animals were played out daily here in the Colosseum for the benefit of city-slicker bureaucrats who got vicarious thrills watching brutes battle to the death. The contests were always free, sponsored by politicians to buy votes or to keep Rome's growing mass of unemployed rabble off the streets.

• *With these scenes in mind, wander around. Climb to the upper deck for a more colossal view. (There are stairs near either long end, and an elevator in the east corner—that is, at the long end which is to your right as you enter.) On the upper level, there's a bookstore at the west corner (that is, at the far end to the left as you enter) and temporary exhibits at the northeast end.*

The exit moves around a bit; it may be opposite the entrance (along Via dei Fori Imperiali where the Colosseo Metro stop is) or at the west corner (to your left as you enter), near the Forum.

After you exit, head to the Arch of Constantine (between the Colosseum and Forum, at the west corner of the Colosseum).

Arch of Constantine

If you are a Christian, were raised a Christian, or simply belong to a so-called "Christian nation," ponder this arch. It marks one of the great turning points in history—the military coup that made Christianity mainstream. In A.D. 312, Emperor Constantine defeated his rival Maxentius in one crucial battle. The night

before, he had seen a vision of
a cross in the sky. Constantine
became sole emperor and
promptly legalized Christianity.
With this one battle, a once-
obscure Jewish sect with a handful of followers was now the
state religion of the entire Western world. In A.D. 300, you could

be killed for being a Christian; later, you could be killed for not
being one. Church enrollment boomed.

By the way, don't look too closely at the reliefs decorating
this arch. By the fourth century, Rome was on its way down.
Rather than struggle with original carvings, the makers of this
arch plugged in bits and pieces scavenged from existing monuments. The arch is newly restored and looking great. But any
meaning read into the stone will be very jumbled.

• *The Roman Forum* (Foro Romano) *is to the right of the arch, 100
meters (330 feet) away. If you're ready for a visit, see the next chapter.*

ROMAN FORUM TOUR

Heart of the Empire

The Forum was the political, religious, and commercial center of the city. Rome's most important temples and halls of justice were here. This was the place for religious processions, elections, important speeches, and parades by conquering generals. As Rome's Empire expanded, these few acres of land became the center of the civilized world.

Orientation

Cost: Free. (There's an €8 charge to visit the Palatine Hill above the Forum; see next chapter.)

Hours: Daily 9:00–19:00, or an hour before dark.

Tip: The ancient paving at the Forum is uneven. Wear sturdy shoes to avoid sore feet.

Getting There: The closest Metro stop is Colosseo. The Forum's main entrance—where this tour begins—is near the Arch of Constantine and the Colosseum.

Information: Street vendors between the Colosseum and Forum sell small *Rome, Past and Present* books with plastic overlays that restore the ruins (marked €11, offer €8). Tel. 06-3974-9907.

Tour: A €4 audioguide helps decipher the rubble (rent at gift shop at entrance on Via dei Fori Imperiali). Guided tours in English are offered once daily (€3.50); ask for information at the ticket booth at the Palatine Hill (near Arch of Titus).

Length of Our Tour: Allow one hour.

Overview

• *Walk through the entrance nearest the Colosseum, hiking up the ramp marked "Via Sacra." Stand next to the triumphal Arch of Titus and look out over the rubble-littered valley called the Forum.*

The hill in the distance with the bell tower is Capitol Hill.

The Forum

1 ARCH OF TITUS
2 BASILICA OF CONSTANTINE
3 THE FORUM'S MAIN SQUARE
4 TEMPLE OF JULIUS CAESAR
5 TEMPLE OF ANTONINUS AND FAUSTINA
6 BASILICA AEMILIA
7 CALIGULA'S PALACE
8 TEMPLE OF VESTA

9 HOUSE OF THE VESTAL VIRGINS
10 CURIA (SENATE HOUSE)
11 ROSTRUM
12 ARCH OF SEPTIMIUS SEVERUS
13 TEMPLE OF SATURN
14 COLUMN OF PHOCAS
15 BASILICA JULIA

Immediately to your left, with all the trees, is Palatine Hill. The valley in-between is rectangular, running roughly east (the Colosseum end) to west (Capitol Hill). The rocky path at your feet is the Via Sacra, which runs through the trees, past the large brick Senate building, and up Capitol Hill.

Picture being here when a conquering general returned to Rome with crates of booty. The valley was full of gleaming white buildings topped with bronze roofs. The Via Sacra—Main Street of the Forum—would be lined with citizens waving branches and carrying torches. The trumpets would sound as the parade began. First came porters, carrying chests full of gold and jewels. Then a parade of exotic animals from the conquered lands—elephants,

giraffes, hippopotamuses—for the crowd to "ooh" and "ahh" at. Next came the prisoners in chains, with the captive king on a wheeled platform so the people could jeer and spit at him. Finally, the conquering hero himself would drive down in his four-horse chariot, with rose petals strewn in his path. The whole procession would go the length of the Forum and up the face of Capitol Hill to the Temple of Saturn (the 8 big columns midway up the hill—#13 on map on page 65), where they'd place the booty in Rome's coffers. They'd continue up to the summit to the Temple of Jupiter (not visible today) to dedicate the victory to the King of the Gods.

Rome—Republic and Empire (500 B.C.–A.D. 500)

Ancient Rome spanned about a thousand years, from 500 B.C. to A.D. 500. During that time, Rome expanded from a small tribe of barbarians to a vast empire, then dwindled slowly to city size again. For the first 500 years, when Rome's armies made her ruler of the Italian peninsula and beyond, Rome was a republic governed by elected senators. Over the next 500 years, a time of world conquest and eventual decline, Rome was an empire ruled by a military-backed dictator.

Julius Caesar bridged the gap between republic and empire. This ambitious general and politician, popular with the people because of his military victories and charisma, suspended the Roman constitution and assumed dictatorial powers around 50 B.C., until he was assassinated by a conspiracy of senators. His adopted son, Augustus, succeeded him, and soon "Caesar" was not just a name but a title.

Emperor Augustus ushered in the Pax Romana, or Roman peace (from A.D. 1–200), a time when Rome reached her peak and controlled an empire that stretched even beyond Eurail—from Scotland to Egypt, from Turkey to Morocco.

1. Arch of Titus *(Arco di Tito)*

The Arch of Titus commemorated the Roman victory over the province of Judea (Israel) in A.D. 70. The Romans had a reputation as benevolent conquerors who tolerated the local customs and rulers. All they required was allegiance to the empire, which could be shown by worshiping the current emperor as a god. No problem for most conquered people, who already had half a dozen gods on their prayer lists. But the Israelites' god was jealous and refused to let his people worship the emperor. Israel revolted. After a short but bitter war, the Romans defeated the rebels, took Jerusalem, sacked their temple, and brought home 50,000 Jewish slaves...who were forced to build this arch.

Roman propaganda decorates the inside of the arch, where a relief shows the emperor Titus in a chariot being crowned by the Goddess Victory. (Thanks to the toll of modern pollution, they both look like they've been through the wars.) The other side shows the sacking of the temple—soldiers carrying a Jewish candelabrum and other plunder. The two (unfinished) plaques on poles were to have listed the conquered cities.

The brutal crushing of this rebellion (and another one 60 years later) devastated the nation of Israel. With no temple as a center for their faith, the Jews scattered throughout the world (the Diaspora). There would be no Jewish political entity again for two thousand years, until modern Israel was created after World War II.

• *Start down the Via Sacra into the Forum. After just a few meters, turn right and follow a path uphill to the three huge arches of the . . .*

2. Basilica of Constantine
(a.k.a. Basilica Maxentius)

Yes, these are big arches. But they represent only one third of the original Basilica of Constantine, a mammoth hall of justice. The arches were matched by a similar set along the Via Sacra side (only a few squat brick piers remain). Between them ran the central hall, which was spanned by a roof 40 meters (130 feet) high—about 17 meters (56 feet) higher than the side arches you see. (The stub of brick you see sticking up once spanned the central hall.) The hall itself was as long as a football field, lavishly furnished with colorful inlaid marble, a gilded bronze ceiling, fountains, and statues, and filled with strolling Romans. At the far (west) end was an enormous marble statue of Emperor Constantine on a throne. (Pieces of this statue, including a hand the size of a man, are on display in Rome's Capitol Hill Museum.)

This basilica was begun by the emperor Maxentius, but after he was trounced in battle (see page 62), the victor—Constantine— completed the massive building. No doubt about it, the Romans built monuments on a more epic scale than any previous Europeans, wowing their neighbors.

• *Now stroll deeper into the Forum, down the Via Sacra. Many of the large basalt stones under your feet were walked on by Caesar Augustus 2,000 years ago. Pass through the trees and between ruined buildings until it opens up to a flat, grassy area.*

3. The Forum's Main Square

The original Forum, or main square, was this flat patch about the size of a football field, stretching to the foot of Capitol Hill. Surrounding it were temples, law courts, government buildings, and triumphal arches.

Rome was born right here. According to legend, twin brothers Romulus (Rome) and Remus were orphaned in infancy and raised by a she-wolf on top of the Palatine. Growing up, they found it hard to get dates. So they and their cohorts attacked the nearby Sabine tribe and kidnapped their women. After they made peace, this marshy valley became the meeting place and then the trading center for the scattered tribes on the surrounding hillsides.

The square was the busiest and most crowded—and often the seediest—section of town. Besides the senators, politicians, and currency exchangers, there were even sleazier types—souvenir hawkers, fortune-tellers, gamblers, slave marketers, drunks, hookers, lawyers, and tour guides.

The Forum is now rubble, no denying it, but imagine it in its prime: blinding white marble buildings with 13-meter-high (40-foot) columns and shining bronze roofs; rows of statues painted in realistic colors; chariots rattling down the Via Sacra. Mentally replace tourists in T-shirts with tribunes in togas. Imagine the buildings towering and the people buzzing around you while an orator gives a rabble-rousing speech from the Rostrum. If things still look like just a pile of rocks, at least tell yourself, "But Julius Caesar once leaned against these rocks."

• *At the near (east) end of the main square (the Colosseum is to the east) sit the foundations of a temple now capped with a peaked wood-and-metal roof...*

4. The Temple of Julius Caesar
(Tempio del Divo Giulio, or "Ara di Cesare")

Julius Caesar's body was burned on this spot—right under the metal roof—after his assassination.

Caesar (100–44 B.C.) changed Rome—and the Forum—dramatically. He cleared out many of the wooden market stalls and began to ring the square with even grander buildings. Caesar's

house was located behind the temple, near that clump of trees. He walked right by here on the day he was assassinated ("Beware the Ides of March!" warned a street-corner Etruscan preacher).

Though popular with the masses, not everyone liked Caesar's urban design or his politics. When he assumed dictatorial powers, he was ambushed and stabbed to death by a conspiracy of senators, including his adopted son, Brutus (*Et tu, Brute?*).

The funeral was held here, facing the main square. The citizens gathered and speeches were made. Mark Antony stood up to say (in Shakespeare's words), "Friends, Romans, countrymen, lend me your ears. I come to bury Caesar, not to praise him." When Caesar's body was burned, the citizens who still loved him threw anything at hand on the fire, requiring the fire department to come put it out. Later, Emperor Augustus dedicated this temple in his name, making Caesar the first Roman to be a god.

• *Behind and to the left of the Temple of Julius Caesar are the eight tall columns of the...*

5. Temple of Antoninus and Faustina

The respected Emperor Antoninus (A.D. 138–161) built this

temple—originally called the Temple of Faustina—in honor of his late beloved wife. After the emperor's death, the temple became a monument to them both.

The 17-meter-tall (56-foot) Corinthian (leafy) columns must have been awe-inspiring to out-of-towners who grew up in thatched huts. Although the temple has been reconstructed as a church, you can still see the basic layout—a staircase led to a shaded porch (the columns), which admitted you to the main building (now a church) where the statue of the god sat. Originally, these columns supported a triangular pediment decorated with sculptures.

Picture these columns whitewashed, with gilded capitals, supporting brightly painted statues in the pediment, and the whole building capped with a gleaming bronze roof. The stately gray rubble of today's Forum is a faded black-and-white photograph of a 3-D Technicolor era.

• *There's a ramp next to the Temple of A. and F. Walk halfway up it and look to the left to view the...*

6. Basilica Aemilia

A basilica was a Roman hall of justice. In a society that was as legal-minded as America is today, you needed a lot of lawyers and a big place to put them. Citizens came here to work out matters such as inheritances and building permits, or to sue somebody.

Notice the layout. It was a long, rectangular building. The stubby columns all in a row form one long, central hall flanked by two side aisles. Medieval Christians required a larger meeting hall for their worship services than Roman temples provided, so they used the spacious Roman

basilica (hall of justice) as the model for their churches. Cathedrals from France to Spain to England, from Romanesque to Gothic to Renaissance, all have the same basic floor plan as a Roman basilica.

• *Return again to the Temple of Julius Caesar. Notice the ruts in the stone street in front of the temple—carved by chariot wheels. To the right of the temple are the three tall Corinthian columns of the Temple of Castor and Pollux. Beyond that is Palatine Hill.*

7. Caligula's Palace (a.k.a. the Palace of Tiberius)

Emperor Caligula (ruled A.D. 37–41) had a huge palace on Palatine Hill overlooking the Forum. It actually sprawled down the hill into the Forum (some supporting arches remain in the hillside), with an entrance by the Temple of Castor and Pollux.

Caligula was not a nice person. He tortured enemies, stole senators' wives, and parked his chariot in handicap spaces. But Rome's luxury-loving emperors only added to the glory of the Forum, with each one trying to make his mark on history.

• *To the left of the Temple of Castor and Pollux, find the remains of a small white circular temple...*

8. The Temple of Vesta

This was Rome's most sacred spot. Rome considered itself one big family, and this temple represented a circular hut, like the kind Rome's first families lived in. Inside, a fire burned, just as in a Roman home. And back in the days before lighters and matches, you never wanted your fire to go out. As long as the sacred flame burned, Rome

would stand. The flame was tended by priestesses known as Vestal Virgins.

• *Around the back of the Temple of Vesta you'll find two rectangular brick pools. These stood in the courtyard of...*

9. The House of the Vestal Virgins

The Vestal Virgins lived in a two-story building surrounding a central courtyard with these two pools at one end. Rows of statues to the left and right marked the long sides of the building. This place was the model—both architecturally and sexually— for medieval convents and monasteries.

The six Vestal Virgins, chosen from noble families before they reached the age of 10, served a 30-year term. Honored and revered by the Romans, the Vestals even had their own box opposite the emperor in the Colosseum.

As the name implies, a Vestal took a vow of chastity. If she served her term faithfully—abstaining for 30 years—she was given a huge dowry, honored with a statue (like the ones at left), and allowed to marry (life begins at 40?). But if they found any Virgin who wasn't, she was strapped to a funeral car, paraded through the streets of the Forum, taken to a crypt, given a loaf of bread and a lamp...and buried alive. Many women suffered the latter fate.

• *Head to the Forum's west end. Stop at the big, reconstructed brick building with the triangular roof. If the door's open, look in.*

10. The Curia

The Senate House (Curia) was the most important political building in the Forum. Though this current building is a 1930s reconstruction, this was the site of Rome's official center of gov-

ernment since the birth of the republic. Three hundred senators, elected by the citizens of Rome, met here to debate and create the laws of the land. Their wooden seats once circled the building in three tiers; the Senate president's podium sat at the far end.

The marble floor is from ancient times. Listen to the echoes in this vast room—the acoustics are great.

Rome prided itself on being a republic. Early in the city's history, its people threw out the king and established rule by elected representatives. Each Roman citizen was free to speak his mind and have a say in public policy. Even when emperors became the supreme authority, the Senate was a power to be reckoned with. (Note: Although Julius Caesar was assassinated in "the Senate," it wasn't here—the Senate was temporarily meeting across town.)

A statue and two reliefs inside the Curia help build our mental image of the Forum. The statue, made of porphyry marble in about A.D. 100, with its head, arms, and feet missing, was a tribute to an emperor, probably Hadrian or Trajan. The two relief panels may have decorated the Rostrum. One shows people standing in line to burn their debt records following a government amnesty. The other shows intact architecture and the latest fashion in togas.

• *Go back down the Senate steps to the metal guardrail and look right to a three-meter-high (10-foot) wall at the base of Capitol Hill marked...*

11. Rostrum *(Rostri)*

Nowhere was Roman freedom more apparent than at this "Speaker's Corner." The Rostrum was a raised platform, three meters high and 25 meters long (10 feet high, 80 feet long), decorated with statues, columns, and the prows of ships *(rostra)*.

Rome's orators, great and small, came here trying to draw a crowd and sway public opinion. Mark Antony rose to offer Caesar the laurel-leaf crown of kingship, which Caesar publicly (and hypocritically) refused while privately becoming a dictator. Men such as Cicero railed against the corruption and decadence that came with the city's newfound wealth. In later years, daring citizens even spoke out against the emperors, reminding them that Rome was once free. Picture the backdrop these speakers would have had—a mountain of marble buildings piling up on Capitol Hill.

At the near (north) end of the Rostrum was the Umbilicus Urbis that marked the center of the city. A column at the far end once told how far it was from here to the distant cities of Rome's vast empire ("Londinium, 851 miles").

In front of the Rostrum are trees bearing fruits that were sacred to the ancient Romans: olives (provided food, light, and preservatives), figs (tasty), and wine grapes (made a popular export product).

• *The big arch to the right of the Rostrum is . . .*

12. Arch of Septimius Severus

In imperial times, the Rostrum's voices of democracy would have been dwarfed by images of empire such as the huge, six-story-high Arch of Septimius Severus (A.D. 203). The reliefs commemorate

the African-born emperor's battles in Mesopotamia. Near ground level, see curly haired Severus marching captured barbarians back to Rome for the victory parade. Despite Severus' efficient rule, Rome's empire was crumbling under the weight of its own corruption, disease, and the constant attacks by foreign "barbarians."

• *Pass underneath the Arch of Septimius Severus and turn left. On the slope of Capitol Hill are the eight remaining columns of the . . .*

Rome Falls

Again, Rome lasted 1,000 years—500 years of growth, 200 years of peak power, and 300 years of gradual decay. The fall had many causes, among them the barbarians who pecked away at Rome's borders. Christians blamed the fall on moral decay. Pagans blamed it on Christians. Marxists blamed it on a shallow economy based on spoils of war. (Pat Buchanan blamed it on Marxists.) Whatever the reasons, the far-flung empire could no longer keep its grip on conquered lands, and it pulled back. Barbarian tribes from Germany and Asia attacked the Italian peninsula and even looted Rome itself in A.D. 410, leveling many of the buildings in the Forum. In 476, when the last emperor checked out and switched off the lights, Europe plunged into centuries of ignorance, poverty, and weak government—the Dark Ages.

But Rome lived on in the Catholic Church. Catholicism was the state religion of Rome's last generations. Emperors became popes (both called themselves Pontifex Maximus), senators became bishops, orators became priests, and basilicas became churches. And remember that the goal for the greatest church building project ever—that of St. Peter's—was to "put the dome of the Pantheon atop the Basilica of Constantine." The glory of Rome remains eternal.

13. Temple of Saturn

These columns framed the entrance to the Forum's oldest temple (497 B.C.). Inside was a humble, very old wooden statue of the god Saturn. But the statue's pedestal held the gold bars, coins, and jewels of Rome's state treasury, the booty collected by conquering generals.

• *Standing here, at one of the Forum's first buildings, look east at the lone, tall . . .*

14. Column of Phocas

This is the Forum's last great monument (A.D. 608), a gift from the powerful Byzantine Empire to a fallen empire—Rome. After Rome's 1,000-year reign, the city was looted by Vandals, the population of a million-plus shrank to 10,000, and the once-grand city center—the Forum—was abandoned, slowly covered up by centuries of silt and dirt. In the 1700s, an English historian named Edward Gibbon stood here. Hearing Christian monks singing at these pagan ruins, he looked out at the few columns poking up from the ground, pondered the "Decline and Fall of the Roman Empire," and thought, "Hmm, that's a catchy title...."

• *There are several ways to exit the Forum:*

East—Return to the Colosseum. Or visit Palatine Hill (the entrance is near the Arch of Titus), see page 77.

West—Climb Capitol Hill. The stairs near the Arch of Septimius Severus are the most direct way, or take the pathway that winds past the Temple of Saturn. (Both lead to the Capitol Hill Museum, see page 120.)

North—The ramp near Basilica Aemilia spills you out on Via dei Fori Imperiali (near Trajan's Forum, see page 86).

South—Passing by the Temple of Castor and Pollux, you climb to a small exit leading to the Theater of Marcellus and the Tiber River.

PALATINE HILL
HILL
TOUR

If you found the Forum absolutely enthralling, you'll be mildly entertained by Palatine Hill. It's certainly jam–packed with history— "the huts of Romulus and Remus," the huge Imperial Palace, a view of the Circus Maximus—but there's only the barest skeleton of rubble left to support all that history. Palatine Hill is recommended for serious sightseers with low expectations.

Orientation
Cost: €8, includes Colosseum visit within 24 hours; also covered by €20 combo–ticket.
Hours: Daily 9:00–19:00 or an hour before dark.
Getting There: Enter the Palatine Hill from within the Forum (the entrance closest to the Colosseum; Metro: Colosseo). Buy your ticket at the booth about 30 meters (100 feet) uphill from the Arch of Titus.
Tour: Audioguides cost €4. Guided tours in English are offered once daily (€3.50); ask for information at the ticket booth.
Length of Our Tour: Allow 90 minutes.

Climbing the Palatine Hill
• *After you buy your ticket, follow the route the ancients walked (up the pathway, not the stairs), straight up the hill. At the top of the hill, keep heading to the gray, modern building housing the museum ("Antaquario Palatino"). You may wish to skip ahead (see page 83) and visit the museum right away. Otherwise, orient with your back to the museum, so you're facing the Forum (roughly north).*

THE IMPERIAL PALACE
You're standing at the center of what was once a huge palace, the residence of emperors for three centuries. Orgies, royal weddings,

Palatine Hill

- EXISTING WALLS
-- ANCIENT OUTLINE

100 YARDS
100 METERS

1 MAIN COURTYARD
2 THRONE ROOM
3 BANQUET HALL
4 STADIUM
5 PRIVATE WING OF PALACE
6 "LOGGIA STATI MATTEI" MUSEUM
7 LOWER COURTYARD
8 CIRCUS MAXIMUS
9 MUSEUM (ANTAQUARIO PALATINO)
10 HOUSE OF LIVIA AND AUGUSTUS
11 PALACE OF TIBERIUS AND CALIGULA (AND CRYPTOPORTICUS TUNNEL)
12 IRON AGE HUTS
13 TEMPLE OF CYBELE

assassinations, concerts, intrigues, births, funerals, banquets, and the occasional Tupperware party took place within these walls.

What walls? The row of umbrella pines to the east (to your right as you face the Forum) now marks one edge of the palace. The reconstructed brick tower (at about 11 o'clock, as you face the Forum) was the northwest corner. The palace also stretched behind you (the area behind the museum) and beneath you, since some of the palace had a lower floor. The area to your left was the official wing of the palace; to your right were the private quarters. All in all, it made a cozy little 14,000-square-meter (150,000-square-foot) pad.

The palace was built by Emperor Domitian around A.D. 81. His family was trying to rid Rome of the bitter taste of Nero, and this palace was a way of one-upping Nero and his Golden House. A poet of the day described it as so grand that it "made Jupiter jealous."

• *To your left (as you face the Forum) is a big rectangular field with an octagonal brick design in the center. Let's start with the Official Wing (Domus Flavia) of the palace: its main courtyard, throne room, and banquet hall.*

1. Main Courtyard *(Peristilio)*

The brick octagon was a sunken fountain in the middle of an

open-air courtyard. Like even the humblest Roman homes, this palace was built around an oasis of peace where you could enjoy the sun, catch the precious rain, and listen to the babble of moving water. The courtyard was lined with columns (notice the fragments) supporting an arcade for shade. Originally, the floor and walls of the courtyard were faced with shiny white marble.

• *Begin circling the courtyard. At the north (Forum) edge of the courtyard, step between the big, brick wall-stumps and enter the . . .*

2. Throne Room

The Throne Room was the official center of power, the nerve center of an empire that controlled some 50 million people from Scotland to Africa. The curved apse of the largest brick stump

(there's now a plaque on it) marks the spot where the emperor sat on his throne for official business.

Imagine being a Roman citizen summoned by the emperor. You'd enter the palace through the main doorway (now a gap) at the far (Forum) end of the room, having climbed up three flights of a monumental staircase. The floor and walls dazzled with green, purple, red, white, and yellow marble. Along the walls were 12 colossal statues of Roman gods. The ceiling towered seven stories overhead. On either side were doorways leading to a basilica and the emperor's private temple.

You'd approach the emperor, who sat on a raised throne in the apse, dressed in royal purple, with a crown of laurel leaves on his head and a scepter cradled in his arm. Big braziers burned on either side, throwing off a flickering light. As you approached, you'd raise your arm to greet him, saying, "*Ave, Cesare!*" The words would echo through the great hall.

• *From the Throne Room, return to the courtyard and continue circling it. At the far (south) end is a square area with a sunken floor now covered with gravel.*

3. Banquet Hall *(Triclinium)*

The floor of the banquet room had a hollow space beneath it (you can see the 2-foot gap between the two original floors), to heat the floor with forced air from underground stoves. At the far end of the room, the platform and curved apse mark the spot where the emperor ate while looking down on his subjects. On either side of the room were windows that the guests could look through to see oval-shaped fountains (these still remain) bubbling in an artificial cavern.

Here, the wealthiest Romans enjoyed the spoils that poured into Rome from their vast empire. Reclining on a couch, waited on by slaves, you'd order bowls of larks' tongues or a roast pig stuffed with live birds, then wash it down with wine. When you were stuffed, but the waiters brought yet another delicacy, you could call for a feather, vomit, and start all over. Dancing, dark-skinned slave girls from Egypt or flute players from Greece enter-

tained. If you fancied one, he or she was yours—the bedrooms were just down the hall.

Or so went the stories. In fact, many emperors were just and simple men, continuing the old Roman traditions of hard work and moderate tastes. But just as many were power-mad scoundrels who used their power to indulge their every urge.

• *The palace's stadium is 100 meters (330 feet) to the east, near the long row of pine trees. Belly up to the railing and look down on the elliptical track.*

4. Stadium *(Hippodromo)*

This cigar-shaped, sunken stadium (150 meters, or 500 feet, long) was the palace's rec room. It looks like a racetrack and may have been used for foot and horse races, but it also held gardens with

strolling paths. The oval running track at the south end was added later. The emperor had a raised box on the 50-yard line, in the curved apse across from you. At the north end were changing rooms, and the marble fragments that litter the ground once held up an arcade.

5. Private Wing *(Domus Augustana)* of the Palace

The area between the stadium and official wing held the private rooms of the emperor and his extended family. Today, a lone umbrella pine on a mound marks the courtyard of this wing. Wander through the maze of brick rooms (many of them reconstructed), noticing:

• The typical Roman building method: Build a rectangular shell of brick, fill it with concrete, then finish it with either plaster (you'll see an occasional faded fresco) or slabs of marble. The small, round pockmarks on many walls show where the marble was fastened.
• The square holes in the walls held wooden beams, used for scaffolding during construction and maintenance, for shelves, and for wooden floors.
• Over the doorways, notice that the bricks in the walls form the pattern of an arch. These "blind arches" were structural elements that allowed the walls to be built higher. The iron bar clamps are recent additions and hold the crumbling walls together.
• Niches and apses once held statues. Every family had their own household gods and displayed small images of these guardian spirits, as well as busts of honored ancestors.
• The fragments of columns, reliefs, and sculpture scattered about suggest the wealth of this great palace.
• Finally, notice the floor plan—a complex, fantasyland maze of small, private, sometimes even curved rooms.

6. *Loggia Stati Mattei* Museum

This museum is located in one of the rooms of the Domus Augustana. From the balcony of this reconstructed room, look down on the original frescoes dug out from the ancient Temple of Isis (located near where the Throne Room was later built).

• *In the south part of the Domus Augustana, you can look down on the ruins of the lower story.*

7. Lower Courtyard *(Peristilio)*

This open-air courtyard has the concave-convex remains of a large fountain that must have been a marvel. Try to mentally reconstruct the palace that surrounded this fountain. The emperors could look down on it from the upper story (where you're standing) or view it from the rooms around it on the lower story, where the emperor and his family ate their meals in private.

The lower story was built into the slope of the hill. The southern part of the palace was an extension of the hillside, supported beneath your feet by big arches.

• *Head to the southern edge of the hill, overlooking a long, wide grassy field—what once was the Circus Maximus. Lean over the railing and you might be able to make out the concave shape of the palace's southern facade.*

8. Circus Maximus

If the gladiator show at the Colosseum was sold out, you could always get a seat at the Circus Max. In an early version of today's demolition derby, Ben Hur and his fellow charioteers once raced recklessly around this oblong course.

The chariots circled around the cigar-shaped mound in the center (notice the lone cypress tree that now marks one end of the mound). Bleachers (now grassy banks) originally surrounded the track (see artist's reconstruction on page 83).

The track was 400 meters (1,300 feet) long, while the whole stadium measured 650 by 220 meters (2,130 by 720 feet) and seated—get this—250,000 people. The wooden bleachers once collapsed during a race, killing 13,000.

The horses started from a starting gate at the west end (to your right), while the public entered at the other end. Races consisted of seven laps (about 5.5 km, or 3.5 miles total). In such a small space, collisions and overturned chariots were common. The charioteers were usually poor low-borns who used this dangerous sport to get rich and famous. Many succeeded.

The public was crazy about the races. There were 12 per day, 240 days a year. Four teams dominated the competition—Reds, Whites, Blues, and Greens—and every citizen was fanatically devoted to one of them. Obviously, the emperors had the best seats in the house; built into the palace's curved facade was a box overlooking the track. For their pleasure, emperors occasionally had the circus floor carpeted with designs in colored powders.

Picture the scene: intact palace; emperor watching; a quarter of a million Romans cheering, jeering, and furiously betting.

Horses raced here for over a thousand years. The track was originally built by Rome's Etruscan kings (c. 600 B.C.), and the spectacles continued into the Christian era, until 549, despite Church disapproval.

From this viewpoint, looking to the left, you can see the ruins of the Baths of Caracalla rising above the trees a kilometer (0.6 mile) away. About 1.5 kilometers (1 mile) beyond that, the Appian Way led from a grand gate in the ancient wall, past the catacombs, to Brindisi.

9. Museum *(Antaquario Palatino)*

The museum contains statues and frescoes that help you imagine the luxury of the imperial Palatine. Upstairs, pause at the statue of "Magna Mater" on her throne. This Great Mother brought life and fertility to the Roman people, who worshiped her at the Temple of Cybele (which we'll see later). Her arms and foot were destroyed by time, but there was always a cavity where her head should be—this was a standard Roman device in which interchangeable heads could be inserted. In this case, the Magna Mater's "head" was actually a sacred, black, cone-shaped meteorite that caused astonishment when it fell from the sky.

Also upstairs, Room V holds frescoes and statues from the Domus Augustana (the private wing of the palace). Room VII has a bust of the notorious Emperor Nero *(Nerone)*. In Room VIII is a statue fragment of a river god's stomach. And finally, back near the entrance is a large statue of a Muse that once decorated the Hippodrome.

Downstairs, there's a helpful model of the round Iron Age huts of Romulus (and a WC).

• *From the museum, head west, crossing the octagonal brick courtyard and continuing through ruins. As you exit the ruins of the Imperial Palace, you'll run into a railing overlooking the sunken remains (with modern corrugated roof) of...*

10. House of Livia and Augustus *(Casa di Livia)*

Augustus, the first emperor, lived in this house (and the neighboring house to the left) with his wife, Livia. Peer down the hallways at the small rooms with honeycomb brick walls that surrounded a small courtyard. This relatively humble dwelling is a far cry from

the later Imperial Palace. There are some fine frescoes inside (usually closed for restoration), but Casa di Livia had little of the lavish marble found in most homes of the wealthy.

Augustus was a modest man who believed in traditional Roman values. His wife and

daughter wove the clothes he wore. He slept in the same small bedroom for 40 years. He burned the midnight oil in his study, reading and writing his memoirs. Augustus set a standard for emperors' conduct that would last... until his death.

• *To the right of Casa di Livia are the Farnese Gardens. These grow over the remains of what was the...*

11. Palace of Tiberius and Caligula (and the Cryptoporticus Tunnel)

Augustus' successors started the trend of fancy imperial homes with a palace that sprawled all the way from here to the Forum. Virtually nothing is visible today. One feature that remains is the underground passageway (Cripto Portico or Cryptoporticus Tunnel) that runs from near Casa di Livia toward the Forum—140 meters (460 feet) long. Look down and see some of the mosaic floor of this once marbled and stuccoed passageway, which is lit by windows

along the side. Emperors used it as a private, convenient way to get around the hill. Caligula may have been murdered in it.

• *Circle clockwise around behind the Casa di Livia to an area with several archaeological sites. Head for the far, southwest corner. Under a corrugated roof are the scant outlines of...*

12. Iron Age Huts—
"The Huts of Romulus and Remus"

Looking down into the pit from the railing (stand at the far right), you can make out some elliptical and rectangular shapes carved into the stony ground—the partial outlines of huts from around 850 B.C. Some have holes that once held the wooden posts of round, thatched huts.

Romulus and Remus were babies orphaned when their mother, a disgraced Vestal Virgin, was executed. (She claimed she was raped by Mars, the War God.) Set adrift on the flooding Tiber, the babes

washed ashore at the foot of Palatine Hill. A shepherd discovered them in a cave just downhill from here, being suckled by a mother wolf. He took them home—maybe right here—and raised them as his own. When Romulus grew up, he killed his brother and built a square wall (Roma Quadrata) around the tiny hill town, founding the city of Rome. (The dusty-orange blocks of volcanic tufa stone may be part of that wall.)

For centuries, the Romans believed this legend. They honored the wolf's cave (called the "Lupercal," where every February 15th men dressed up in animal skins and whipped women), as well as the spot where Romulus lived. Lo and behold, in the 1940s, these huts were unearthed, and the legend became history.

• *Over your right shoulder are the rectangular walls of the . . .*

13. Temple of Cybele *(Templo di Cibele)*, or Temple of the Magna Mater

The statue of the Mother of the Gods, built to thank her for saving Rome from Hannibal and his elephants (c. 200 B.C.), once sat at the far end of this temple. (It's now in the museum.)

March 22 was a festive day at the temple, as new priests joined the Magna Mater's cult by castrating themselves and draping their testicles over the altar, helping the goddess fertilize the world.

Here at Rome's birthplace, reflect on the rise of this great culture—from thatched hut to the modest house of Augustus to the massive Imperial Palace of Domitian, with its stadium and view over the Circus Maximus. It's no wonder that the hill's name gave us our English word "palace."

• *A good way to complete your Palatine visit is to stroll through the Farnese Gardens (Horti Farnesini), admiring the exotic plants, fountains, underground grotto, and pavilions. When you see the view of the Forum from here, you'll know why the Palatine was Rome's best address.*

TRAJAN'S
COLUMN,
FORUM &
MARKET

Rome's expansion peaked under Emperor Trajan (ruled A.D. 98–117)—the empire stretched from Scotland to the Sahara, from Spain to Asia. A triumphant Trajan returned to Rome with his booty and shook it all over the city. He extended the Forum by building his own commercial, political, and religious center nearby, complete with temples, law courts, squares lined with shops, and a monumental column.

Orientation

Cost and Hours: Trajan's Column and Forum are free and always viewable; Trajan's Market, including access to part of the forum, costs €6.20 (summer Tue–Sun 9:00–18:30, winter Tue–Sun 9:00–16:30, closed Mon, tel. 06-679-0048).

Getting There: Trajan's Column is just a few steps off Piazza Venezia, on Via dei Fori Imperiali, across the street from the Victor Emmanuel Monument. Trajan's Forum stretches southeast of the column toward the Colosseum. The entrance to Trajan's (dull) Market is uphill from the column on Via IV Novembre.

Length of Our Tour: Thirty minutes, or an hour if you also enter Trajan's Market.

Trajan's Column

Rising 42 meters (140 feet) and decorated with a spiral relief of 2,500 figures trumpeting Trajan's exploits, this is the world's grandest column from antiquity. The ashes of Trajan and his wife were once held in the base, and the sun once glinted off a polished bronze statue of Trajan at the top. (Today, St. Peter is on top.) Built as a stack of 17 marble doughnuts, the column is hollow (note the small window slots) with a spiral staircase inside, leading up to the balcony.

The relief unfolds like a scroll, telling the story of Trajan's conquest of Dacia (modern–day Romania). It starts at the bottom with a trickle of water that becomes a river and soon picks up boats full of supplies. Then come the soldiers themselves, who spill out from the gates of the city. A river god (bottom band, south side) surfaces to bless the journey. Along the way (second band), they

build roads and forts to sustain the vast enterprise, including (third band, south side) Trajan's kilometer–long (0.6-mile) bridge over the Danube, the longest for a thousand years. (Find the 3 tiny, crisscross rectangles representing the wooden span.) Trajan himself (fourth band, in military skirt with toga over his arm) mounts a podium to fire up the troops. They hop into

a Roman galley ship (fifth band) and head off to fight the valiant Dacians in the middle of a forest (eighth band). Finally, at the very top, the Romans hold a sacrifice to give thanks for the victory, while the captured armor is displayed on the pedestal.

Originally, the entire story was painted in bright colors. If you unwound the scroll, it would stretch over two football fields—it's far longer than the frieze around the Greek Parthenon. (An unscrolled copy is in E.U.R.'s Museum of Roman Civilization.)

• *The best place to view the ruins of Trajan's Forum is on the pedestrian walkway (70 meters, or 230 feet, southeast of the column) that cuts right across the heart of the forum.*

Trajan's Forum *(Foro di Traiano)*

Trajan's Forum starts at Trajan's Column and runs about 120 meters (400 feet) southeast toward the Colosseum. It's mostly rubble today. The highlight of the forum, then and now, is Trajan's Market—the big, crescent–shaped brick structure that rises up the flank of Quirinal Hill.

In Roman times, you would have entered at the Colosseum end through a triumphal arch and been greeted in the main square by a large statue of the soldier–king on a horse. Continuing on, you'd enter the Basilica Ulpia (the gray granite columns near Trajan's Column), the largest law court of its day. Finally, at the far end you would have found Trajan's Column, flanked by two libraries that contained the world's knowledge in Greek and Latin. Balconies on the libraries gave close–up looks at the upper reliefs of the column, in case anyone doubted the outcome of Trajan's war.

Trajan's Forum

Trajan's Forum was a crucial expansion of the old Roman Forum, which was too small and ceremonial to fill the commercial needs of a booming city of over a million people. Built with the staggering haul of gold plundered from Dacia (Romania), this was the largest forum ever—its opulence astounded even the jaded Romans.

To build his forum, Trajan literally moved mountains. He cut away a ridge that once connected the Quirinal and Capitol Hills, creating this artificial valley. Trajan's Column marks the hill's original height—42 meters (140 feet).

Trajan's Market

Nestled into the cutaway curve of the hill is the semicircular brick complex of Trajan's Market. Part shopping mall, part warehouse, part administration office, it was a place Romans gravitated to and a popular spot to bring out–of–town guests.

At ground level, the 13 tall arches housed (shallow) shops selling fresh fruit, vegetables, and flowers to shoppers who passed by on the street. The 26 arched windows (above) lighted a covered walkway lined with shops that sold wine and olive oil. On the roof (now lined

with a metal railing) runs a
street that held still more
shops, making about 150
in all. Shoppers could
browse through goods from
every corner of Rome's vast
empire—exotic fruits from
Africa, spices from Asia, fish
and chips from Londinium.

Above the semicircle,
the upper floors of the complex housed bureaucrats in charge of
a crucial element of city life—doling out free grain to unemployed citizens, who lived off the wealth plundered from distant
lands. Better to pacify them than risk a riot. Above the offices,
at the very top, rises a tower added in the Middle Ages.

Going inside the market (which costs €6.20) is worth it only
for those with a good imagination, stamina for stairs, or a Masters
in Food Distribution. As you walk by the shops in the welcome
shade of the arcade, you'll get a better sense of how inviting the
market must have been in its heyday. Today, only one shop is
"furnished"—crammed with the clay jugs used to store olive oil
(upstairs from ticket booth). Throughout the market, you'll get
expansive views of the ancient forum and modern Victor
Emmanuel Monument.

The market was beautiful and functional, filling the space of
the curved hill perfectly and echoing the curved side of the forum's
main courtyard. (The wall of rough tufa stones on the ground
once extended into a semicircle.) Unlike most Roman buildings,
the brick facade was never covered with plaster or marble. The
architect liked the simple contrast between warm brick and the
white stone lining the arches and windows.

Trajan's conquest of the Dacians was Rome's last and greatest foreign conquest. It produced this forum, which stood for
centuries as a symbol of a truly cosmopolitan civilization.

PANTHEON TOUR

If your imagination is fried from trying to reconstruct ancient buildings out of today's rubble, visit the Pantheon, Rome's best-preserved monument. Engineers still admire how the Romans built such a mathematically precise structure without computers, fossil-fuel machinery, or electricity. (Having unlimited slave-power didn't hurt.) Stand under the Pantheon's solemn dome to gain a new appreciation for the enlightenment of these ancient people.

Several interesting churches are clustered near the Pantheon. We'll visit these after the Pantheon.

Orientation

Cost: Free.

Hours: Mon–Sat 8:30–19:30, Sun and holidays 9:00–18:00.

Getting There: Walk (it's a 10– to 15–min walk from the Forum), take a taxi, or catch a bus. Bus #64 runs daily and frequently between the train station and Vatican City, stopping at Largo Argentina, a few blocks south of the Pantheon. The *electrico* minibus #116 runs between Campo de' Fiori and Piazza Barberini via the Pantheon (daily except Sun).

Information: Tel. 06-6830-0230. Small gift shop inside entrance. Nearest WCs at bars and McDonald's on the square.

Length of Our Tour: Allow 45 minutes.

Cuisine Art: You'll find Rome's best gelato at Gelateria della Palma, two blocks in front of the Pantheon (Via della Maddalena 20); for lunch or dinner ideas, see page 244.

Pantheon Exterior

The Pantheon was a Roman temple dedicated to all *(pan)* the gods *(theos)*. First built in 27 B.C. by Augustus' son-in-law (find "M. Agrippa" on the facade), it was completely rebuilt around

A.D. 120 by the emperor Hadrian.
Some say that Hadrian, an amateur
architect, helped design it.

The Pantheon looks like a
pretty typical temple from the out-
side, but this is perhaps the most
influential building in art history.
Its dome was the model for the
Florence cathedral dome, which launched the Renaissance, and for
Michelangelo's dome of St. Peter's, which capped it all off. Even
Washington, D.C.'s Capitol Building was inspired by this dome.

Back up or step to one side to look above the triangular pediment to the building itself. You'll see the beginnings of a roofline
that was abandoned in mid-construction. The pediment was originally intended to be higher, but when the support columns arrived,
they were shorter than ordered. Even the most enlightened can
forget to "measure twice, cut once."

• *Pass between the enormous, one–piece (too–short) granite columns (most
are original) and through the enormous, 2,000-year-old bronze door.
Take a seat and take it all in.*

Pantheon Interior

The dome, which was the largest made until the Renaissance,
is set on a circular base. The
mathematical perfection of this
dome-on-a-base design is a
testament to Roman engineering. The dome is as high as it is
wide—44 meters (142 feet) from
floor to rooftop and from side to side. To picture it, imagine a
basketball set inside a wastebasket so that it just touches bottom.

The dome is made from concrete that gets lighter and thinner
as it reaches the top. The walls at the base are seven meters (23 feet)
thick and made from heavy travertine concrete, while near the top
they're less than two meters (5 feet) thick and made of a light vol-

canic rock. Both Brunelleschi and
Michelangelo studied this dome
before building their own (in Florence and in the Vatican). Remember, St. Peter's Cathedral is really
only "the dome of the Pantheon
atop the Basilica of Constantine."

The oculus, or eye–in–the–sky,
at the top, the building's only light

source, is almost 10 meters (30 feet) across. The 1,800-year-old floor has holes in it and slants toward the edges to let the rainwater drain. The marble floor is largely restored, though the designs are close to the originals.

In ancient times, this was a one–stop–shopping temple where you could worship any of the gods whose statues decorated the niches. Early in the Middle Ages the Pantheon became a Christian church (from "all the gods" to "all the martyrs"), which saved it from architectural cannibalism and ensured its upkeep through the Dark Ages. The only major destruction came in the 17th century, when the pope took the bronze plating from the ceiling of the entry porch and melted it down—some was used to build the huge bronze canopy over the altar at St. Peter's.

About the only new things in the interior are the decorative statues and the tombs of famous people, such as the artist Raphael (to the left of the main altar, in the glass case) and modern Italy's first two kings, Victor Emmanuel II (to the right) and Umberto I (to the left). Under Umberto lies his Queen, Margherita, for whom pizza Margherita is named.

The Pantheon is the only continuously used ancient building in Rome. When you leave, you'll notice how the rest of the city has risen on 20 centuries of rubble.

The Pantheon also contains the world's greatest Roman column. There it is, spanning the entire 44 meters (144 feet) from heaven to earth—the pillar of light from the oculus.

CHURCHES NEAR THE PANTHEON
Francesi, Gesu, Sopra Minerva, and St. Ignazio
* *These four churches are all less than 10 minutes' walk from the Pantheon.*

Church of San Luigi dei Francesi
The one truly *magnifique* sight in the French national church is the chapel in the far left corner, which was decorated by Caravaggio (free, but bring coins to buy light, Fri–Wed 7:30–12:30 & 15:30–19:00, Thu 7:30–12:30, sightseers should avoid Mass at 7:30 and 19:00, modest dress recommended).

The Calling of St. Matthew (left wall of chapel)
Matthew and his well–dressed, tax–collecting cronies sit in a dingy bar and count the money they've extorted. Suddenly, two men in robes and bare feet enter from the right—Jesus and Peter. Jesus' "Creation–of–Adam" hand emerges from the darkness to point at Matthew. A shaft of light extends the gesture, lighting up the face of bearded Matthew, who points to himself Last Supper–style to

Churches near the Pantheon

ask, "You talking to me?" Jesus came to convince Matthew to leave his sleazy job and preach Love. Matthew did.

In this, his first large–scale work, 29–year–old Caravaggio (1571–1610) shocked critics and clerics by showing a holy scene in a down–to–earth location. Lower–class people in everyday clothes were his models; his setting was a dive bar (which he knew well). Christ's teeny gold halo is the only hint of the supernatural, as Caravaggio makes a bold proclamation—that miracles are natural events experienced in a profound way.

St. Matthew and the Angel (center wall)

Matthew followed Christ's call, traveled with Him, and (supposedly) wrote His life's story (the Gospel of Matthew). Here, Matthew is hard at work when he's interrupted by an angel with a few suggestions. Matthew's bald head, wrinkled face, and grizzled beard make him an all–too–human saint. Even the teen angel lacks a holy glow—he just hangs there. Caravaggio paints a dark background, then shines a dramatic spotlight on the few things that tell the story.

The Martyrdom of St. Matthew (right wall)

Matthew lies prone, while a truly scary man straddles him and brandishes a sword. The bystanders shrink away from this angry executioner. Caravaggio shines his harsh third–degree spotlight on Matthew and the killer, who are the focus of the painting. The other figures swirl around them in a circle (with the executioner's arm as the radius). Matthew, who thought he had given up everything to follow Christ, now gives up his life as well.

When the chapel was unveiled in 1600, Caravaggio's ultra-realism shocked Rome. (Find his bearded self–portrait in the background.) Although he died only 10 years later, his uncompromising details, emotional subjects, odd compositions, and dramatic lighting set the tone for later Baroque painters.

Il Gesu Church

The center of the Jesuit order and the best symbol of the Catholic Counter-Reformation, the Gesu Church is packed with overblown art and underappreciated history (free, daily 7:00–12:30 & 16:00–19:15, modest dress recommended).

Exterior

The facade looks ho–hum, like a thousand no–name Catholic churches scattered from Europe to Southern California...until you realize that this was the first, the model for the others. Its scroll–like shoulders were revolutionary, breaking up the rigid rectangles of Renaissance architecture and signaling the coming of Baroque.

The building to the right of the church is where Ignatius of Loyola, the founder of the Jesuits, lived, worked, and died.

• *Step inside the church and look up at the huge painting on the ceiling.*

1. Ceiling Fresco and Stucco— The Triumph of the Name of Jesus (by Il Baciccia)

Gesu

The church's sunroof opens, and we can see right up to heaven. A glowing cross, with the "I.H.S." of the Society of Jesus, astounds the faithful and sends the infidels plunging down-ward. The twisted tangle of bodies—the Damned— spills over the edge of the painting's frame on their way to Hell. The painted bodies mingle with 3-D stucco bodies and a riot of decoration in a classic example of Baroque multimedia.

During the Counter-Reformation, when Catholics fought Protestants for the hearts and minds of the world's Christians, art became propaganda. The moral here is clear—this is the fate of Protestant heretics who dared pervert the true teachings of Jesus.

1 CEILING FRESCO AND STUCCO
2 NAVE
3 TOMB AND ALTARPIECE OF ST. IGNATIUS
4 "RELIGION VANQUISHING UNTRUTH"
5 TOMB AND ALTARPIECE OF ST. FRANCIS XAVIER
6 BUST OF CARDINAL BELLARMINE
7 MANGER SCENE

2. The Nave

When the church was originally built (1568), the walls were white and the decor was simple. It was designed for what the Jesuits did best—teaching. The Jesuits wanted to educate Catholics to prepare them for the onslaught of probing Protestant questions. The church's nave is like one big lecture hall, with no traditional side aisles.

In the 1500s, the best way to keep Protestants from stealing your church members was to reason with them. By the 1600s, it was easier to kill them, and the Thirty Years' War raged across Europe. The church became crusted over with the colorful, bombastic, jingoistic Baroque we see today.

3. Tomb and Altarpiece of
St. Ignatius of Loyola (left transept)
The gleaming statue of Ignatius spreads his arms wide and
gazes up, receiving a vision from on high. Ignatius (1491–1556)
was a Spanish soldier during the era of conquistadores. Then,
at age 30, he was struck down by a cannonball. While convales-
cing, he was seized by the burning desire to change his life.
He wandered Europe and traveled to Jerusalem. He meditated
with monks. He lived in a cave. At 33, he enrolled in a school
for boys to pick up the knowledge he'd missed. He studied in
Paris and in Rome. Finally, after almost two decades of learning
and seeking, he found a way to combine his military training
with his spiritual aspirations.

In 1540, the pope gave approval to Ignatius and his small
band of followers—the Society of Jesus (Jesuits). These monks,
organized like a military company, vowed complete obedience to
their "General," and placed themselves at the service of the pope.
Their mission? To be the intellectual warriors doing battle with
heretics. They were in the right place at the right time—Ignatius
and Luther were almost exact contemporaries.

Ignatius' body lies in the small coffin beneath the statue
(near ground level). This simple, intense man might have been
embarrassed by the lavish memorial to him, with its silver, gold,
green marble, and lapis lazuli columns. Above Ignatius, a statue
of God stands near a lapis lazuli globe (the biggest in the world)
and gestures as though to say, "Go and spread the Word to every
land"...which the Jesuits tried to do.

4. *Religion Vanquishing Untruth*
(marble statue group to the right of Ignatius)
This statue (and a similar one to the left of Ignatius) shows
the Church as an angry nun hauling back with a whip and just
spanking a bunch of miserable Protestants. Not too subtle.

Yes, the Jesuits got a reputation for unfeeling dedication to
truth above all else, but their weapons were words, ideas, and
critical reasoning. They taught and defended the recently
revamped doctrines of the Council of Trent (1545–1563).

5. Tomb and Altarpiece of St. Francis Xavier
(right transept)
This was also the Age of Discovery, when Spain and Portugal
were colonizing and Christianizing the world, using force if
necessary. Francis Xavier joined a Portuguese expedition and
headed out to convert the heathen. He touched down in Africa,
India, Indonesia, China, and Japan. Along the way, he learned

new languages and customs as he tried to communicate a strange, monotheistic religion to puzzled polytheists.

He had been on the road more than a decade (1552) when he died on an island off China (see the painting over the altar). Thanks largely to zealous Jesuits such as Francis, Catholicism became a truly worldwide religion.

6. Bust of Cardinal Roberto Bellarmine— by Gian Lorenzo Bernini

The great sculptor Bernini attended this church and honored Bellarmine with a bust. The Jesuits produced some great, open-minded thinkers, from the poet Gerard Manley Hopkins to modern mystic Teilhard de Chardin. But they also caught flak for being closed-minded to new ideas. In the 1700s, several countries expelled them, and finally (1773), the pope even banned the Society. Chastened, they were brought back (1814) and today fill the staff of many a Catholic college.

7. Manger Scene

Don't leave before pressing the button to see water run, comets shoot, and angels fly. It's cheesy, but it carries on the Baroque tradition of using whiz-bang effects to make the supernatural seem tangible to the masses.

Church of Santa Maria sopra Minerva

Exterior

From the outside, survey the many layers of Rome: An Egyptian obelisk sits on a Baroque elephant in front of a Gothic church built over *(sopra)* a pre-Christian, pagan Temple of Minerva (free, daily 7:00–12:00 & 15:30–19:00, modest dress recommended).

Before stepping in, notice the high-water-mark plaques *(Alluvione)* on the wall to the right of the door. Inside, you'll see that the lower parts of some frescoes were lost to floods. (After the last great flood, in 1870, Rome built the present embankments, finally breaking the spirit of the Tiber River.)

Nave

This is the only Gothic church you'll see in Rome. The ceiling has pointed, crisscross arches in a starry blue sky. When this

Dominican church was built, Gothic was the rage in northern Europe, but Rome was almost a ghost town. Little was built during this time. Much of what was built was later redone in the Baroque style. This church is a refreshing exception.

Main Altar

The body of St. Catherine lies under the altar (her head is in Siena). In the 1300s, this Italian nun was renowned for her righteousness and her visions of a mystical marriage with Jesus. Her impassioned letters convinced the pope to return from France to Rome, thus saving Italy from untold chaos.

In 1634, a frail, 70-year-old Galileo knelt at this altar on the way to his trial before the Inquisition in the Sopra Minerva monastery. Facing the fierce Dominican lawyers, he renounced his heretical belief that the earth moved around the sun. (Legend has it that as he walked out, he whispered, "But it *does* move.")

Left of the altar stands a little-known Michelangelo statue, *Christ Bearing the Cross*. Michelangelo gave Jesus an athlete's body (a striking contrast to the docile Christ of medieval art), but he left the face to one of his pupils. Originally, Christ was buck naked, but was later given a golden girdle by Counter-Reformation prudes.

The tomb of the great early Renaissance painter (and Dominican brother) Fra Angelico ("Beato Angelico 1387–1455") is farther to the left, just up the three stairs.

Over in the right (south) transept, pop in a coin for light, and enjoy a Filippino Lippi fresco showing scenes of the great Dominican scholar St. Thomas Aquinas (big man in black and white).

• *Exit the church via its rear door (behind the Michelangelo statue), walk down Fra Angelico lane (spy any artisans at work), turn left, and walk to the next square. On your right, you'll find the . . .*

Church of St. Ignazio

This church is a riot of Baroque illusions (free, daily 7:00–12:30 & 15:30–19:00, modest dress recommended).

In the nave, look up at the large, colorful ceiling fresco. St. Ignatius (in the center) is having a vision of Christ with the Cross. Heavenly light from the vision bounces off his chest, and the rays beam to the four corners of the earth (including America, to the left, depicted as a bare-breasted Indian maiden spearing naked men). Now fix your eyes on the arch at the far end of the painting. Walk up the nave, and watch the arch grow and tower over you.

Before you reach the center of the church, stop at the small yellow disk on the floor and look up into the central (black) dome. Watching the dome, walk under and past it. Building project runs out of money? Hire a painter to paint a fake, flat dome.

Back outside, the church faces the yellow headquarters of the Carabinieri police force, forming a square with several converging streets that has been compared to a stage set. Sit on the church steps, admire the theatrical yellow backdrop, and watch the "actors" enter one way and exit another, in the human opera that is modern Rome.

BATHS OF DIOCLETIAN
TOUR

Of all the marvelous structures built by the Romans, their public baths were the grandest, and the Baths of Diocletian were the granddaddy of them all. These baths sprawled over 10 acres—roughly twice the area of the entire Forum—and could cleanse 3,000 Romans at once. Today, there are several sections you can visit:

The **Church of Santa Maria degli Angeli**, housed in the former main hall of the baths, is the single most impressive place. The entrance is on Piazza Repubblica (free, Mon–Sat 7:00–18:30, Sun 8:00–19:30, closed to sightseers during Mass).

The **Octagonal Hall** (Aula Ottagona), also facing Piazza Repubblica, is a well-preserved rotunda that now displays sculpture from the baths. As you face the church entrance, the Octagonal Hall is 100 meters (328 feet) to your left (free, Tue–Sat 9:00–14:00, Sun 9:00–13:00, closed Mon, borrow the English-description booklet, handy WC hidden in the back corner through an unmarked door).

The **Museum of the Bath** (Museo Nazionale Romano Terme di Diocleziano) contains tons of Roman tombstones and inscriptions. The entrance faces the Termini train station (€5, covered by €20 combo-ticket, Tue–Sun 9:00–19:45, last entry 45 min before closing, closed Mon, Viale E. De Nicola 79, tel. 06-4782-6152).

Energetic architecture wonks can even walk the perimeter of the baths: from Via Torino to Piazza dei Cinquecento to Via Volturno to Via XX Settembre.

SANTA MARIA DEGLI ANGELI

From Piazza Repubblica, step through the curved brick wall of the ancient baths and into the church.

Baths of Diocletian

GREAT CLOISTER
←ENTRY
GARDEN
VIA GAETA
MUSEUM OF THE BATH
PIAZZA DEI CINQUE-CENTO
FRIGI-DARIUM
SANTA MARIA DEGLI ANGELI
EXHIBITION HALL
CENTRAL HALL
TO TERMINI STATION
VIA PARIGI
VIA CERNAIA
TEPI-DARIUM
ENTRY
VIALE EINAUDI
OCTAGONAL HALL
FOUNTAIN
CALDARIUM
VIA ORL.
VIA TERME DIOCLEZIANO
PIAZZA REPUBBLICA
Ⓜ
SAN BERNARDO
N
DCH
TO VICTOR EMMANUELE MONUMENT
— EXISTING WALLS
-- ANCIENT OUTLINE
100 YARDS
100 METERS

The Church's Entry Hall—The Baths' Tepidarium

This round-domed room with an oculus (open skylight) was once the cooling-off room of the baths where medium, "tepid" temperatures were maintained. Romans loved to sweat out last night's indulgences at the baths. After stripping in the locker rooms,

they'd enter the steam baths of the *caldarium*, located where Piazza Repubblica is today. The *caldarium* had wood furnaces—stoked by slaves—under the raised floors to heat the floors and hot tubs. The ceiling was low to keep the room steamy.

Next, you'd pass into

this *tepidarium*, where masseuses would rub you down and scrape you off with a stick (Romans didn't use soap). Finally, you'd continue on to the central area of the baths...

The Church's Large Transept— The Baths' Central Hall

This hall retains the grandeur of the ancient baths. It's the size of a football field and seven stories high—originally higher, since the old floor was five meters (about 15 feet) below its present level. The ceiling's crisscross arches were an architectural feat unmatched for a thousand years. The eight red granite columns are original—stand next to one and feel its 1.5-meter (5-foot) girth. (Only the 8 in the transept proper are original. The others are made of plastered-over brick.) The original hall was covered with mosaics, marble, and gold, and lined with statues.

From here, Romans could continue (through what is now the apse, near altar) into a large, open-air courtyard to take a dip in the large 3,000-square-meter (32,000-square-foot) swimming pool (in the *frigidarium*) that paralleled this huge hall. Many other rooms, gardens, and courtyards extended beyond what we see here. The baths were built in only 10 years (around A.D. 300)—amazing when you think of the centuries it took builders of puny medieval cathedrals, such as Paris' Notre-Dame.

Mentally undress your fellow tourists and churchgoers, and imagine hundreds of naked or togaed Romans wrestling, doing jumping jacks, singing in the baths, networking, or just milling about.

The baths were more than washrooms. They were health clubs with exercising areas, equipment, and swimming pools. They had gardens for socializing. Libraries, shops, bars, fast-food vendors, pedicurists, depilators, and brothels catered to every Roman need. Most important, perhaps, the baths offered a spacious, cool-in-summer/warm-in-winter place for Romans to get out of their stuffy apartments, schmooze, or simply hang out.

Admission was virtually free, requiring only the smallest coin. Baths were open to men and women—and during Nero's reign, coed bathing was popular—but generally there were either separate rooms or separate entry times. Most Romans went daily.

The church we see today was designed by Michelangelo (1561), who placed the entry at the right end of the long hall, using it as the nave. Later, when Piazza Repubblica became an important Roman intersection, another architect reoriented it, turning Michelangelo's nave into a long transept, so people could enter from the piazza.

Step into the sacristy (free, left of main altar) for an explanation of the church's architectural history and copies of Michelangelo's drawings.

Notice the immensity and height of the Roman brickwork in this room (and just outside in the courtyard). Large building projects like this were political security: They provided employment and fed the masses.

Diocletian (ruled A.D. 285–305) struggled with a system to rule his unwieldy empire. He broke it into zones ruled by four "tetrarchs." Later, Constantine divided the empire into east and west halves. During Diocletian's "tetrarchs" period, architecture and art were grandiose, but almost a caricature of greatness—meant to proclaim to Romans that their city was still the power it no longer was.

The baths were one of the last great structures built before Rome's 200-year fall. They functioned until A.D. 537, when barbarians cut the city's aqueducts, plunging Rome into a thousand years of poverty, darkness, and B.O.

OCTAGONAL HALL *(AULA OTTAGONA)*

This octagonal building, capped by a dome with a hole in the top, may have served as a cool room *(frigidarium)*, with small pools of cold water for plunging into. Or, because of its many doors, it may simply have been a large intersection, connecting other parts of the baths. Either way, it's one of the best-preserved rooms. Originally, the floor was seven meters (23 feet) lower—as you can see through the glass-covered hole in the floor. The graceful iron grid supported the canopy of a 1928 planetarium. Today, the hall's a free gallery showing off fine bronze and marble statues, some of which once decorated the Baths of Caracalla. Of the statues (mostly Roman copies of Greek originals—athletes, gods, Herculeses, satyrs, and portraits), two merit a close look:

The Boxer at Rest—*Pugilatore,* First Century B.C.

An exhausted boxer sits between rounds and gasps for air. See the brass-knuckle-type Roman boxing gloves. Textbook Hellenistic, this bronze statue is realistic and full of emotion. His face is scarred, his back muscles are knotted, and he's got cauliflower ears. He's losing.

Slumped over, he turns with a questioning look ("Why am I losing again?"), and eyes that once held glass now make him look empty indeed. I coulda been a contender.

Roman Aristocrat

The aristocrat's face is older than his body. This bronze-casted statue is typical of the day: Take a body of Alexander the Great and pop on a portrait bust.

MUSEUM OF THE BATH

The museum is separated into three parts: Epigraphy (most interesting), History of the Proto-Latin People (dull pre-Roman vases, etc.), and the Michelangelesque cloister (yawn). If you're killing time at Termini station, the museum becomes more interesting.

Epigraphy

Epigraphy means the study of inscribed objects, and ancient Rome was big on writing, from tombs to laws to graffiti to propaganda. This museum is difficult to appreciate quickly, and most travelers will find more history presented on a grander scale at the nearby National Museum of Rome. Here, you'll see many fragments, and it takes time and patience to read the English descriptions.

The building, with its white walls and suspended walkways, has a light, airy feeling, but the only reminder of the baths is in the museum's name.

Ground floor: The first room contains pottery, bronze vases, and votive offerings found in tombs and at altars. Notice the display case (far end) containing the artifacts from a warrior's grave: swords, a helmet, and a remarkably well-preserved anatomical breastplate (475 B.C.).

In the side hall (loaded with tombstones), look for the two pottery cups in a small glass case (to the left) titled "Catiline and Cato Seeking Votes" (63 B.C.). In hopes of getting elected, candidates would write their names on cups, fill the cups with food or drink, then pass them out to people on the street. Cato's bowl is bigger—he won. Politicians (and voters) haven't changed much.

First Floor: On the first floor (which holds more tombstones), follow the walkways—lined with even more tombstones—to a room holding several statues and the sarcophagus of a man who supervised gladiators (A.D. 270). On his tomb, the peaceful country scene of sheep and shepherds is disturbed by huge, hungry lions gobbling sheep (at the sides of the tomb), while charioteer babies race along the top.

Second Floor: Along the walkway, you'll find some early Christian inscriptions (third century), one showing the sign of the fish (symbolizing Jesus) and an anchor (representing the cross). Near the back of the hall (and the WCs) are tombs showing Romans in action: cobbling shoes, spinning yarn, dancing, working with marble, and fighting gladiators.

In the uppermost room, a painted marble bas-relief shows the god Mithras, in a red cloak, stabbing a bull. The cult of Mithras believed this act brought life to the universe (though it didn't do much for the bull). It's thought that much marble sculpture was once painted.

History of the Proto-Latin People
The two wings of this section, which overlook the cloister, would be more interesting if air-conditioned. One wing tells the history of the pre-Roman people and the other displays articles found in tombs (from the 11th to sixth century B.C.). Although ancient Rome was impressive, this part of the museum reminds us that the Roman civilization built upon a solid foundation.

Michelangelesque Cloister
So named because it was based on a drawing by the great Renaissance artist, this large, elegant cloister was built in 1565. As you enter the courtyard, look left to see the lifelike monk. There's no need to walk around the cloisters, unless you like mediocre statuary.

PIAZZA DELLA REPUBBLICA
The piazza, shaped like an exedra (a semicircular recess in a wall or building), echoes the wall of a stadium adjoining the original baths. It was called Piazza Exedra until Italian unification. The thundering Via Nazionale starts at what was an ancient door. Look down it (past the almost erotic nymphs of the Naiad fountain) to the Victor Emmanuel Monument. The Art Nouveau fountain of the four water nymphs created quite a stir when unveiled in 1911. The nymphs were modeled after a set of twins, who kept coming to visit as late as the 1960s for a reminder of their nubile youth.

NATIONAL MUSEUM OF ROME TOUR

Museo Nazionale Romano
Palazzo Massimo alla Terme

Rome lasted a thousand years, and so do most Roman history courses. But if you want a breezy overview of this fascinating society, there's no better place than the Palazzo Massimo.

Rome took Greek culture and wrote it in capital letters. Thanks to this lack of originality, ancient Greek statues were preserved for our enjoyment today. But the Romans also pioneered an unheard-of path in art—sculpting painfully realistic portraits of emperors and important citizens.

Think of this museum as a walk back in time. As you gaze at the same statues the Romans swooned over, Rome comes alive—from Romulus sucking a wolf's teat to Julius Caesar's murder to Caligula's incest to the coming of Christianity.

Orientation

Cost: €6, covered by €20 combo–ticket.

Hours: Tue–Sun 9:00–19:45, last entry 45 min before closing, closed Mon, open some summer Sat until 23:00.

Getting There: The museum is about 100 meters (330 feet) from the Termini train station (Metro: Termini). As you leave the station, it's the sandstone-brick building ahead on your left. Enter at the far end, at Largo di Villa Peretti.

Information: Tel. 06-481-4144.

Tours: An audioguide costs €4 (buy ticket first, then get audioguide at bookshop). To see the fresco collection on the second floor, you must reserve an entry time for a free, 45-minute tour led by an Italian- (and sometimes English-) speaking guide. If interested, book the next available tour when you buy your ticket.

Length of Our Tour: Allow two hours.

Starring: The Discus Thrower, Roman emperor busts, original Greek statues, and fine Roman copies.

THE MUSEUM

The Palazzo Massimo is now the permanent home of the major Greek and Roman statues that were formerly scattered in other museums. However, some famous statues once in the collection (*The Boxer at Rest*, *Gaul Killing His Wife*, and *Ludovisi Throne*) are still located elsewhere. With its long name, Palazzo Massimo seems to be searching for a convenient nickname to distinguish it from other "Museo Nazionales" around town.

The museum is rectangular, with rooms and hallways built around a central courtyard. The ground-floor displays follow Rome's history as it changes from democratic republic to dictatorial empire. The first-floor exhibits take Rome from its peak to its slow fall. The second floor houses rare frescoes and fine mosaics (reservation for a free tour required), and the basement displays coins and everyday objects. As you tour this museum, note that "room" is *sala* in Italian and "hall" is *galleria*.

GROUND FLOOR—FROM SENATORS TO CAESARS

• *Buy your ticket and pass through the turnstile, where you'll find . . .*

Minerva

It's big, it's gaudy, it's a weird goddess from a pagan cult. Welcome to the Roman world. The statue is also a good reminder that all the statues in this museum—now missing limbs, scarred by erosion, or weathered down to the bare stone—were once whole and painted to look as lifelike as possible.

• *Continuing to the right, you'll stand at the head of . . .*

Gallery I—Portrait Heads from the Republic, 500–1 B.C.

Stare into the eyes of these stern, hardy, no-nonsense, farmer-stock people who founded Rome. The wrinkles and crags of these original "ugly Republicans" tell the story of Rome's roots as a small agricultural tribe that fought neighboring tribes for survival.

These faces are brutally realistic, unlike more idealized Greek statues. Romans honored their ancestors and worthy citizens in the "family" (*gens*) of Rome. They wanted lifelike statues to remember them by, and to instruct the young with their air of moral rectitude.

In its first 500 years, Rome was a republic ruled by a Senate of wealthy landowners. But as Rome expanded throughout Italy and the economy shifted from farming to booty, changes were needed.

• *Enter Room I* (Sala I). *Along the wall, between the doorways, find the bust of . . .*

National Museum—Ground Floor

1 MINERVA
2 PORTRAIT HEADS
3 JULIUS CAESAR
4 AUGUSTUS
5 FOUR FRESCOES
6 LIVIA
7 TIBERIUS
8 CALIGULA
9 ALEXANDER THE GREAT
10 SOCRATES
11 NIOBID
12 GREEK-MANIA

Julius Caesar *(Rilievo con Ritratto c.d. Cesare)*, c. 100–44 B.C.

The prominent brow, the strong nose, the male-pattern baldness with the forward comb-over... these features identify the man who changed Rome forever. (Or some think it may be a look-alike.)

When this charismatic general swept onto the scene, Rome was in chaos. Rich landowners were fighting middle-class plebs, who wanted their slice of the plunder. Slaves such as Spartacus were picking up hoes and hacking up masters. And renegade generals—the new providers of wealth and security in a booty economy—were becoming dictators. (Notice the **life-size statue** of an unknown but obviously once-renowned general.)

Caesar was a people's favorite. He conquered Gaul (France), then sacked Egypt, then impregnated Cleopatra. He defeated rivals and made them his allies. He gave great speeches. Chicks dug him.

With the army at his back and the people in awe, he took the reins of government, instituted sweeping changes, made himself the center of power... and antagonized lovers of freedom everywhere.

A band of Republican assassins surrounded him in a Senate meeting. He called out for help as one by one they stepped up to take turns stabbing him. The senators sat and watched in silence. One of the killers was his adopted son, Brutus, and Caesar died saying, "*Et tu, Brute?*"

• *At the end of the hall, turn left, then left again, into the large glassed-in Room V, with a life-size statue of Augustus.*

Room V—Augustus and Rome's Legendary Birth

Statue of Augustus as Pontifex Maximus
(Ritratto di Augusto in Vesta di Offerente)

Julius Caesar died, but his family name, his politics, and his flamboyance lived on. Julius had adopted his grandnephew, Octavian, who united Rome's warring factions and became the first emperor, Augustus.

Here, 50-year-old Emperor Augustus has taken off his armor and laurel-leaf crown, donning the simple hooded robes of a priest. He's retiring to a desk job after a lifetime of fighting to reunite Rome. He killed Brutus and eliminated his rivals, Mark Antony and Cleopatra. For the first time in almost a century of fighting, one general reigned supreme. Octavian took the title "Augustus" ("He who just keeps getting bigger") and became the first of the emperors who would rule Rome for the next 500 years.

In fact, Augustus was a down-to-earth man who lived simply, worked hard, read books, listened to underlings, and tried to restore traditional Roman values after the turbulence of Julius Caesar's time. He outwardly praised and defended the Senate and the republic while actually becoming a dictator. Despite the excesses of his descendants, Augustus' reign marked the start of 200 years of peace and prosperity, the "Pax Romana."

See if the statue matches a description of Augustus by a contemporary—the historian Seutonius: "He was unusually handsome. His expression was calm and mild. He had clear, bright eyes, in which was a kind of divine power. His eyebrows met. His hair was slightly curly and somewhat golden." Any variations were made by sculptors who idealized features to make him almost godlike.

Augustus proclaimed himself a god—not arrogantly or

blasphemously, as Caligula later did, but as the honored "father" of the "family" of Rome. As the empire expanded, the vanquished had to worship the emperor's statue as a show of loyalty. Augustus even claimed he was descended from Romulus and Remus. Such propaganda solidified the emperor's hold over Rome as both political and spiritual head.

• *At this crucial dividing point in Roman history—from republic to empire—let's refresh our memory of Rome's legendary origins. At the opposite end of Room V, find...*

Four Frescoes of Rome's Mythical Origins
(*Fregio Pittorico*, etc.)

These cartoon-strip frescoes (read right to left) tell the story of Augustus' legendary forebears.

1. Upper right fresco: Aeneas (red skin and sword) arrives in Italy from Troy and fights the locals for a place to live.

2. Upper left: His wife (far left, seated, in purple) and son build a city wall around Rome. The womenfolk are safe and the city prospers.

3. Lower right: Several generations later, the God of War (lounging in center, with red skin) lies in wait to rape and impregnate a Vestal Virgin.

4. Lower left: Her disgraced babies, Romulus and Remus, are placed in a basket (center) and set adrift on the Tiber River. They wash ashore, are suckled by a wolf, and finally (far left) taken in by a shepherd. These legendary babies, of course, grow up to found the city that makes real history.

• *Cross the hallway into Room IV. The bust next to the door is the empress Livia.*

Room IV—The Julio-Claudian Family: Rome's First Emperors, c. 50 B.C.–A.D. 68

Julius Caesar's descendants ruled Rome for a century after his death, turning the family surname "Caesar" into a title.

Livia

Augustus' wife, Livia, was a major power behind the throne. Her stern, thin-lipped gaze withered rivals at court. Her hairstyle—bunched up in a peak, braided down the center, and tied in back—became the rage of Europe, as her face appeared everywhere in statues and on coins. Notice that by the next generation (Antonia Minore, Livia's daughter-in-law), a simpler bun was chic. And by the following generation, it was tight curls. Empresses dictated fashion like emperors dictated policy.

Livia bore Augustus no sons. She lobbied hard for Tiberius, her own son by a first marriage, to succeed as emperor. Augustus didn't like him, but Livia was persuasive. He relented, ate some bad figs, and died—the gossip was that Livia poisoned him to seal the bargain. The pattern of succession was established—adopt a son from within the extended family—and Tiberius was proclaimed emperor.

• *Over your left shoulder, in the corner of the room, is ...*

Tiberius *(Tiberio)*, ruled A.D. 14–37

Scholars speculate that acne may have soured Tiberius to the world. Shy and sullen but diligent, he worked hard to be the easygoing leader of men Augustus had been. Early on, he was wise and patient, but he suffered personal setbacks. Politics forced him to divorce his only beloved and marry a slut. His favorite brother died, then his son. Embittered, he let subordinates run things and retired to Capri, where he built a villa with underground dungeons. There he hosted orgies of sex, drugs, torture, really loud music, and execution. At his side was his young grandnephew, who he adopted as next emperor.

• *To your right, in the glass case, is the small bust of ...*

Caligula *(Caligola)*, ruled A.D. 37–41

This emperor had sex with his sisters, tortured his enemies, stole friends' wives during dinner, then returned to rate their performance in bed, crucified Christians, tore up parking tickets, and had men kneel before him as a god. Caligula has become the archetype of a man with enough power to act out his basest fantasies.

Politically, he squandered Rome's money, then taxed and extorted from the citizens. Perhaps he was made mad by illness, perhaps he was the victim of vindictive historians, but still, no one mourned when assassins ambushed him and ran a sword through his privates. Rome was tiring of this family dynasty's dysfunction. Augustus must have been rolling in his grave ... and they hadn't even seen Nero yet.

Before leaving the room, look around and see if you can spot a family resemblance. Livia's thin lips and Augustus' strong nose? Eh, maybe.

• *Continue down the hall and turn left. Lining the hallway are busts of ...*

Gallery III—Rome's Greek Mentors

Rome's legions easily conquered the less-organized but more-cultured Greek civilization that had dominated the Mediterranean for centuries. Romans adopted Greek gods, art styles, and fashions, and sophisticated Romans sprinkled their conversation with Greek phrases.

Alexander the Great *(Alessandro Magno)*

Alexander the Great (356–323 B.C.) single-handedly created an empire by conquering, in just a few short years, lands from Greece to Egypt to Persia, spreading Greek culture and language along the way. Later, when the Romans conquered Greece (c. 200 B.C.), they inherited this preexisting collection of cultured, Greek-speaking cities ringing the Mediterranean.

Alexander's handsome statues set the standard for those of later Roman emperors. His features were chiseled and youthful, and he was adorned with pompous decorations, like a golden sunburst aura (which was fitted into holes). The greatest man of his day, he ruled the known world by the age of 30.

Alexander, a Macedonian, had learned Greek culture from his teacher, none other than the philosopher Aristotle. Aristotle's teacher was Plato, whose mentor was Socrates.

• *To Alexander's left is . . .*

Socrates *(Socrate)*

This nonconformist critic of complacent thinking is the father of philosophy. The Greeks were an intellectual, introspective, sensitive, and artistic people. The Romans were practical, no-nonsense soldiers, salesmen, and bureaucrats. Many a Greek slave—warning a Roman senator not to wear a plaid toga with a polka-dot robe—was more cultured than his master.

• *Enter room VII between Alexander and Socrates.*

Room VII—Pure Greek Beauty in Greek Originals

Niobid *(Niobide Ferita)*, 440 B.C.

The Romans were astonished by the beauty of Greek statues. This woman's smooth skin contrasts with the rough folds of her clothing. Her pose is angular but still balanced—notice how she twists naturally around an axis running straight up and down. She looks like a classical goddess awakening from a beautiful dream. But . . .

Circle around back. The hole bored in her back, right in that itchy place you can't quite reach, once held a golden arrow. The woman has been shot by Artemis, goddess of hunting, because her mother dared to boast to the gods about her kids. The Niobid reaches back in vain, trying to remove the arrow before it drains her of life.

Romans ate this stuff up: the sensual beauty, the underplayed pathos, the very

Greekness of it. They crated up centuries-old statues like this and brought them home to their gardens and palaces. Appreciate the beauty in this room, since these are some of the world's rare, surviving Greek originals.

• *Continue down the hall and into...*

Room VIII—Greek Mania

Rome was in the grip of a "Neo-Attic" (Nouveau Greek) craze, and there weren't enough old statues to meet the demand. Crafty Greeks began cranking out knock-offs of Greek originals for mass consumption. Though copies, the works in this room were of extremely high quality, while others were more like cheesy fake *Davids* in a garden store.

To the Romans, this "art" was just furniture for their homes. An altar from a Greek temple became a place to set your wine, a sacred basin was a rain catcher, a statue of Athena took your olive pits. Different styles from different historical periods were mixed and matched to suit Roman tastes. The rich Roman who bought *Afrodite Pudica*, signed along the base by "Menophantos," would not have known or cared that the artist was copying a one-of-a-kind original done by the great Praxiteles 400 years before, back when Greece was Golden.

Rome conquered Greece, but the Greeks conquered the Romans.

• *We've covered Rome's first 500 years. At the end of the hall are the stairs up to the first floor.*

FIRST FLOOR

As we saw, Augustus' family did not always rule wisely. Under Nero (ruled A.D. 54–68), the debauchery, violence, and paranoia typical of the Julio-Claudians festered to a head. When the city burned in the great fire of 64, the Romans suspected Nero of torching it himself to clear land for his enormous luxury palace.

Enough. Facing a death sentence, Nero committed suicide with the help of a servant. An outsider was brought in to rule.

• *At the top of the stairs, enter Room I. To your right is Vespasian.*

Room I—The Flavian Family

Vespasian *(Vespasianus)*, **ruled A.D. 69–79**

Balding and wrinkled, with a big head, a double chin, and a shy smile, Vespasian was a common man. The son of a tax collector, he rose through the military ranks with a reputation as a competent drudge. As emperor, he restored integrity, raised taxes, started the Colosseum, and suppressed the Jewish rebellion in Palestine.

National Museum—First Floor

1 VESPASIAN	**9** DISCUS THROWER
2 DOMITIAN	**10** HERMAPHRODITE
3 DOMITIA	**11** SEPTIMIUS SEVERUS
4 NERVA	**12** CARACALLA
5 TRAJAN	**13** BALBINUS
6 HADRIAN	**14** GORDIANUS III
7 APHRODITE CROUCHING	**15** SARCOPHAGUS
8 APOLLO	**16** CHRIST TEACHING

• *In the center of the room is . . .*

Domitian *(Domitianus)*
Vespasian's son, Domitian (emperor A.D. 81–96), used his father's
tax revenues to construct the massive Imperial Palace on Palatine
Hill, home to emperors for the next three centuries. Shown with
his lips curled in a sneering smile, he was a moralistic prude who
executed several Vestal ex-Virgins, while in private he took one
mistress after another. Until . . .
• *Over your left shoulder, find . . .*

Domitia
. . . until his stern wife found out and hired a servant to stab him in
the groin. Domitia's hairstyle is a far cry from the "Livia" cut, with
a high crown of tight curls.
• *In the corner opposite Domitia is . . .*

Nerva
Nerva (ruled A.D. 96–98) realized that the Flavian dynasty was
no better than its predecessors. Old and childless, he made a

bold, far-sighted move—he adopted a son from outside of Rome's corrupting influence.

• *Entering Room II, Trajan is on the left wall.*

Room II—A Cosmopolitan Culture

Trajan *(Traianus-Hercules)*, ruled A.D. 98–117

Born in Spain, this conquering hero pushed Rome's borders to their greatest extent, creating a truly worldwide empire. The spoils of three continents funneled into a city of a million-plus people. Trajan could dress up in a lion's skin, presenting himself as a "new Hercules," and no one found it funny. Romans felt a spirit of Manifest Destiny: "The gods desire that the City of Rome shall be the capital of all the countries of the world." (Livy)

• *On the opposite wall . . .*

Hadrian *(Hadrianus)*, ruled A.D. 117–138

Hadrian was a fully cosmopolitan man. His beard—the first we've seen—shows his taste for foreign things; he poses like the Greek philosopher he imagined himself to be.

Hadrian was a voracious tourist, personally visiting almost every corner of the vast empire, from Britain (where he built Hadrian's Wall) to Egypt (where he sailed the Nile), from Jerusalem (where he suppressed another Jewish revolt) to Athens (where he soaked up classical culture). An omnivorous learner, he scaled Sicily's Mount Etna just to see what made a volcano tick. Back home, he beautified Rome with the Pantheon and his Villa at Tivoli, a microcosm of places he'd visited.

Hadrian is flanked here by the two loves of his life. His wife, **Sabina** (left), with modest hairstyle and scarf, kept the home fires burning for her traveling husband. Hadrian was 50 years old when he became captivated by a teenage boy named **Antinous** (right), with his curly hair and full, sensual lips. Together they traveled the Nile, where Antinous drowned. Hadrian wept. This public display of emotion, somewhat embarrassing to the stoic Romans, became a legend among Greeks, who erected Antinous statues everywhere.

Hadrian spent his last years at his lavish villa outside Rome, surrounded by buildings and souvenirs that reminded him of his traveling days.

• *Backtrack through room I and turn right, down a hall that leads into the large Room V.*

Rooms V and VI—Rome's Grandeur

Pause at Rome's peak to admire the things the Romans found beautiful. Imagine these statues in their original locations, in the pleasure gardens of the Roman rich—surrounded by greenery, with the splashing sound of fountains, the statues all painted in bright, lifelike colors. Though executed by Romans, the themes are mostly Greek, with godlike humans and human-looking gods.

• *In the center of Room V is...*

Aphrodite Crouching (Afrodite Accovacciata)

The goddess of beauty crouches while bathing, then turns to admire herself. This sets her whole body in motion—one thigh goes down, one up; her head turns clockwise while her body goes reverse—yet she's perfectly still. The crouch creates a series of symmetrical love handles, molded by the sculptor into the marble like wax. Hadrian had good taste—he ordered a copy of this Greek classic for his bathroom.

• *Nearby, find the large statue of...*

Apollo

The god of light appears as a slender youth, not some burly, powerful, autocratic god. He stands *contrapposto*—originally he was leaning against the tree—in a relaxed and very human way. His curled hair is tied with a headband, with strands that tumble down his neck. His muscles and skin are smooth. (The rusty stains come from the centuries Apollo spent submerged in the Tiber.) Apollo is in a reflective mood, and the serenity and intelligence in his face show off classical Greece as a nation of thinkers.

• *At the end of the room is...*

The Discus Thrower (Discobolo)

An athlete winds up, about to unleash his pent-up energy and hurl the discus. The sculptor has frozen the moment for us, so we can examine the inner workings of the wonder called man. The perfect pecs and washboard abs make this human godlike. Geometrically, you could draw a perfect circle around him, with his hipbone at the center. He's natural yet ideal, twisting yet balanced, moving while at rest. For the Greeks, the universe was a rational place, and the human body was the perfect embodiment of the order found in nature.

This statue is the best-preserved Roman copy (not one member is missing—I checked) of the original Greek work by Myron (450 B.C.). Statues of athletes like this commonly stood in the baths, where Romans cultivated healthy bodies, minds, and social skills, hoping to live well-rounded lives. *The Discus Thrower*, with his geometrical perfection and godlike air, sums up all that is best in the classical world.

• *Continue into Room VII, where you'll run into a sleeping statue.*

Room VII

Hermaphrodite Sleeping (Ermafrodito Dormiente)

After leaving the baths, a well-rounded Roman may head post-haste to an orgy, where he might see a reclining nude like this, be titillated, circle around for a closer look, and say, "Hey! (Insert your own reaction here)!"

• *Exit Room VII at the far end and turn left. Then turn right into Room XIII, and look to the right to find the bust of Septimius Severus.*

Room XIII—Beginning of the End

Septimius Severus, ruled A.D. 193–211

Rome's sprawling empire was starting to unravel, and it took a disciplined, emperor-warrior like this African to keep it together. Severus' victories on the frontier earned him a grand triumphal arch in the Forum, but here he seems to be rolling his eyes at the chaos growing around him.

• *Next to Severus is his son . . .*

Caracalla, ruled A.D. 211–217

The stubbly beard, cruel frown, and glaring eyes tell us that Severus' son was bad news. He murdered his little brother, Geta, to seize power, then proceeded to massacre thousands of loyal citizens on a whim. The army came to distrust rulers whose personal agenda got in their way, and Caracalla was stabbed in the back by a man whose brother had just been executed. Rome's long slide had begun.

Room XIV—The Fall

There are a lot of scared, serious faces in this room. People who grew up in the lap of luxury and security were witnessing the unthinkable—the disintegration of a thousand years of tradition. Rome never recovered from the chaos of the third century. Disease, corruption, revolts from within, and "barbarians" pecking away at the borders were body blows that sapped Rome's strength.

• *At the near end of this long room, find...*

Balbinus, ruled A.D. 238

This old man was appointed emperor by the Senate, but he was
no soldier, and the army didn't like him. He was one of some
20 emperors in the space of 40 years who was saluted, then murdered, at the whim of soldiers of fortune. At one point, the office
of emperor was literally auctioned to the highest bidder. Balbinus,
with his stubbly beard and forlorn look, knows he's lost the army's
confidence, and he waits for the ax to fall. Next.

Gordianus III, ruled A.D. 238–244

The 13-year-old Gordianus, with barely a wisp of facial hair, was
naive and pliable, the perfect choice—until he got old enough to
question the generals. His assassins had no problem sneaking up
on him because, as you can see, he had no ears.

Sarcophagus of a Procession
(Sarcofago con Corteo, etc.), A.D. 270

This coffin shows a parade of
dignitaries accompanying a
new Roman leader. As they
march up Capitol Hill, they
huddle together, their backs
to the wall, looking around
suspiciously for assassins.
Their faces reflect the fear of
the age. Rome would stagger
on for another 200 years, but the glory of old Rome was gone.
The city was becoming a den of thugs, thieves, prostitutes,
barbarians... and Christians.

• *Farther along, on the right-hand wall, find the small...*

Seated Statuette of Christ Teaching
(Cristo Docente), A.D. 350

Christ sits like a Roman senator—in a toga, holding a scroll,
dispensing wisdom like the law of the land. The statue comes
from those delirious days when formerly persecuted Christians
could now "come out" and worship in public. Emperor Constantine (ruled 306–337) legalized Christianity, and within two generations it was Rome's official religion.

Whether Christianity invigorated or ruined Rome is debated,
but the fall was inevitable. Rome's once-great legions backpedaled,
until even the city itself was raped and plundered by foreigners
(410). In 476, the last emperor sold his title for a comfy pension

plan, and "Rome" was just another dirty city with a big history. The barely flickering torch of ancient Rome was passed on to medieval Christians: Senators became bishops, basilicas became churches, the Pontifex Maximus (Emperor) became the Pontifex Maximus (Pope)... and the artistic masterpieces now in this museum became buried under rubble.

THE REST OF THE MUSEUM

The **second floor** contains frescoes and mosaics that once decorated the walls and floors of Roman villas. The frescoes (in black, red, yellow, and blue) show a few scenes of people and animals but are mostly architectural designs, with fake columns and "windows" that "look out" on landscape scenes. Granted, the collection is impressive, but the tour is in Italian (the guides *might* speak a little English), and it's a 45-minute commitment.

More interesting stuff is in the **basement**, housing coins and everyday objects from ancient Rome. In A.D. 300, one denar bought one egg. Evaluate Roman life by studying Diocletian's wage and price controls (glass case 21).

Find your favorite emperor or empress on the **coins** using remote-controlled magnifying glasses: Julius Caesar (case 8, #41–44), Augustus (case 8, #65, and case 9, #1–38), Augustus' system of denars (case 10), Tiberius (case 10, #1), Caligula (case 10, #17–28), and Nero (case 11, #2).

The displays trace Europe's money from denars to euros, including the monetary unit that is now history—lire.

CAPITOL HILL MUSEUM
TOUR

Recently reopened, this museum is a joy. Perched on the top of Capitol Hill Square, its two buildings (Palazzo dei Conservatori and Palazzo Nuovo) are now connected by an underground passage—which leads to the Tabularium and panoramic views of the Roman Forum.

Orientation

Cost: €8.

Hours: Tue–Sun 9:00–20:00, last entry 60 min before closing, closed Mon, Jan 1, May 1, and Dec 25.

Getting There: From Piazza Venezia or the Forum, walk uphill to the top of Capitol Hill (Campidoglio in Italian; pron. cahm-pee-DOHL-yoh).

Information: You'll find some English descriptions within the museum. Free baggage check. Tel. 06-3996-7800.

Tour: The €4 audioguide, available only at the Palazzo dei Conservatori entrance, is good.

Length of Our Tour: Allow one hour.

Cuisine Art: Great view café—called Café Capitolino—upstairs in Palazzo dei Conservatori (accessed from within museum, also has exterior entrance for public—facing museum entrance, go to your right around building).

Starring: Ancient Greek and Roman statuary, plus 14th– to 17th–century paintings and Forum views.

Museum Overview

To identify the museum's two buildings, face the equestrian statue on Capitol Hill Square (with your back to the grand stair-way leading up to the square). The Palazzo Nuovo is on your left, the Palazzo dei Conservatori is on your right (closer to the river).

Capitol Hill Museum Overview

Ahead is the Palazzo Senatorio (mayoral palace, not open to public); below it—and out of sight—are the Tabularium and underground passage connecting the two museum buildings.

You can buy a ticket at either museum. And, with your ticket, you can enter either museum (or connect the buildings underground). The ticket, valid for three hours, "starts" when it's scanned by the ticket taker.

Note that this museum is also referred to as the Capitoline Museums or Musei Capitolini. Same place.

• *Start at the …*

PALAZZO NUOVO

• *After your ticket is scanned, walk down the hall to the small courtyard on your left. Behind the glass is …*

Marcus Aurelius

This is the greatest surviving equestrian statue of antiquity. Marcus Aurelius was a Roman philosopher-emperor (ruled A.D. 161–180), known more for his *Meditations* than his prowess on the battlefield. Notice that he doesn't use stirrups. An Asian invention, those newfangled devices wouldn't arrive in Europe for another 500 years.

Dark-Age Christians thought the statue's hand was raised in blessing, which probably led to their misidentifying him as Constantine, the first Christian emperor. While most pagan statues were destroyed by Christians, "Constantine" was spared. It graced several prominent locations in medieval Rome, including the papal palace at San Giovanni in Laterano.

In 1538, Michelangelo placed this gilded bronze statue in the center of the square he designed, Capitol Hill Square, directly outside this museum. During the last few years, the statue was moved inside and restored, while a copy was placed on the square.

• *Go up the stairs. The first room at the top contains one of the museum's most famous pieces.*

Dying Gaul

A first-century-B.C. copy of a Greek original, this was sculpted to celebrate the Greeks' victory over the Galatians. It's thought this statue may have been part of a larger sculpture group (long since lost).

Wounded in battle, the dying Gaul holds himself upright, but barely. Minutes earlier, before he was stabbed in the chest, he'd been in his prime. Now he can only watch helplessly as his life ebbs away.

His sword is useless against this last battle. With his messy hair, downcast eyes, and crumpled position, he poignantly reminds us that every victory means a defeat.

• *In the next few rooms, take a quick look at . . .*

Ancient Roman Statues and Busts

A reddish faun glories in grapes and life, oblivious to the loss of his penis (at least he still has his tail). The statue, found in a couple dozen pieces in Hadrian's Villa, was skillfully restored. Check out the ceilings in this room and elsewhere; this building is truly a palazzo (palace).

More sculpture from Hadrian's Villa (and elsewhere) fills the next room, the large hall. Notice the *Wounded Amazon* (near the window) plucking her delicate dress away from her breast. This is a Roman copy of a fifth-century Greek original by Polycletus.

Roll through two rooms lined with busts—the Room of Philosophers (Socrates, Homer, Euripides, Cicero, and many more) and the Hall of Emperors (Constantine's mom Helena sits center stage, resting after her journey to Jerusalem to find Christ's Cross). In this 3-D yearbook of ancient history, there are few labels. If you knock into anything, heads will roll, but you won't know whose.

• *Enter the hallway and start down the hall. The small octagonal room— off to your left—contains one of the museum's treasures.*

Capitoline *Venus*

This is a Roman copy of a Greek fourth-century original by the master Praxiteles. Venus, leaving the bath, is suddenly aware that someone is watching her. As she turns to look, she reflexively covers up (nearly). Her blank eyes hold no personality or emotion. Her fancy hairstyle is the only complicated thing about her. She is simply beautiful—generically erotic.

• *Farther down the hallway, enter the small room to your left. Displayed on the wall is the . . .*

Mosaic of Doves

Four doves perch on the rim of a bronze bowl as one drinks water from the bowl. Minute bits make up this small, exquisite work. Found in the center of a floor in one of the rooms in Hadrian's Villa, this second-century A.D. mosaic was based on an earlier work done, of course, by the Greeks.

• *Head down the stairs to reach the underground passage (and WC). Follow signs back up one flight to the . . .*

TABULARIUM

Built in the first century A.D., these sturdy, vacant rooms once held the archives of ancient Rome. The word Tabularium comes from "tablet," on which laws were written. Inside the Tabularium, you can look to your right to see the remains of an earlier temple, look up to see two huge white hunks of a temple overhang, and look down to see an underground passage, but the irresistible urge is to look out—at the Forum. his head-on view does justice to the Forum, giving you a more complete picture of the sprawl of ancient Rome.

The arcade of the Tabularium used to have more overlooks, but some of the arches were bricked up during the Middle Ages.
• *Leave the Tabularium by going back down the stairs, then take the underground passage and stairs up to Palazzo Conservatori.*

PALAZZO DEI CONSERVATORI

In the courtyard, enjoy the massive chunks of Constantine: his head, hand, and foot. When intact, this giant held the place of honor in the Basilica of Constantine in the Forum.
• *Go up the staircase (the one in the corner of the courtyard) to the first floor. In the room at the top of the stairs, you'll find . . .*

Huge Statues, Huge Art—Roman Style

Here are more hunks of another statue of Constantine: head, finger, and a globe he held in his hand. The large wall paintings in this room commemorate the founding of Rome, from its wolfish origins (the twins Romulus and Remus nursed by a she-wolf) to the bloody battles fought with nearby tribes for supremacy. Everything about this room—the gargantuan *Constantine*, the gilded *Hercules*, and even the larger-than-life pope—is about power wielded by men.
• *For a contrast, power yourself straight ahead into the corner room to see one of the museum's highlights.*

Boy Extracting a Thorn (Spinario)

He's just a boy, intent only on picking a thorn out of his foot. As he bends over to reach his foot, his body sticks out at all angles, like a bony chicken wing. He's even scuffed up, the way small boys get. At this moment, nothing matters to him but that splinter. Our lives are filled with these mundane moments (when we'd give anything for tweezers) rarely captured in art.

Art scholars speculate that the boy's head, tilted unnaturally down, and his body are from two separate statues spliced together.
• *In the next room . . .*

Capitoline *She-Wolf*
The original bronze *She-Wolf* suckles the twins Romulus and Remus. The wolf is Etruscan from the fifth century B.C., the boys an invention of the Renaissance, the result—the symbol of Rome. Look into the eyes of the wolf. An animal looks back, with ragged ears, sharp teeth, and staring eyes. This wild animal, teamed with the wildest creatures of all—hungry babies—makes a powerful symbol for the tenacious city/empire of Rome.
• *In the next room . . .*

From Michelangelo to Medusa
Along with a kindly bust of Michelangelo, this room contains Bernini's scary bust of Medusa—even she looks stressed by the writhing snakes on her head. This goes way beyond a bad hair day.
• *Walk between Michelangelo and Medusa to the next room to discover the remarkable bust of . . .*

Commodus as Hercules
This arrogant emperor brat used to run around the palace in animal skins. Here he wears a lion's head over his own, and drapes the lion's paws over his chest. This lion king made a bad emperor.
• *Go upstairs to the . . .*

Painting Gallery
Wander among works by Van Dyck, Velázquez (self-portrait near entry), Titian, Tintoretto, and Bellini. The highlights are two Caravaggios: *St. John the Baptist* and an earlier work, *The Fortune Teller* (both in the large Santa Petronilla room).
• *Head upstairs to the café.*

VIEW CAFÉ

You've earned the café. Its huge outdoor view patio overlooks
the domes of Rome. From the Tabularium, you saw the Forum,
the heart of ancient Rome. From here, you see the churches,
representing the religion that remained after Rome fell. Be
here at sunset—it's divine.

BORGHESE GALLERY TOUR

Galleria Borghese

More than just a great museum, Galleria Borghese is a beautiful villa set in the greenery of surrounding gardens. You get to see art commissioned by the luxury-loving Borghese family displayed in the very rooms they were created for. Frescoes, marble, stucco, and interior design enhance the masterpieces. This is a place where—regardless of whether you learn a darn thing—you can sit back and enjoy the sheer beauty of the palace and its art.

Orientation

Cost: €8.

Hours: Tue–Sun 9:00–19:30, sometimes on Sat until 23:00 June–Sept, closed Mon.

Reservations: Reservations are mandatory and easy to get in English by booking online (www.ticketeria.it) or calling 06-32810 (if you get an Italian recording, press 2 for English; office hours: Mon–Fri 9:00–19:00, Sat 9:00–13:00, office closed Sat in Aug). Every two hours, 360 people are allowed to enter the museum. Entry times are 9:00, 11:00, 13:00, 15:00, and 17:00 (plus 19:00 and 21:00 if open late on Sat June–Sept). Reserve a *minimum* of several days in advance for a weekday visit, at least a week ahead for weekends. When you reserve, request a day and time, and you'll get a claim number. While you'll be advised to come 30 minutes before your appointed time, you can arrive a few minutes beforehand. But don't be late, as no-show tickets are sold to stand-bys.

If you don't have a reservation, try calling to see if there are any openings, or just show up and hope for a cancellation. Reservations are tightest at 11:00 and on weekends. No-shows are released a few minutes after the top of the hour. Generally, out of 360 reservations, a few will fail to show (but more than a few may be waiting to grab them).

Borghese Gallery—Ground Floor

1 - CANOVA - Pauline Bonaparte as Venus
2 - BERNINI - David
3 - BERNINI - Apollo Chasing Daphne
4 - BERNINI - Rape of Proserpine,
           Diana the Hunter,
           & other marbles

5 - BERNINI - Aeneas
6 - Theater of the Universe
7 - CARAVAGGIO paintings
8 - Enter Basement below for tickets,
    info, shop, WC, and stairs up to
    Pinacoteca (Painting Gallery)

Visits are strictly limited to two hours. Concentrate on the first floor, but leave yourself 30 minutes for the paintings of the Pinacoteca upstairs; highlights are marked by the audioguide icons. The fine bookshop and cafeteria are best visited outside your two-hour entry window.

Getting There: The museum is in the Villa Borghese park. A taxi can get you within 100 meters (330 feet) of the museum (tell the cabbie your destination: gah-leh-REE-ah bor-GAY-zay). Otherwise, Metro to Spagna and take a 15-minute walk through the park.

Tours: Guided English tours are offered at 9:10 and 11:10 for €5; reserve with entry reservation (or consider the excellent audioguide tour for €4).

Length of Our Tour: Two hours maximum.

Checkroom: Baggage check is free and mandatory.

Cuisine Art: A café is on-site.
Photography: No photos are allowed.
Starring: Sculptures by Bernini and paintings by Caravaggio, Raphael, and Titian.

Portico

Ancient Roman reliefs (at either end), topped by Michelangelo-designed panels, capture the essence of the collection—a gathering of beautiful objects from every age and culture inside a lavish 17th-century villa. Cardinal Borghese built the villa, collected ancient works, and hired the best artists of his day. In pursuing the optimistic spirit of the Renaissance, they invented Baroque.

Main Entry Hall

Five Roman mosaics decorate the floor with colorful, festive scenes of slaughter. Gladiators fight animals and each other with swords, whips, and tridents. The Greek letter θ (theta) marks the dead. Notice some of the gladiators' pro-wrestler nicknames: "Cupid(-o)," "Serpent(-ius)," "Licentious(-us)."

On the wall is a thrilling first-century Greek sculpture of a horse falling. The Renaissance-era rider was added by Pietro Bernini, father of the famous Bernini.

Room I

Statue of *Pauline Bonaparte as Venus* *(Paolina Borghese Bonaparte)*—**Antonio Canova (1808)**

Napoleon's sister went the full monty for the sculptor Canova, scandalizing Europe. ("How could you have done such a thing?!" she was asked. She replied, "The room wasn't cold.") With the famous nose of her conqueror brother, she strikes the pose of Venus as conqueror of men's hearts. Her relaxed afterglow and slight smirk say she's already had her man. The light dent she puts in the mattress makes this goddess human.

Notice the contrasting textures that Canova gets out of the pure-white marble: the rumpled sheet versus her smooth skin.

The satiny-smooth pillows and mattress versus the creases in them. Her porcelain skin versus the hint of a love handle. Canova polished and waxed the marble until it looked as soft and pliable as cloth.

The mythological

pose, the Roman couch, the ancient hairdo, and the calm harmony make Pauline the epitome of the neoclassical style.

Room II

David—Gian Lorenzo Bernini (1624)

Duck! David twists around to put a big rock in his sling. He purses his lips, knits his brow, and winds his body like a spring as

his eyes lock onto the target—Goliath, who's somewhere behind us, putting us right in the line of fire.

In this self-portrait, 25-year-old Bernini is ready to take on the world. He's charged with the same fighting energy that fueled the missionaries and conquistadores of the Counter-Reformation.

Compared with Michelangelo's *David*, this is gritty realism—an unbalanced pose, bulging veins, unflattering face, and armpit hair. Bernini slays the pretty-boy Davids of the Renaissance and

prepares to invent Baroque.

To David's left, find the ancient sarcophagus on the wall with the ***Labors of Hercules*** (A.D. 160, at chest level). The twisting, bodybuilders' poses were the Hellenistic inspiration for Bernini's Baroque. In the last scene, Hercules pauses while subduing a centaur to adjust himself.

Room III

Apollo and Daphne (Apollo e Dafne)—Bernini (1625)

Apollo—made stupid by Cupid's arrow of love—chases after Daphne, who has been turned off by the "arrow of disgust." Just as he's about to catch her, she calls to her father to save her. Magically, her fingers begin to sprout leaves, her toes become roots, her skin turns to bark, and she transforms into a tree. Frustrated Apollo will end up with a handful of leaves.

Stand behind the statue to experience it as Bernini originally intended. It's only when you circle around to the front that he reveals the story's surprise ending.

Gian Lorenzo Bernini (1598–1680)

A Renaissance man in Counter-Reformation times, Bernini almost personally invented the Baroque style, transforming the city of Rome. If you're visiting Rome, you will see Bernini's work, guaranteed.

Bernini was a child prodigy in his father's sculpting studio, growing up among Europe's rich and powerful. His flamboyant personality endeared him to his cultured employers—the popes in Rome, Louis XIV in France, and Charles I in England. He was extremely prolific, working fast and utilizing an army of assistants.

Despite the fleshiness and sensuality of his works, Bernini was a religious man, seeing his creativity as an extension of God's. In stark contrast to the Protestant world's sobriety, Bernini shamelessly embraced pagan myths and nude goddesses, declaring them all part of the "Catholic"—that is, universal—Church.

Bernini, a master of multimedia, was a . . .

- Sculptor (Borghese Gallery, *St. Teresa in Ecstasy*—page 36)
- Architect (elements of St. Peter's—see "Bernini Blitz," page 176, and the Church of Sant' Andrea al Quirinale)
- Painter (Borghese Gallery)
- Interior decorator (the *baldacchino* canopy and other stuff in St. Peter's, page 174)
- Civic engineer (he laid out St. Peter's Square—page 165, and designed and renovated Rome's fountains in Piazza Navona—page 54, Piazza Barberini, Piazza di Spagna, and more).

Even works done by other artists a century later (such as the Trevi Fountain) can be traced indirectly to Bernini, the man who invented Baroque, the "look" of Rome for the next two centuries.

Walk slowly around. Apollo's back leg defies gravity. Bernini has chipped away more than half of the block of marble, leaving airy, open spaces. The statue was two years in restoration (described to me as being something like dental work). The marble leaves at the top ring like crystal when struck. Notice the same scene, colorized, painted on the ceiling above.

Bernini carves out some of the chief features of Baroque

art: He makes a supernatural event seem realistic. He freezes it
at the most dramatic, emotional moment. The figures move and
twist in unusual poses. He turns the wind machine on, sending
Apollo's cape billowing behind him. It's a sculpture group of
two, forming a scene, rather than a stand-alone portrait. And
the subject is classical. Even in strict Counter-Reformation
times, there was always a place for groping, if the subject matter
had a moral—this one taught you not to pursue fleeting earthly
pleasures. And, besides, Bernini tends to show a lot of skin,
but no genitals.

Room IV

The Rape of Proserpine (Il Ratto di Proserpina)— Bernini (1622)

Pluto strides into the Underworld and
shows off his catch—the beautiful daughter of the earth goddess. His three-headed
guard dog, Cerberus, barks triumphantly.
Pluto is squat, thick, and uncouth, with
knotted muscles and untrimmed beard.
He's trying not to hurt her, but she pushes
her divine molester away and twists to call
out for help. Tears roll down her cheeks.
She wishes she could turn into a tree.

　　Bernini was the master of marble.
Look how Pluto's fingers dig into her
thigh like it was real flesh. Bernini picked
out this Carrara marble knowing that its
relative suppleness and ivory hue would
lend itself to a fleshy statue.

• *In a niche over Pluto's right shoulder, find . . .*

Diana the Hunter (Artemide)— Artist Unknown

The goddess has been running through the forest. Now she's
spotted her prey, and slows down, preparing to string her
(missing) bow with an arrow. Or is she smoking a (missing)
cigarette? Scholars debate it.

　　The statues in the niches are classical originals. *Diana
the Hunter* is a rare Greek original, with every limb and
finger intact, from the second century B.C. The traditional
contrapposto pose (weight on one leg) and idealized grace were
an inspiration for artists such as Canova, who grew tired of
Bernini's Baroque bombast.

The Marbles in Room IV

Appreciate the beauty of the different types of marble in the room: Bernini's ivory Carrara, Diana's translucent white, purple porphyry emperors, granite-like columns that support them, wood-grained pilasters on the walls, and the different colors on the floor—green, red, gray, lavender, and yellow, some grainy, some "marbled" like a steak. Some of the world's most beautiful and durable things have been made from the shells of sea creatures layered in sediment, fossilized into limestone, then baked and crystallized by the pressure of the earth—marble.

Room VI

Aeneas (Enea che fugge, etc.)—Bernini (1620)

Aeneas' home in Troy is in flames, and he escapes with the three most important things: his family (decrepit father on his shoulder, baby boy), his household gods (the statues in dad's hands), and the Eternal Flame (carried by son). They're all in shock, lost in thought, facing an uncertain future. Aeneas isn't even looking where he's going; he just puts one foot in front of the other. Little do they know that eventually they'll wind up in Italy, where—according to legend—Aeneas will found the city of Rome and house the flame in the Temple of Vesta.

Bernini was still a teenager when he started this, his first life-size work. He was probably helped by his dad, who nurtured the child prodigy much like Leopold mentored Mozart, but without the rivalry. Bernini's portrayal of human flesh—from baby fat to middle-age muscle to sagging decrepitude—is astonishing. Still, the flat-footed statue just stands there—not nearly as interesting as the reliefs up at the ceiling, with their dancing, light-footed soldiers with do-si-do shields.

Room VII

The "Theater of the Universe"

The room's decor sums up the eclectic nature of the villa. There are Greek statues and Roman mosaics. There are fake "Egyptian" sphynxes and hieroglyphs (perfectly symmetrical in good neoclassical style). Look out the window past the sculpted gardens, at the mesh domes of the aviary once filled with exotic birds. Cardinal Borghese's vision was to make a place where art, history, music, nature, and science from every place and time would come together . . . "a theater of the universe."

Room VIII

Caravaggio

The paintings in this room change often, but you'll likely find at least one or two by the Baroque innovator Caravaggio (1571–1610). Caravaggio brought Christian saints and Greek gods down to earth with gritty realism. His saints are balding and wrinkled. His Bacchus (a self-portrait) is pale and puffy-faced. David sticks Goliath's severed head (a self-portrait) right in your face. The Madonnas scarcely glow. The boy Jesus is buck naked. Ordinary people were his models. People emerge from a dark background, lit by a harsh, unflattering light, which highlights part of the figure, leaving the rest in deep shadows. Caravaggio's straightforwardness can be a refreshing change in a museum full of (sometimes overly) refined beauty.

• *To reach the Pinacoteca, go outside and return to the basement where you got your ticket, follow signs to the Pinacoteca, show your ticket to the guard, and climb the long spiral stairway.*

Pinacoteca—Painting Gallery

Remember, you're limited to only 30 minutes in the Pinacoteca, and you must visit it within the two-hour window of time printed on your ticket. Most visitors wait until the last half hour to see the Pinacoteca, so that's when it's most crowded (and the ground floor is less crowded). If you see the paintings first, remember that given a two-hour visit, the ground floor with the sculpture is worth most of that time.

• *Along the long wall of Room XIV you'll find a number of statues and paintings, many of them by Bernini.*

Room XIV

Bust of Cardinal Borghese
(Ritr. del Card. Scipione Borghese)—Bernini (1632)

Say *grazie* to the man who built this villa, assembled the collection, and hired Bernini to sculpt masterpieces. The cardinal is caught turning as though to greet someone at a party. There's a twinkle in his eye, and he opens his mouth to make a witty comment. This man of the cloth was, in fact, a sophisticated hedonist.

Notice that there are two identical versions of this bust. The first one started cracking along the forehead (visible) just as

Bernini was finishing it. *No problema*, Bernini whipped out a
replacement in three days.
• *On the wall above the table, find these paintings...*

Two Bernini Self-Portraits (*Autoritratto Giovanile*, 1623; and *Autoritratto in Eta Matura*, 1630/35)
Bernini was a master of many media, including painting. The young-
er Bernini looks out a bit hesitantly, as if he's still finding his way in
high-class society. His jet-black eyes came from his Southern Italian
mother who, it's said, also gave him his passionate personality.

In his next self-portrait, with a few masterpieces under his
belt, Bernini shows himself with more confidence and facial hair—
the dashing, flamboyant man who would rebuild Rome in Baroque
style, from St. Peter's Square to the fountains that dot the piazzas.
• *On the table nearby, find the smaller...*

Bust of Pope Paul V
The cardinal's uncle was a more sober man, but he was also a
patron of the arts with a good eye for talent who hired Bernini's
father. When Pope Paul saw sketches made by little Lorenzo, he
announced: "This boy will be the Michelangelo of his age."
• *Also nearby, find a small statue of...*

Two Babies Milking a Goat
Bernini may have been as young as 10 years old when he did
this. That's about the age when I mastered how to make a
Play-Doh snake.
• *Room IX is back near the top of the staircase you came up on.*

Room IX

Deposition (Deposizione di Cristo)— Raphael (Raffaelo Sanzio)
Jesus is being taken from the cross. The men support him while the

women support Mary (in purple),
who has fainted. Mary Magdalene
rushes up to take Christ's hand.
The woman who commissioned
the painting had recently lost her
son. She wanted to show the death
of a son and the grief of a mother.
We see two different faces of
grief—mother Mary faints at the
horror while Mary Magdalene still
can't quite believe he's gone.

In true Renaissance style, Raphael orders the scene with geo-metrical perfection. The curve of Jesus' body is echoed by the swirl of Mary Magdalene's hair, and then by the curve of Calvary Hill, where he met his fate.

Room X

Danae—Correggio

Cupid strips Danae as she spreads her legs, most unladylike, to re-ceive a trickle of gold from the smudgy cloud overhead—this was Zeus' idea of intercourse with a human. The sheets are rumpled, and Danae looks right where the action is with a smile on her face. It's hard to believe that a suppos-edly religious family would display such an erotic work. But the Borgheses felt that the Church was truly "catholic" (universal), and that all forms of human expression—including physical passion—glorified God.

• *Backtrack through the room of the two cardinal busts, then turn left and travel to the farthest room.*

Room XX

Sacred and Profane Love (Amor Sacrae, Amor Profane)— Titian (Tiziano Vecello)

The clothed woman at left was recently married, and she cradles a vase filled with jewels representing the riches of earthly love. Her naked twin on the right holds the burning flame of eternal, heav-enly love. Baby Cupid, between them, playfully stirs the waters.

Symbolically, the steeple on the right points up to the love of heaven, while on the left, soldiers prepare to "storm the castle" of the new bride. Miss Heavenly Love looks jealous.

This exquisite painting expresses the spirit of the Renaissance—that earth and heaven are two sides of the same coin. And here in

the Borghese Gallery, that love of earthly beauty can be spiritually uplifting—as long as you feel it within two hours.

VATICAN MUSEUM TOUR

Musei Vaticani

The glories of the ancient world displayed in a lavish papal palace, decorated by the likes of Michelangelo and Raphael...the Musei Vaticani. Unfortunately, many tourists see the Vatican Museum only as an obstacle between them and its grand finale, the Sistine Chapel. True, this huge, confusing, and crowded mega-museum can be a jungle—but with this book as your vine, you should swing through with ease, enjoying the highlights and getting to the Sistine just before you collapse. On the way, you'll enjoy some of the less appreciated but equally important sections of this warehouse of Western civilization.

Orientation

Cost: €10, free on last Sun of each month.

Dress Code: Modest dress (no short shorts or bare shoulders) is appropriate and often required.

Hours: March–Oct Mon–Fri 8:45–15:45; Sat 8:45–13:45; Nov–Feb Mon–Sat 8:45–13:45, closed Sun except last Sun of the month (when it's free, crowded, and open 8:45–13:45). Last entry is about 90 minutes before the closing time (12:20 when museum closes at 13:45, 14:20 when museum closes at 15:45).

The museum is closed on many holidays (mainly religious ones) including—for 2003: Jan 1 and 6, Feb 11, March 19, Easter and Easter Monday (April 20 and 21 in 2003), May 1 and 29, June 19, Aug 14 and 15, Nov 1, and Dec 8 and 25.

The Sistine Chapel may close 30 minutes before the museum does. Some individual rooms close at odd hours, especially after 13:00. TV screens inside the entrance lists closures. The rooms described here are usually open. The museum is generally hot and crowded. Saturday, the last Sunday of the month, and Monday are the worst; afternoons are best.

Vatican Museum Overview

Getting There: From the nearest Metro stop, Cipro-Musei Vaticani, it's a 10-minute walk. From St. Peter's Square, it's about a 15-minute walk (follow the Vatican Wall). Taxis are reasonable (hop in and say "moo-ZAY-ee vah-tee-KAHN-ee").

Information: In the entry, look for the *i* (it's probably in the bank of windows to your left, under "Special Permits"; some English spoken). You'll find a book kiosk in the lobby, another up the stairs, and others scattered throughout the museum. Some exhibits have English explanations. The museum has signs to four color-coded self-guided visits (A—the Sistine blitz, B—highlights, C—a good tour, D—everything). Tel. 06-6988-4947 or 06-6988-3333 (www.vatican.va). For more on the Vatican City, see page 166.

Exchange windows with sinful rates are in the entry and exit. The post office is upstairs.

Tour: A tour in English is offered once daily at 11:00 (€16.50, 2 hrs, call 06-6988-4466 to reserve). You can rent a €5 audioguide (but if you do, you lose the option of taking the shortcut from the Sistine Chapel to St. Peter's, because the audioguide must be returned at the Vatican Museum entrance).

Length of Our Tour: Until you expire, or 2.5 hours, whichever comes first.

Cuisine Art: A cafeteria is upstairs. Cheaper choices: The great Via Andrea Doria produce market is three blocks north of the entrance (head across the street, down the stairs, and continue straight) and inexpensive Pizza Rustica shops line Viale Giulio Cesare. Good restaurants are nearby (see page 260).

Photography: No photos are allowed in the Sistine Chapel. Elsewhere in the museum, photos without a flash are permitted.

Starring: World history, Michelangelo, Raphael, *Laocoön*, the Greek masters, and their Roman copyists.

The Pope's Collection

With the Fall of Rome, the Catholic (or "universal") Church became the great preserver of civilization, collecting artifacts from cultures dead and dying. Renaissance popes (15th and 16th centuries) collected most of what we'll see. Those lusty priests-as-Roman-emperors loved the ancient world. They built these palaces and decorated them with classical statues and Renaissance paintings. They combined the classical and Christian worlds, finding the divine in the creations of man.

We'll concentrate on classical sculpture and Renaissance painting. But along the way (and there's a lot of along-the-way here), we'll stop to leaf through a few yellowed pages from this 5,000-year-old scrapbook of humankind.

This heavyweight museum is shaped like a barbell—two buildings connected by a long hall. The entrance building covers the ancient world (Egypt, Greece, Rome). The one at the far end covers its "rebirth" in the Renaissance (including the Sistine Chapel). The halls there and back are a mix of old and new. Move quickly—don't burn out before the Sistine Chapel at the end—and see how each civilization borrows from and builds on the previous one.

• *Leave Italy by entering the doors. You may need to go through a security check (like at an airport). Go upstairs (or take the elevator) to buy your ticket, punch it in the turnstiles, then take the long escalator or spiral stairs up, up, up.*

At the top: To your right is the café and the Pinacoteca painting gallery (consider touring the Pinacoteca now if you want the option of taking the shortcut from the Sistine Chapel directly to St. Peter's; for information on the Pinacoteca, see the end of this chapter). To your left, the beginning of our tour. Go left, then take another left up a flight of stairs to reach the first-floor Egyptian Rooms (Museo Egizio). Don't stop until you find your mummy.

EGYPT (3000–1000 B.C.)

Egyptian art was for religion, not decoration. A statue or painting preserved the likeness of someone, giving him a form of eternal life. Most of the art was for tombs, where they put the mummies. Notice that the art is only realistic enough to get the job done. You can recognize that it's a man, a bird, or whatever, but these are stiff, two-dimensional, schematic figures—functional rather than beautiful.

Mummies

This woman died three millennia ago. Her corpse was disemboweled, and her organs were placed in a jar like those you see nearby. Then the body was refilled with pitch, dried with natron (a natural sodium carbonate), wrapped in linen,

The Ancient World

- TO NEW WING" (CLASSICAL SCULPTURE)
- WC
- ←SUMERIAN WRITING
- ROMAN PINE CONE
- OCTAGONAL COURTYARD
- HALL OF ANIMALS
- ANIMALS
- MUMMIES
- ← EGYPTIAN ROOMS
- (ETRUSCAN ROOMS ONE FLOOR ABOVE)
- FROM ENTRANCE
- DCH
- UPSTAIRS TO "THE LONG MARCH"

1 - Egyptian statues
2 - Apollo Belvedere
3 - Laocoon
4 - Belvedere Torso
5 - Hercules statue
6 - Porphyry basin
7 - Mrs. Constantine's sarcophagus

and placed in a wood coffin, which went inside a stone coffin, which was placed in a tomb. (Remember that the pyramids were just big tombs.) In the next life, the spirit was homeless without its body, and you wanted to look your best—notice the henna job on her hair.

Notice also, painted inside the coffin lid, what the deceased "packed" for the journey to eternity. The coffins were decorated

with magical spells to protect the body from evil and to act as crib notes for the confused soul in the netherworld.

• *In the next room are . . .*

Egyptian Statues

Even in the Romanized versions, it's clear that Egyptian statues are stiff and unnatural. They walk awkwardly like they're carrying heavy buckets, with arms straight down at their sides. Each was made according to an established set of proportions. Little changed over the centuries. These had a function and they worked. In Egyptian belief, a statue like this could be a stable refuge for the wandering soul of a dead man.

Various Egyptian Gods as Animals

Before technology made humans top dogs on earth, it was easier to appreciate our fellow creatures. The Egyptians saw the superiority of animals and worshiped them as incarnations of the gods. Wander through a pet store of Egyptian animal gods. Find Anubis, a jackal in a toga. The lioness portrays the fierce goddess Sekhmet. The clever baboon is the god of wisdom, Thot. At the end of the hall is Bes, the patron of pregnant women (and beer-bellied men).
• *Continue through a curved corridor of animal gods, then through three more rooms, pausing at the glass case in the third room, which contains brown clay tablets.*

Sumerian Writing

Even before Egypt, civilizations flourished in the Middle East. The Sumerian culture in Mesopotamia (the ancestors of the ancient Babylonians and of Saddam Hussein) invented writing around 3000 B.C. The clay tablets were written on by pressing into the wet clay with a wedge-shaped (cuneiform) pen. Also notice the ingenious cylindrical seals, with which they made impressions in soft clay to seal documents and mark property.
• *Go with the flow to a balcony with a view of Rome out the window, then turn left into an octagonal courtyard.*

SCULPTURE—GREECE AND ROME (500 B.C.–A.D. 500)

This palace wouldn't be here, this sculpture wouldn't be here, and you'd be spending your vacation in South Dakota at Reptile Gardens if it weren't for a few thousand Greeks in a small city about 450 years before Christ. Athens set the tone for the rest of the West. Democracy, theater, economics, literature, and art all got their start in Athens during a 50-year "Golden Age." Greek culture was then appropriated by Rome and revived again 1,500 years later, during the Renaissance. The Renaissance popes built and decorated these palaces, re-creating the glory of the classical world.

Apollo Belvedere

Apollo, the god of the sun and of music, is hunting. He's been running through the woods, and now he spots his prey. Keeping his eye on the animal, he slows down and prepares to put a (missing) arrow into his (missing) bow. The optimistic Greeks conceived of their gods in human form... and buck naked.

The Greek sculptor Leochares, following the style of the

greater Greek sculptor Praxiteles, has fully captured the beauty of the human form. The anatomy is perfect, his pose is natural. Instead of standing at attention, face forward with his arms at his sides (Egyptian style), Apollo is on the move, coming to rest, with his weight on one leg.

The Greeks loved balance. A well-rounded man was both a thinker and an athlete, a poet and a warrior. In art, the *Apollo Belvedere* balances several opposites. Apollo eyes his target, but hasn't attacked yet. He's moving, but not out of control. He's also a balance between a real person and an ideal god. And the smoothness of his muscles is balanced by the rough folds of his cloak. The only sour note: his recently added left hand. Could we try a size smaller?

During the Renaissance, when this Roman copy of the original Greek work was discovered, it was considered the most perfect work of art in the world. The handsome face, eternal youth, and the body that seems to float just above the pedestal made *Apollo Belvedere* an object of wonder and almost worship. Apollo's grace was something superhuman, divine, and godlike, even for devout Christians.

• *In the neighboring niche to the right, a bearded old Roman river god lounges in the shade. This pose inspired Michelangelo's* Adam, *in the Sistine Chapel (coming soon). While there are a few fancy bathtubs in this courtyard, most of the carved boxes you see are sarcophagi—Roman coffins and relic holders, carved with the deceased's epitaph in picture form.*

Laocoön

Laocoön (lay-AWK-oh-wahn) was a pagan high priest of Troy, the ancient city attacked by the Greeks. When the Greeks brought the Trojan Horse to the gates as a ploy to get inside the city walls, Laocoön tried to warn his people not to bring it inside. But the gods wanted the Greeks to win, so they sent huge snakes to crush him and his two sons to death. We see them at the height of their terror, when they realize that, no matter how hard they struggle, they—and their entire race—are doomed.

The *Laocoön* is Hellenistic, done four centuries after the Golden Age, after the scales of "balance" had been tipped. Where *Apollo* is a balance between stillness and motion, this is unbridled motion. Where *Apollo* is serene, this is emotional. Where *Apollo* is idealized grace, this is powerful and gritty realism. The figures (carved from 4 blocks of marble pieced together seamlessly) are powerful, not light and graceful. The poses are as twisted as possible, accentuating every rippling muscle and bulging vein. Follow the line of motion from *Laocoön*'s left foot, up his leg, through his body, and out his right arm (which some historians used to think extended straight out—until the elbow was dug up early in the 1900s). Goethe used to stand here and blink his eyes rapidly, watching the statue flicker to life.

Laocoön—the most famous Greek statue in ancient Rome and considered "superior to all other sculpture or painting"—was lost for over a thousand years. Then, in 1506, it was unexpectedly unearthed in the ruins of Nero's Golden House near the Colosseum. The discovery caused a sensation. They cleaned it off and paraded it through the streets before an awestruck populace. No one had ever seen anything like its motion and emotion, having been raised on a white-bread diet of pretty-boy *Apollo*s. One of those who saw it was the young Michelangelo, and it was a revelation to him. Two years later, he started work on the Sistine Chapel, and the Renaissance was about to take another turn.

• *Leave the courtyard. Swing around the Hall of Animals, a jungle of beasts real and surreal, to the limbless* Torso *in the middle of the next large hall.*

Belvedere Torso

My entire experience with statues consists of making snowmen. But standing face to face with this hunk of shaped rock makes you appreciate the sheer physical labor involved in chipping a figure out of solid rock. It takes great strength, but at the same time, great delicacy.

This is all that remains of an ancient statue of Hercules seated on a lion skin. Michelangelo loved this old rock. He knew he was the best sculptor of his day. The ancients were his only peers—and his rivals. He'd caress this statue lovingly and tell people, "I am the pupil of the *Torso*." To him, it contained all the beauty of classical sculpture. But it's not beautiful. It's ugly. Compared with the pure grace of the *Apollo*, it's downright hideous.

But Michelangelo, an ugly man himself, was looking for a new kind of beauty—not the beauty of idealized gods, but the innate beauty of every person, even so-called ugly ones. With its knotty lumps of muscle, the *Torso* has a brute power and a distinct personality despite—or because of—its rough edges. Remember this *Torso*, because we'll see it again later on.

• *Enter the next, domed room.*

Round Room

This room, modeled on the Pantheon interior, gives some idea of Roman grandeur. Romans often took Greek ideas and made them bigger, like the big bronze statue of Hercules with his club, found near the Theater of Pompey (by modern-day Campo de' Fiori). The mosaic floor re-creates an ancient Roman villa, and the enormous Roman hot tub/birdbath/vase, made of purple porphyry marble, is also likely from a villa. Purple was a rare, royal, expensive, and prestigious color in pre-Crayola days.

• *Enter the next room.*

Sarcophagi

These two large porphyry marble coffins were made (though not used) for the Roman emperor Constantine's mother and daughter. They were Christians— and therefore outlaws—until Constantine made Christianity legal (A.D. 312).

• *See how we've come full circle in this building—the Egyptian Rooms are ahead on your left. Go upstairs and prepare for the Long March down the hall lined with statues, toward the Sistine Chapel and Raphael Rooms.*

Overachievers may first choose to pop into the Etruscan wing— "Museo Etrusco"—located a few steps up from the "Long March" level. (Others have permission to save their aesthetic energy for the Sistine.)

THE ETRUSCANS (800–300 B.C.)

Room I

The chariot is from 550 B.C., when crude Romans were ruled by their more civilized neighbors to the north—the Etruscans. Imagine the chariot racing around the dirt track of the Circus Maximus, through the marshy valley of the newly drained Forum, or up Capitol Hill to the Temple of Jupiter—all originally built by Rome's Etruscan kings.

Room II

The golden breastplate (*Pectoral*, 650 B.C., immediately to the right), decorated with tiny winged angels and animals, shows off the sophistication of the Etruscans. Though unwarlike and politically decentralized, these people were able to "conquer" all of central Italy around 650 B.C. through trade, offering tempting metalwork goods like this.

The Etruscan vases done in the Greek style remind us of the other great pre-Roman power—the Greek colonists who settled in southern Italy (Magna Graecia). The Etruscans traded with the Greeks, adopting their fashions. Rome, cradled between the two, grew up learning from both cultures.

A Greek-style bowl (far corner of the room) depicting a man and woman in bed together would have scandalized early Roman farmers. He's peeing in a chamberpot, she's blowing a flute. Etruscan art often showed husbands and wives at ease together, giving them a reputation among the Romans as immoral, flute-playing degenerates.

Room III

This bronze warrior, whose head was sawed off by lightning, has a rare inscription that's readable (on armor below the navel). It probably refers to the statue's former owner: "Aha! Trutitis gave [this] as [a] gift." Archaeologists understand the Etruscans' Greek-style alphabet and some individual words, but they've yet to fully crack the code. As you look around at beautiful bronze pitchers, candlesticks, shields, and urns, ponder yet another of Etruria's unsolved mysteries—no one is sure where these sophisticated people came from.

Room IV

Most of our knowledge of the Etruscans is from sarcophagi and art in Etruscan tombs. Their funeral art is solemn, but hardly morbid—check out the sarcopha-guy with the bulging belly, enjoying a banquet for all eternity.

The Etruscans' origins are obscure, but their legacy is clear. In 509 B.C., the Etruscan king's son raped a Roman. The king was thrown out, the republic was declared, Etruscan cities were conquered by Rome's legions, and their culture was swallowed up in

Roman expansion. By Julius
Caesar's time, the few remaining ethnic Etruscans were
reduced to serving their masters as flute players, gold-
smiths, surgeons, and street-
corner preachers, like the
one that Caesar brushed aside

when he called out, "Beware the Ides of March ... "
• *Backtrack, returning to the long hall leading to the Sistine Chapel
and Raphael Rooms.*

THE LONG MARCH—SCULPTURE, TAPESTRIES, MAPS, AND VIEWS

This half-kilometer (0.3 mile) walk gives you a sense of the scale that
Renaissance popes built on. Remember, this building was originally
a series of papal palaces. The popes loved beautiful things—statues,
urns, marble floors, friezes, stuccoed ceilings—and, as heirs of imperial Rome, they felt they deserved such luxury. The palaces and
art represent both the peak and the decline of the Catholic Church
in Europe. It was extravagant spending like this that inspired Martin
Luther to rebel, starting the Protestant Reformation.

Gallery of the Candelabra— Classical Sculpture

In the second "room" of the long hall, stop at
the **statue *Diana the Huntress*** on the left.
Here, the virgin goddess goes hunting. Roman
hunters would pray and give offerings to statues like this to get divine help in their search
for food.

Farmers might pray
to another version of the
same goddess, ***Artemis***,
on the opposite wall. This billion-breasted
beauty stood for fertility. "Boobs or bulls'
balls?" Some historians say that bulls were
sacrificed and castrated, with the testicles
draped over the statues as symbols of fertility.
• *Shuffle along to the next "room" on the left and
the* Bacchus *with a baby on his shoulders.*

Fig Leaves

Why do the statues have fig leaves? Like ***Bacchus***, many of these
statues originally looked much different than they do now. First

The Long March

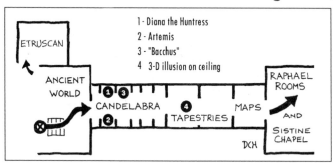

1 - Diana the Huntress
2 - Artemis
3 - "Bacchus"
4 3-D illusion on ceiling

ETRUSCAN

ANCIENT WORLD

RAPHAEL ROOMS

CANDELABRA

TAPESTRIES

MAPS

AND SISTINE CHAPEL

DCH

off, they were painted, usually in gaudy colors. *Bacchus* may have had brown hair, rosy cheeks, purple grapes, and a leopard-skin sidekick at his feet. Even the *Apollo Belvedere*, whose cool gray tones we now admire as "classic Greek austerity," may have had a paisley pink cloak for all we know. Also, many statues had glass eyes like *Bacchus*.

And the fig leaves? Those came from the years 1550 to 1800, when the Church decided that certain parts of the human anatomy were obscene. (Why they didn't pick the feet, which are universally ugly, I'll never know.) Perhaps Church leaders associated these full-frontal statues with the outbreak of Renaissance humanism that reduced their power in Europe. Whatever the cause, they reacted by covering classical crotches with plaster fig leaves, the same leaves Adam and Eve had used when the concept of "privates" was invented.

Note: The leaves could be removed at any time if the museum officials were so motivated. There are suggestion boxes around the museum. Whenever I see a fig leaf, I get the urge to pick-it. We could start an organ-ized campaign....

• *Cover your eyes in case they forgot a fig leaf or two and continue to the tapestries.*

Tapestries

Along the left wall are tapestries designed by Raphael's workshop and made in Brussels. They show scenes from the life of Christ, starting with the baby Jesus in the manger.

Check out the beautiful sculpted reliefs on the ceiling, especially the lavender panel near the end of the first tapestry room

showing a centurion ordering Eskimo pies from a vendor. Admire
the workmanship of this relief, then realize that it's not a relief at
all—it's painted on a flat surface! Illusions like this were proof that
painters had mastered the 3-D realism of ancient statues.

Map Gallery and View of Vatican City

This gallery still feels like a pope's palace.
The crusted ceiling of colorful stucco and
paint is pure papal splendor. The maps on
the walls are decorations from the 16th century. You can plan the next leg of your trip
with the two maps of Italy at the far end
of the hall—"New Italy" and "Old Italy"—
both with a smoking Mount Vesuvius next to
Napoli/Neapolis/Naples. There's an interesting old map of Venice on the right as you exit.

The windows give you your best look at the tiny country
of Vatican City, formed in 1929. It has its own radio station
(KPOP), as you see from the tower on the hill. What you see
here is pretty much all there is—these gardens, the palaces you're
in, and St. Peter's.

If you lean out and look left you'll see the dome of St. Peter's
the way Michelangelo would have liked you to see it—without
the bulky Baroque facade.

• *Exit the map room and take a breather in the next small tapestry hall
before turning left into the crowded rooms leading to the Raphael Rooms.*

RENAISSANCE ART

Raphael Rooms—Papal Wallpaper

We've seen art from the ancient world; now we'll see its rebirth
in the Renaissance. We're entering the living quarters of the great
Renaissance popes—where they slept, worked, and worshiped.
The rooms reflect the grandeur of their position. They hired
the best artists—mostly from Florence—to paint the walls and
ceilings, combining classical and Christian motifs.

• *Entering, you'll immediately see . . .*

The huge non-Raphael painting shows **Sobieski liberating
Vienna** from the Muslim Turks in 1683, finally tipping the tide in
favor of a Christian Europe. See the Muslim tents on the left and
the spires of Christian Vienna on the right.

The second room's paintings celebrate the doctrine of the
Immaculate Conception, establishing that Mary herself was
conceived free from original sin. This medieval idea wasn't actually
made dogma until a century ago. The largest fresco shows how

Raphael Rooms

1 - Sobieski Liberating Vienna
2 - Room of the Immaculate Conception
3 - Story of Constantine
4 - RAPHAEL - The Liberation of St. Peter
5 - RAPHAEL - The School of Athens and Disputa
6 - "Fire in the Borgia" room

the inspiration came straight from heaven (upper left) in a ray of light directly to the pope.

• *Next, you'll pass along an outside ramp overlooking a courtyard (is that the pope's Fiat?), finally ending up in the first of the Raphael Rooms—the Constantine Room.*

Constantine Room

The frescoes (by Raphael and assistants) celebrate the passing of the baton from one culture to the next. Remember, Rome was a pagan empire persecuting a new cult from the East—Christianity.

Then, on the night of October 27, A.D. 312 (left wall), as General Constantine (in gold, with crown) was preparing his troops for a coup d'état, he looked up and saw something strange. A cross appeared in the sky with the words, "You will conquer in this sign."

The next day (long wall), his troops raged victoriously into battle with the Christian cross atop their Roman eagle banners. There's Constantine in the center with a smile on his face, slashing through the enemy, while God's warrior angels ride shot-gun overhead.

Constantine even stripped (right wall) and knelt before the pope to be baptized a Christian (some say). As emperor, he legalized Christianity and worked hand in hand with the pope (window wall). When Rome fell, its glory lived on through the Dark Ages in the pomp, pageantry, and learning of the Catholic Church.

Look at the ceiling painting. A classical statue is knocked backward, crumbling before the overpowering force of the cross. Whoa! Christianity triumphs over pagan Rome. (This was painted, I believe, by Raphael's surrealist colleague, Salvadorus Dalio.)

RAPHAEL

Raphael was only 25 when Pope Julius II invited him to paint the walls of his personal living quarters. Julius was so impressed by Raphael's talent that he had the work of earlier masters scraped off and gave Raphael free rein to paint what he wanted.

Raphael lived a charmed life. He was handsome and sophisticated, and soon became Julius' favorite. He painted masterpieces effortlessly. In a different decade, he might have been thrown out of the Church as a great sinner, but his love affairs and devil-may-care personality seemed to epitomize the optimistic pagan spirit of the Renaissance. His works are graceful but never lightweight or frilly—they're strong, balanced, and harmonious in the best Renaissance tradition. When he died young in 1520, the High Renaissance died with him.

• *Continue through the next room and bookshop. In the following room, block the sunlight with your hand to see . . .*

The Liberation of St. Peter

Peter, Jesus' right-hand man, was thrown into prison in Jerusalem for his beliefs. In the middle of the night, an angel appeared and rescued him from the sleeping guards (Acts 12). The chains miracu-

lously fell away (and were later brought to the St. Peter-in-Chains Church in Rome, see page tk) and the angel led him to safety (right) while the guards took hell from their captain (left). This little "play" is neatly divided into three separate acts that make a balanced composition.

Raphael makes the miraculous event even more dramatic with the use of three kinds of light illuminating the dark cell—half-moonlight, the captain's torch, and the radiant angel. Raphael's mastery of realism, rich colors, and sense of drama made him understandably famous.

• *Enter the next room. Here in the pope's private study, Raphael painted...*

The School of Athens

In both style and subject matter, this fresco sums up the spirit of the Renaissance, which was not only the rebirth of classical art, but a rebirth of learning, discovery, and the optimistic spirit that man is a rational creature. Raphael pays respect to the great thinkers and scientists of ancient Greece, gathering them together at one time in a mythical school setting.

In the center are Plato and Aristotle, the two greatest. Plato points up, indicating his philosophy that mathematics and pure ideas are the source of truth, while Aristotle points down, showing his preference for hands-on study of the material world. There's their master, Socrates (midway to the left, in green), ticking off arguments on his fingers. And in the foreground at right, bald Euclid bends over a slate to demonstrate a geometrical formula.

Raphael shows that Renaissance thinkers were as good as the ancients. There's Leonardo da Vinci, whom Raphael worshiped, in the role of Plato. Euclid is the architect Bramante, who designed St. Peter's. Raphael himself (next to last on the far right, with the black beret) looks out at us. And the "school" building is actually an early version of St. Peter's Basilica (under construction at the time).

Raphael balances everything symmetrically—thinkers to the left, scientists to the right, with Plato and Aristotle dead center—showing the geometrical order found in the world. Look at the square floor tiles in the foreground. If you laid a ruler over them and extended the line upward, it would run right to the center of the picture. Similarly, the tops of the columns all point down to the middle. All the lines of sight draw our attention to Plato and Aristotle, and to the small arch over their heads—a halo over these two secular saints in the divine pursuit of knowledge.

While Raphael was painting this room, Michelangelo was at work down the hall in the Sistine Chapel. Raphael popped in on

the sly to see the master at work. He was astonished. When he saw
Michelangelo's powerful figures and dramatic scenes, he began to
beef up his delicate, graceful style to a more heroic level. In *The
School of Athens*, perhaps Raphael's greatest work, he tipped his
brush to the master by adding Michelangelo to the scene—the
brooding, melancholy figure in front, leaning on a block of marble.
• *On the opposite wall...*

The Disputa

As if to underline the
new attitude that pre-
Christian philosophy and
Church thinking could
coexist, Raphael painted
The Disputa facing *The
School of Athens*. Christ
and the saints in heaven
are overseeing a discus-
sion of the Eucharist
(the communion wafer) by mortals below. The classical-looking
character in blue looks out as if to say, "The pagans had their
School of Athens, but us Christians (pointing up) have the School
of Heaven." Balance and symmetry reign, from the angel trios in
the upper corners to the books littering the floor.

In Catholic terms, the communion wafer miraculously becomes
the body of Christ when it's consecrated by a priest, bringing a little
bit of heaven into the material world. Raphael's painting also connects heaven and earth, with descending circles: Jesus in a halo, down
to the dove of the Holy Spirit in a circle, which enters the communion wafer in its holder. The composition drives the point home.
By the way, these rooms were the papal library, so themes featuring
learning, knowledge, and debate were appropriate.

Moving along, the last Raphael Room (called the "Fire in the
Borgia" Room) shows work done mostly by Raphael's students,
who were influenced by the bulging muscles and bodybuilder
poses of Michelangelo.
• *Get ready. It's decision time. From here, there are two ways to get to
the Sistine Chapel. Leaving the final Raphael Room, you'll soon see two
arrows—one pointing left to the Sistine (Cappella Sistina) and one
pointing right to the Sistine. Left goes directly to the Sistine.*

*But going right (5 min and a few staircases longer) leads to a quiet
room at the foot of the stairs with a bench where you can sit in peace and
read ahead before entering the hectic Sistine Chapel. Also, you get to stroll
through the impressive Modern Religious Art collection on the way (signs
will direct you to the Sistine). Your call.*

THE SISTINE CHAPEL

The Sistine Chapel contains Michelangelo's ceiling and his huge *Last Judgment*. The Sistine is the personal chapel of the pope and the place where new popes are elected. When Pope Julius II asked Michelangelo to take on this important project, he said, "No, *grazie*."

Michelangelo insisted he was a sculptor, not a painter. The Sistine ceiling was a vast undertaking, and he didn't want to do a half-vast job. But the pope pleaded, bribed, and threatened until Michelangelo finally consented, on the condition he be able to do it all his own way.

Julius had asked for only 12 apostles along the sides of the ceiling, but Michelangelo had a grander vision—the entire history of the world until Jesus. He spent the next four years (1508–1512) craning his neck on scaffolding six stories up, covering the ceiling with frescoes of Bible scenes.

In sheer physical terms, it's an astonishing achievement: 500 square meters (5,400 square feet), and every human figure done by his own hand. (Raphael only designed most of his rooms, letting assistants do the grunt work.)

First, he had to design and erect the scaffolding. Any materials had to be hauled up on pulleys. Then, a section of ceiling would be plastered. With fresco—painting on wet plaster—if you don't get it right the first time, you have to scrape the whole thing off and start over. And if you've ever struggled with a ceiling light fixture or worked underneath a car for even five minutes, you know how heavy your arms get. The physical effort, the paint dripping in his eyes, the creative drain, and the mental stress from a pushy pope combined to almost kill Michelangelo.

But when it was finished and revealed to the public, it simply blew 'em away. Like the *Laocoön* statue discovered six years earlier, it was unlike anything seen before. It both caps the Renaissance and turns it in a new direction. In perfect Renaissance spirit, it mixes Old Testament prophets with classical figures. But the style is more dramatic, shocking, and emotional than the balanced Renaissance works before it. This is a very personal work—the Gospel according to Michelangelo—but its themes and subject matter are universal. Almost without exception, art critics concede that the Sistine ceiling is the single greatest work of art by any one human being.

The Sistine Schematic

PROPHETS

GENESIS
SCENES

ANCESTORS

THE
SISTINE
CEILING

DCH

The Sistine Ceiling—Understanding What You're Standing Under

The ceiling shows the history of the world before the birth of Jesus. We see God creating the world, creating man and woman, destroying the earth by flood, and so on. Along the sides (where the ceiling starts to curve) we see the Old Testament prophets and pagan Greek prophetesses that foretold the coming of Christ. Dividing these scenes and figures are fake niches (a painted 3-D illusion) decorated with nude, statue-like figures with symbolic meaning.

The key is to see three simple divisions in the tangle of bodies:
1. The central spine of nine rectangular Bible scenes
2. The line of prophets on either side
3. The triangles between the prophets showing the ancestors of Christ

• *Ready? Within the chapel, grab a seat along the side (if there's room). Face the altar with the big* Last Judgment *on the wall (more on that later). Now look up to the ceiling and find the central panel of . . .*

The Creation of Adam

God and man take center stage in this Renaissance version of creation. Adam, newly formed in the image of God, lounges dreamily in perfect naked innocence. God, with his entourage, swoops in in a swirl of activity (which—with a

The Sistine Ceiling

ENTER FROM RAPHAEL ROOMS /OR MODERN RELIGIOUS ART...

EXIT TO LONG MARCH BACK TO PINACOTECA AND ENTRY LOBBY - A 10-15 MINUTE WALK.

EXIT TO ST PETER'S

little imagination—looks like a cross-section of a human brain... quite a strong humanist statement). Their reaching hands are the center of this work. Adam's is limp and passive; God's is strong and forceful, His finger twitching upward with energy. Here is the very moment of creation, as God passes the spark of life to man, the crowning work of His creation.

This is the spirit of the Renaissance. God is not a terrifying giant reaching down to puny and helpless man from way on high. Here they are on an equal plane, divided only by the diagonal patch of sky. God's billowing robe and the patch of green upon which Adam is lying balance each other. They are like two pieces of a jigsaw puzzle, or two long-separated continents, or like the

yin and yang symbols finally coming together—uniting, comple-
menting each other, creating wholeness. God and man work
together in the divine process of creation.

• *This celebration of man permeates the ceiling. Notice the Adonises-
come-to-life on the pedestals that divide the central panels. And then
came woman.*

The Garden of Eden: Temptation and Expulsion

In one panel, we see two scenes from
the Garden of Eden. On the left is the
leafy garden of paradise where Adam
and Eve lie around blissfully. But the
devil comes along—a serpent with a
woman's torso—and winds around the
forbidden Tree of Knowledge. The
temptation to gain new knowledge is
too great for these Renaissance
people. They eat the forbidden fruit.

At right, the sword-wielding
angel drives them from Paradise into
the barren plains. They're grieving, but they're far from helpless.
Adam's body is thick and sturdy, and we know they'll survive in
the cruel world. Adam firmly gestures to the angel, like he's saying,
"All right, already! We're going!"

The Nine Scenes from Genesis

Take some time with these central scenes to understand the story
the ceiling tells. They run in sequence, starting at the front:

1. God, in purple, divides the light from darkness.
2. God creates the sun (burning orange) and the moon (pale
   white, to the right). Oops, I guess there's another moon.
3. God bursts toward us to separate the land and water.
4. *The Creation of Adam*
5. God creates Eve, who dives into existence out of Adam's
   side.
6. *The Garden of Eden: Temptation and Expulsion*
7. Noah kills a ram and stokes the altar fires to make a sacrifice to God.
8. The great Flood, sent by God, destroys the wicked, who
   desperately head for higher ground. In the distance, the Ark
   carries Noah's family to safety. (The fresco itself suffered
   water damage not long after Michelangelo painted it.)
9. Noah's sons see their drunk father. (Perhaps Michelangelo
   chose to end it with this scene as a reminder that even the
   best of men are fallible.)

Prophets

You'll notice that the figures at the far end of the chapel are a bit smaller than those over the *Last Judgment*.

By 1510, Michelangelo had finished the first half of the ceiling (the far end). When they took the scaffolding down and could finally see what he'd been working on for two years, everyone was awestruck—except Michelangelo. As powerful as his figures are, from the floor they didn't look dramatic enough for Michelangelo. For the other half, he pulled out all the stops.

Compare the many small figures in the Noah scenes with, say, Adam and God at the other end. Or compare an early prophet with a later one. Isaiah ("Esaias," in purple) is a stately, sturdy, balanced, composed Renaissance Man. Jeremiah ("Hieremias"), in the corner by the *Last Judgment*, the prophet who witnessed the destruction of Israel, is a dark, brooding figure. He slumps his chin in his hand and ponders the fate of his people. The difference between them is like the difference between the stately *Apollo Belvedere* and the excited *Laocoön*. Michelangelo added a new emotional dimension to Renaissance painting.

The Cleaning Project

The ceiling and the *Last Judgment* have been cleaned, removing centuries of preservatives, dirt, and soot from candles, oil lamps, and the annual Papal Barbecue (just kidding). The bright, bright colors that emerged are a bit shocking, forcing many art experts to reevaluate Michelangelo's style. Notice the very dark patches left in the corner above the *Last Judgment* and imagine how dreary and dark it was before the cleaning.

The Last Judgment

When Michelangelo was asked to paint the altar wall 23 years later (1535), the mood of Europe—and of Michelangelo—was completely different. The Protestant Reformation had forced the Catholic Church to clamp down on free thought, and religious wars raged. Rome had recently been pillaged by roving bands of

mercenaries. The Renaissance spirit of optimism was fading. Michelangelo himself had begun to question the innate goodness of mankind.

It's Judgment Day, and Christ—the powerful figure in the center, raising his arm to spank the

The Last Judgment

1 - Christ with Mary at his side
2 - Trumpeting Angels
3 - The dead come out of their graves, the righteous ascend
4 - One of the damned
5 - Charon in his boat
6 - The demon/critic of nudity
7 - St. Bartholomew with flayed skin containing Michelangelo's self-portrait

wicked—has come to find out who's naughty and who's nice. Beneath him, a band of angels blows its trumpets Dizzy Gillespie–style, giving a wake-up call to the sleeping dead. The dead at lower left leave their graves and prepare to be judged. The righteous, on Christ's right hand (the left side of the picture), are carried up to the glories of Heaven. The wicked on the other side are hurled down to Hell, where demons wait to torture them. Charon, from the underworld of Greek mythology, waits below to ferry the souls of the damned to Hell.

It's a grim picture. No one, but no one, is smiling. Even many of the righteous being resurrected (lower left) are either skeletons or cadavers with ghastly skin. The angels have to play tug-of-war with subterranean monsters to drag them from their graves.

Over in Hell, the wicked are tortured by gleeful demons. One of the damned (to the right of the trumpeting angels) has an utterly lost expression, as if saying, "Why did I cheat on my wife?!" Two demons grab him around the ankles to pull him down to the bowels of Hell, condemned to an eternity of constipation.

But it's the terrifying figure of Christ who dominates this scene. He raises his arm to smite the wicked, sending a ripple of fear through everyone. Even the saints around him—even Mary beneath his arm (whose interceding days are clearly over)—shrink back in terror at loving Jesus' uncharacteristic outburst. His expression is completely closed, and he turns his head, refusing to even listen to the whining alibis of the damned. Look at Christ's bicep. If this muscular figure looks familiar to you, it's because you've seen it before—the *Belvedere Torso.*

When *The Last Judgment* was unveiled to the public in 1544, it caused a sensation. The pope is said to have dropped to his knees and cried, "Lord, charge me not with my sins when thou shalt come on the Day of Judgment."

And it changed the course of art. The complex composition, with more than 300 figures swirling around the figure of Christ, was far beyond traditional Renaissance balance. The twisted figures shown from every imaginable angle challenged other painters to try and top this master of 3-D illusion. And the sheer terror and drama of the scene was a striking contrast to the placid optimism of, say, Raphael's *School of Athens.* Michelangelo had Baroque-en all the rules of the Renaissance, signaling a new era of art.

With the Renaissance fading, the fleshy figures in *The Last Judgment* aroused murmurs of discontent from Church authorities. Michelangelo rebelled by painting his chief critic into the scene—in Hell. He's the jack-assed demon in the bottom right corner wrapped in a snake. Look how Michelangelo covered his privates. Sweet revenge.

(After Michelangelo's death, there was no defense, and prudish Church authorities painted the wisps of clothing we see today.)

Now move up close. Study the details of the lower part of the painting from right to left. Charon, with Dr. Spock ears and a Dalí moustache, paddles the damned in a boat full of human turbulence. Look more closely at the J-Day band. Are they reading music, or is it the Judgment Day tally? Before the cleaning, these details were lost in murk.

The Last Judgment marks the end of Renaissance optimism

epitomized in *The Creation of Adam*, with its innocence and exaltation of man. There, he was the wakening man-child of a fatherly God. Here, man cowers in fear and unworthiness before a terrifying, wrathful deity.

Michelangelo himself must have wondered how he would be judged—had he used his God-given talents wisely? Look at St. Bartholomew, the bald, bearded guy at Christ's left foot (our right). In the flayed skin he's holding is a barely recognizable face—the twisted self-portrait of a self-questioning Michelangelo.

• *There are two exits from the Sistine Chapel. If you exit through the side door next to the screen, you'll soon find yourself facing the Long March back to the museum's entrance (10–15 min away). You're one floor below the long corridor you walked to get here.*

Or, if you're planning to visit St. Peter's Basilica next, consider the Sistine-to-St. Peter's shortcut: In the back corner of the Sistine Chapel, there's an exit that shortcuts directly to St. Peter's Basilica, saving a 30-minute walk (10–15 min back to Vatican Museum entry/exit, then a 15-min walk to St. Peter's). Though this corner exit is ostensibly only for tour groups, you can just slide through with the crowds. Note that if you take this shortcut, you'll miss the Pinacoteca art gallery (unless you toured it at the beginning).

THE LONG MARCH BACK

Along this corridor, you'll see some of the wealth amassed by the popes, mostly gifts from royalty. Find your hometown on the map of the world from 1529—look in the land labeled "Terra Incognita." The elaborately decorated library that branches off to the right contains rare manuscripts.

• *The corridor eventually spills out back outside. Follow signs to the . . .*

PINACOTECA (PAINTING GALLERY)

How would you like to be Lou Gehrig—always batting behind Babe Ruth? That's the Pinacoteca's lot in life, following Sistine & Co. But after the Vatican's artistic feast, this little collection of paintings is a delicious, 15-minute after-dinner mint.

See this gallery of paintings as you'd view a time-lapse blossoming of a flower, walking through the evolution of painting from medieval to Baroque with just four stops.

• *Enter and stroll up to Room IV.*

Pinacoteca

1 - DA FORLI - Musician angels
2 - RAPHAEL - The Transfiguration
3 - LEONARDO DA VINCI - St. Jerome
4 - CARAVAGGIO - Deposition
5 - View of the dome

Melozzo Da Forli—Musician Angels
Salvaged from a condemned church, this playful series of frescoes shows the delicate grace and nobility of Italy during the time known fondly as the Quattrocento (1400s). Notice the detail in the serene faces, the soothing primary colors, bright even light, and the classical purity given these religious figures. Rock on.

• *Walk on to the end room (Room VIII) where they've turned on the dark to let Raphael's* Transfiguration *shine. Take a seat.*

Raphael—*The Transfiguration*
Christ floats above a stumpy mountaintop, visited in a vision by the prophets Moses and Elijah. Peter, James, and John cower in awe under Jesus, "transfigured before them, his face shining as the sun, his rainment white as light" (as described by the evangelist

Matthew—who can be seen taking notes in the painting's lower left).

Raphael composes the scene in three descending tiers: Christ, the holiest, is on top, then Peter-James-John, and finally, the nine remaining apostles who try in vain to heal a boy possessed by demons. Jesus is gone, leaving them in disarray, but "Lady Faith" in the center gives them a pep talk.

Raphael died in 1520, leaving this final work to be finished by his pupils. The last thing Raphael painted was the beatific face of Jesus, perhaps the most beautiful Christ in existence.

• *Heading back down the parallel corridor, stop in Room IX at the brown, unfinished work by Leonardo.*

Leonardo da Vinci—*St. Jerome* (c. 1482)

Jerome squats in the rocky desert. He's spent too much time alone, fasting, and meditating on his sins. His soulful face is echoed by his friend, the roaring lion.

This unfinished work gives us a glimpse behind the scenes at Leonardo's technique. Even in the brown undercoating we see the psychological power of Leonardo's genius. Jerome's emaciated body on the rocks expresses his intense penitence while his pleading eyes hold a glimmer of hope for divine forgiveness. Leonardo wrote that a good painter must paint two things: "man and the movements of his spirit." (The patchwork effect is due to Jerome's head having been cut out and used as the seat of a stool in a shoemaker's shop.)

• *Roll on through the sappy sweetness of the Mannerist rooms into the gritty realism of Caravaggio (Room XII).*

Caravaggio—*Deposition*

Christ is being buried. In the dark tomb, the faces of his followers emerge, lit by a harsh light. Christ's body has a death-like color. We see Christ's dirty toes and Nicodemus' wrinkled, sunburned face.

Caravaggio was the first painter to intentionally shock his viewers. By exaggerating the contrast between light and dark, shining a brutal third-degree-interrogator-type light on his subjects, and using everyday models in sacred scenes, he takes a huge leap away from the Raphael-pretty past and into the "expressive realism" of the modern world.

A tangle of grief looms out of the darkness as Christ's heavy, dead body nearly pulls the whole group with him from the cross into the tomb. After this museum, I know how he feels.

• *Walk through the rest of the gallery's canvas history of art, enjoy one last view of the Vatican grounds and Michelangelo's dome, then follow the grand spiral staircase down. Go in peace.*

ST. PETER'S BASILICA TOUR

St. Peter's is the greatest church in Christendom. It represents the power and splendor of Rome's 2,000-year domination of the Western world. Built on the memory and grave of the first pope, St. Peter, this is where the grandeur of ancient Rome became the grandeur of Christianity.

Orientation

Cost: Free (€5 to climb dome).

Dress Code: The dress code is strictly enforced. No shorts or bare shoulders (applies to men, women, and children), and no miniskirts.

Hours: Daily May–Sept 7:00–19:00, Oct–April 7:00–18:00. Mass is held daily (Mon–Sat 8:30, 10:00, 11:00, 12:00, and 17:00, Sun and holidays 9:00, 10:30, 12:10, 13:00, 16:00, and 17:30). The lift to the dome opens daily at 8:30 and closes one hour before the church closes. The best time to visit the church is early or late.

Getting There: Subway to Ottaviano, then a 10-minute walk south on Via Ottaviano. Several city buses go right to St. Peter's Square (#64 is convenient for pickpockets, the #40 express is less crowded). Taxis are reasonable (Termini train station to St. Peter's is about €10).

Information: The TI on the left (south) side of the square is excellent (Mon–Sat 8:30–19:00, closed Sun, free Vatican and church map, tel. 06-6988-1662). WCs are to the right and left (near TI) of the church and on the roof. Drinking fountains are at the obelisk and near WCs. The post office is next to the TI.

Tour: Ninety-minute tours in English are offered daily at 14:15 and also at 15:00 on Mon, Wed, and Fri; meet at the TI outside the entrance to the basilica (free, confirm schedule at TI, tel. 06-6988-1662).

Length of Our Tour: One hour, plus another hour if you climb the dome (elevator plus 300 steps one-way).

Checkroom: Free, usually mandatory bag check is outside at right of entrance.

Starring: Michelangelo, Bernini, St. Peter, a heavenly host, and, occasionally, the pope.

OLD ST. PETER'S

• *Find a shady spot where you like the view under the columns around St. Peter's oval-shaped "square." If the pigeons left a clean spot, sit on it.*

Nearly 2,000 years ago, this area was the site of Nero's Circus—a huge Roman chariot racecourse. The obelisk you see in the middle of the square stands where the chariots made their hairpin turns. The Romans had no marching bands, so for half-time entertainment they killed Christians. This persecuted minority was forced to fight wild animals and gladiators, or they were simply crucified. Some were tarred up, tied to posts, and burned—human torches to light up the evening races.

One of those killed here, around A.D. 65, was Peter, Jesus' right-hand man, who had come to Rome to spread the message of love. Peter was crucified on an upside-down cross at his own request because he felt unworthy to die as his master had. His remains were buried in a nearby cemetery where, for 250 years, they were quietly and secretly revered.

When Christianity was finally legalized in 313, the Christian emperor Constantine built a church on the site of the martyrdom of this first "pope," or bishop of Rome, from whom all later popes claimed their authority as head of the Church. "Old St. Peter's" lasted 1,200 years (A.D. 329–1500).

By the time of the Renaissance, old St. Peter's was falling apart and was considered unfit to be the center of the Western Church. The new, larger church we see today was begun in 1506 and was actually built around the old one. As the project was completed 120 years later, after many changes of plans, old St. Peter's was dismantled and carried out the doors of the new one.

• *Ideally, you should head out to the obelisk to view the square and read this. But let me guess—it's 95 degrees, right? OK, read on in the shade of these stone sequoias.*

ST. PETER'S SQUARE

St. Peter's Square, with its ring of columns, symbolizes the arms of the church "maternally embracing Catholics, heretics, and the faithless." It was designed by the Baroque architect Bernini, who also did much of the work we'll see inside. Numbers first: 284 columns, 17 meters (56 feet) high, in stern Doric style. Topping

Vatican City

This tiny independent country of just over 100 acres, contained entirely within Rome, has its own postal system, armed guards, helipad, mini–train station, and radio station (KPOP). Politically powerful, the Vatican is the religious capital of 800 million Roman Catholics. If you're not a Catholic, become one for your visit.

Small as it is, Vatican City has two huge sights: St. Peter's Basilica (with Michelangelo's *Pietà*) and the Vatican Museum (with the Sistine Chapel). A helpful TI is just to the left of St. Peter's Basilica (Mon–Sat 8:30–19:00, closed Sun, tel. 06-6988-1662; Vatican switchboard tel. 06-6982, www.vatican.va). The thief-infested bus #64 stops right at the basilica. The nearest Metro stops are a 10-minute walk away from either sight: For St. Peter's, the closest stop is Ottaviano; for the Vatican Museum, it's Cipro-Musei Vaticani.

Post Office: The Vatican post, with offices on St. Peter's Square (next to TI) and in the Vatican Museum, is more reliable than Italy's mail service (Mon–Sat 8:30–19:00). The stamps are a collectible bonus. Vatican stamps are good throughout Rome, but to use the Vatican's mail service, you need to mail your cards from the Vatican; write your postcards ahead of time. (Note that the Vatican won't mail cards with Italian stamps.)

Tours: The Vatican TI conducts free 90-minute tours of St. Peter's (depart daily from TI at 14:15, also Mon, Wed, and Fri at 15:00, confirm schedule at TI, tel. 06-6988-1662). Tours are the only way to see the Vatican Gardens; book at least a day in advance by calling 06-6988-4466 (€9, Mon–Sat 10:00–12:00, tours start at Vatican Museum tour desk and finish on St. Peter's Square). To tour the necropolis of St. Peter's and the saint's tomb, call the

them are Bernini's 90 favorite saints, each three meters (10 feet) tall. The "square" itself is elliptical, 200 by 150 meters (660 by 500 feet).

The obelisk in the center is 27 meters (90 feet) of solid granite weighing over 300 tons. Think for a second about how much history this monument has seen. Erected originally in Egypt over 2,000 years ago, it witnessed the fall of

Excavations Office at 06-6988-5318 (€8, 2 hrs, office open Mon–Fri 9:00–17:00).

Seeing the Pope: Your best chances for a sighting are on Sunday and Wednesday. The pope usually gives a blessing at noon on Sunday from his apartment on St. Peter's Square (except

Vatican City Overview

Aug–Sept, when he speaks at his summer residence at Castel Gandolfo, 40 km, or 25 miles, from Rome; train leaves Rome's Termini station at 8:35, returns after his talk). On Wednesday at 10:30, the pope blesses the crowds at St. Peter's from a balcony or canopied platform on the square (except in winter, when he speaks at 11:00 in the 7,000-seat Aula Paola VI Auditorium, next to St. Peter's Basilica). To find out the pope's schedule or to book a free spot for the Wednesday blessing (either for a seat on the square or in the auditorium), call 06-6988-4631. The weekly entertainment guide *Roma c'è* always has a "Seeing the Pope" section. If you don't want to see the pope, minimize crowd problems by avoiding these times.

the pharaohs to the Greeks and then to the Romans. It was then moved to imperial Rome by the emperor Caligula, where it stood impassively watching the slaughter of Christians at the racecourse and the torture of Protestants by the Inquisition (in the yellow and rust building just outside the square, to the left of the church). Today, it watches over the church, a reminder that each civilization builds on the previous ones. The puny cross on top reminds us that our Christian culture is but a thin veneer over our pagan origins.

• *Now venture out across the burning desert to the obelisk, which provides a narrow sliver of shade.*

Face the church, then turn about-face and say "*Grazie, Benito.*"

St. Peter's Square

BRAMANTE + MICHELANGELO GREEK CROSS PLAN →

(DOME)

ST. PETER'S CHURCH

MADERNO'S ADDITION →

WC

FOUNTAINS

1 - Obelisk
2 - Pope's apartments (top story, right)
3 - Sistine Chapel
4 - "Centro del Colonnato" plaque
5 - Post Office, Tourist Info, bookstore and WC
6 - Swiss Guard at Vatican City entrance
7 - Post Office and WC

N

VATICAN WALL
VIA DI PTA. ANGELICA → TO SUBWAY "OTTAVIANO" (15 MIN.)
↓
VATICAN MUSEUM (15 MIN.)

VIA DEL CONCILIAZIONE

I don't make a habit of thanking fascist dictators, but in the 1930s, Benito Mussolini did open up this broad boulevard, finally letting people see the dome of St. Peter's, which had been hidden for centuries by the facade. From here at the obelisk, Michelangelo's magnificent dome can only peek its top over the bulky Baroque front entrance.

The gray building at two o'clock to the right (as you face the church), rising up behind Bernini's colonnade, is where the pope lives. The last window on the right of the top floor is his bedroom. The window to the left of that is his study, where he appears occasionally to greet

the masses. If you come to the square at night as a Poping Tom, you might see the light on—the pope burns much midnight oil.

On more formal occasions (which you may have seen on TV), the pope appears from the church itself, on the small balcony above the central door.

The Sistine Chapel is just to the right of the facade—the small gray-brown building with the triangular roof, topped by an antenna. The tiny chimney (the pimple along the roofline midway

up the left side) is where the
famous smoke signals announce
the election of each new pope.
If the smoke is black, a 75 percent majority hasn't been reached.
White smoke means a new pope
has been selected.

Walk to the right, five pavement plaques from the obelisk,
to one marked "Centro del Colonnato." From here, all of Bernini's
columns on the right side line up.
The curved Baroque square still
pays its respects to Renaissance
mathematical symmetry.

• *Climb the gradually sloping pavement past crowd barriers and the
huge statues of St. Paul with his two-edged sword and St. Peter with
his bushy hair and keys.*

You'll pass two of the entrances to Vatican City—one to the
left of the facade, one to the right in the crook of Bernini's "arm."
Guarding this small but powerful country's border crossing are the
mercenary guards from Switzerland. You have to wonder if they
really know how to use those pikes. Their colorful uniforms are
said to have been designed by Michelangelo, though he was not
known for his sense of humor.

• *Enter the atrium (entrance hall) of the church. You'll pass by the
dress-code enforcers and a gaggle of ticked-off guys in shorts.*

THE BASILICA

The Atrium

The atrium is itself bigger than most churches. Facing us are the
five famous bronze doors, leading into the main church. The central door, made from the melted-down bronze of the original door
of old St. Peter's, is only opened on special occasions.

The far-right entrance is the Holy Door, opened only during
Holy Years. On Christmas Eve every 25 years, the pope knocks
three times with a silver hammer and the door opens, welcoming
pilgrims to pass through. After opening the door on Christmas
Eve, 1999, he bricked it up again with a ceremonial trowel a year
later to await another 24 years. (A plaque above the door fudges a
bit for effect: it says that Pope "IONNES PAULUS II" opened
the door in the year "MM"—2000—and closed it in "MMI.") On
the door itself, note Jesus' shiny knees, polished by pious pilgrims
who touch them for a blessing.

St. Peter's Basilica

DCH

⊗ ENTER

ST. PETER'S SQUARE

1 - Holy Door
2 - Site of Charlemagne's coronation, 800 AD
3 - Extent of the original "Greek Cross" church plan
4 - St. Andrew statue (view the dome from here)
5 - Main altar directly over Peter's tomb. BERNINI's 70-foot bronze canopy covers the altar
6 - Stairs down to the crypt: the foundation of old St. Peter's, chapels and tombs of popes
    (the entrance moves around)
7 - Statue of St. Peter with irresistibly kissable toe
8 - BERNINI - Dove window and "St. Peter's Throne"
9 - Site of Peter's crucifixion
10 - Museum entrance
11 - RAPHAEL - "Transfiguration" mosaic
12 - Blessed Sacrament Chapel
13 - MICHELANGELO - Pieta
14 - Elevator to roof and dome-climb
    (this entrance moves around - sometimes it is even outside)

The other doors are modern, reminding us that amid all this tradition, the Catholic Church has changed enormously even within our lifetimes. Door #2 (second from left) commemorates the kneeling pope, John (Giovanni) XXIII, who opened the landmark Vatican II Council in the early 1960s. This meeting of Church leaders brought the medieval Church into the modern

age—they dropped outdated rituals, such as the use of Latin in the Mass—and made old doctrines "relevant" to modern times.
• *Now for one of Europe's great "wow" experiences. Enter the church. Gape for a while. But don't gape at Michelangelo's famous* Pietà *(on the right). That's this tour's finale. I'll wait for you at the round maroon pavement stone on the floor near the central doorway.*

The Church

While ancient Rome fell, its grandeur survived. Roman basilicas became churches, senators became bishops, and the Pontifex Maximus (Emperor)...remained the Pontifex Maximus (Pope). This church is appropriately huge.

Size before beauty: The golden window at the far end is two football fields away. The dove in the window above the altar has the wingspan of a 747 (OK, maybe not quite, but it is big). The church covers six acres—if planted with wheat, it could feed a small city. The babies at the base of the pillars along the main hall (the nave) are adult size. The lettering in the gold band along the top of the pillars is two meters (6 feet) high. Really. The church has a capacity of 60,000 standing worshipers (that's more than 1,200 tour groups).

The church is huge and it feels huge, but everything is designed to make it seem smaller and more intimate than it really is. For example, the statue of St. Teresa near the bottom of the first pillar on the right is five meters (15 feet) tall.

The statue above her near the top looks the same size, but is actually two meters (6 feet) taller, giving the impression that it's not so far away. Similarly, the fancy bronze canopy over the altar at the far end is as tall as a seven-story building. That makes the great height of the dome seem smaller.

Looking down the nave, we get a sense of the grandeur of ancient Rome that was carried on by the Catholic Church. The floor plan is based on the ancient Roman basilica, or law-court building, with a central aisle (nave) flanked by two side aisles.

The goal of this unprecedented building project was to "put the dome of the Pantheon atop the Forum's Basilica of Constantine." If you've seen these two Roman structures, you have an idea of this megavision. In fact, many of the stones used to build St. Peter's were scavenged from the ruined law courts of ancient Rome.

On the floor near the central doorway is a round slab of

porphyry stone in the maroon color of ancient Roman officials. This is the spot where, on Christmas night in A.D. 800, the French king Charlemagne was crowned "Holy Roman Emperor." Even in the Dark Ages, when Rome was virtually abandoned and visitors reported that the city "had more thieves and wolves than decent people," its imperial legacy made it a fitting place to symbolically establish a briefly united Europe.

St. Peter's was very expensive to build and decorate. The popes financed it by selling "indulgences," allowing the rich to literally buy forgiveness from the Church. This kind of corruption inspired an obscure German monk named Martin Luther to rebel and start the Protestant Reformation.

The ornate Baroque-style interior—a riot of marble, gold, stucco, mosaics, columns of stone, and pillars of light—was part of the Church's "Counter-" Reformation. Baroque served as cheery propaganda, impressing followers with the authority of the Church, and giving them a glimpse of the heaven that awaited the faithful.

• *Now, walk straight up the center of the nave toward the altar.*

"Michelangelo's Church"—The Greek Cross

The plaques on the floor show where other, smaller churches of the world would end if they were placed inside St. Peter's: St. Paul's Cathedral in London (Londinense), the Florence Cathedral, and so on.

You'll also walk over circular golden grates. Stop at the second one (at the third pillar from the entrance). Look back at the entrance and realize that if Michelangelo had had his way, this whole long section of the church wouldn't exist. The nave was extended after his death.

Michelangelo was 70 years old when the pope persuaded him to take over the church project and cap it with a dome. He agreed, intending to put the dome over Bramante's original "Greek Cross" floor plan (+), with four equal arms. In optimistic Renaissance times, this symmetrical arrangement symbolized perfection—the orderliness of the created world and the goodness of man (who was created in God's image). But Michelangelo was a Renaissance Man in Counter-Reformation times. The Church, struggling against Protestants and its own corruption,

opted for a plan designed to impress the world with its grandeur—
the Latin cross of the Crucifixion with its nave extended to accommodate the grand religious spectacles of the Baroque period.
• *Continue toward the altar, entering "Michelangelo's Church." Park
yourself in front of the statue of St. Andrew to the left of the altar, the
guy holding an X-shaped cross. Like Andrew, gaze up into the dome,
and also like him, gasp. (Never stifle a gasp.)*

The Dome

The dome soars higher than a football field on end, 130 meters
(430 feet) to the top of the lantern. It glows with light from its
windows, the blue and gold mosaics creating a cool, solemn
atmosphere. In this majestic vision of heaven, we see (above the
windows) Jesus, Mary, and a ring of saints, more rings of angels
above them, and, way up in the ozone, God the Father (a blur of
blue and red, without binoculars).

Listen to the hum of visitors echoing through St. Peter's.
Churches are an early form of biofeedback where we can become
aware of ourselves, hear our own human sounds, and reflect on
our place in the cosmos. Half animal, half angel, stretched between
heaven and earth, born to live only a short while, a bubble of foam
on a great cresting wave of humanity.
• *But I digress.*

Peter

The base of the dome is ringed with a gold banner telling us in massive blue letters why this church is so important. According to Catholics, Peter was selected by Jesus to head the church. The banner in
Latin quotes from the Bible where Jesus says to him, "You are Peter
(*Tu es Petrus*) and upon this rock I will build my church" (Matthew
16:18). Peter was the first bishop of Rome, and his authority has supposedly passed in an unbroken chain to each succeeding bishop of
Rome—that is, the 250-odd popes that followed.

Under the dome, under the bronze canopy, under the altar,
some seven meters (23 feet) under the marble floor, rest the bones
of St. Peter, the "rock" upon which this particular church was built.

Go to the railing and look
down into the small, lighted
niche below the altar with
a box containing bishops'
shawls—a symbol of how
Peter's authority spread to
the other churches. Peter's
tomb is just below this box.
Are they really the bones

of Jesus' apostle? According to a papal pronouncement: definitely maybe. The traditional site of his tomb was sealed up when Old St. Peter's was built on it in A.D. 326, and it remained sealed until 1940, when it was opened for archaeological study. Bones were found, dated from the first century, of a robust man who died in old age. His body was wrapped in expensive cloth. Various inscriptions and graffiti in the tomb indicate that second- and third-century visitors thought this was Peter's tomb. Does that mean it's really Peter? Who am I to disagree with the pope? Definitely maybe.

If you line up the cross on the altar with the dove in the window, you'll notice that the niche below the cross is just off-center compared with the rest of the church. Why? Because Michelangelo built the church around the traditional location of the tomb, not the actual location—about a half meter (2 feet) away—discovered by modern archaeology.

Back in the nave sits a bronze statue of Peter under a canopy. This is one of a handful of pieces of art that was in the earlier

church. In one hand he holds the keys, the symbol of the authority given him by Christ, while with the other he blesses us. He's wearing the toga of a Roman senator. It may be that the original statue was of a senator and the bushy head and keys were added later to make it Peter. His big right toe has been worn smooth by the lips of pilgrims and foot-fetishists. Stand in line and kiss it, or, to avoid foot-and-mouth disease, touch your hand to your lips, then rub the toe. This is simply an act of reverence with no legend attached, though you can make one up if you like.

The Main Altar

The main altar beneath the dome and canopy (the white marble slab with cross and candlesticks) is used only when the pope himself says Mass. He sometimes conducts the Sunday morning service when he's in town, a sight worth seeing. I must admit, though, it's a little strange being frisked at the door for weapons at the holiest place in Christendom.

The tiny altar would be lost in this enormous church if it weren't for Bernini's seven-story bronze canopy, which "extends" the altar upward and reduces the perceived distance between floor and ceiling.

Gian Lorenzo Bernini (1598–1680) is the man most responsible for the interior decoration of the church. The altar

area was his masterpiece, a "theater"
for holy spectacles. Bernini did: (1) the
bronze canopy; (2) the dove window
in the apse surrounded by bronzework
and statues; (3) the statue of lance-
bearing St. Longinus ("The hills are
alive . . . "), which became the model
for the other three statues; (4) the balconies above the four statues, incorpo-
rating the actual corkscrew columns
looted from Solomon's Temple in
Jerusalem; and (5) much of the marble
floor decoration. Bernini, the father of

Baroque, gave an impressive unity to an amazing variety of pillars,
windows, statues, chapels, and aisles.

The bronze canopy (like a "four-poster bed") is his crowning
touch. The corkscrew columns are modeled after the ancient
columns from Solomon's Temple. Some of the bronze used here
was taken and melted down from the ancient Pantheon. On the
marble base of the columns are three bees on a shield, the symbol
of the Barberini family, who commissioned the work and ordered
the raid on the Pantheon. As the saying went, "What the barbarians didn't do, the Barberini did."

Starting from the column
to the left of the altar, walk
clockwise around the canopy.
Notice the female faces on the
marble bases, about eye level
above the bees. Someone in
the Barberini family was pregnant during the making of the
canopy, so Bernini put the
various stages of childbirth on the bases. Continue clockwise to
the last base to see how it came out.

• *Walk into the apse (it's the front area with the golden dove window)
and take a seat.*

The Apse

Bernini's dove window shines above the smaller front altar used
for everyday services. The Holy Spirit, in the form of a two-meter-
high (6-foot) dove, pours sunlight onto the faithful through the
alabaster windows, turning into artificial rays of gold and reflecting
off swirling gold clouds, angels, and winged babies. This is the
epitome of Baroque—a highly decorative, glorious, mixed-media
work designed to overwhelm the viewer.

Bernini Blitz

Nowhere is there such a conglomeration of works by the flamboyant genius who remade the church—and the city— in the Baroque style. Here's your scavenger-hunt list. You have 20 minutes. Go.

1. St. Peter's Square: design and statues
2. Constantine equestrian relief (right end of atrium)
3. Decoration (stucco, gold leaf, marble, etc.) of side aisles (flanking the nave)
4. Tabernacle (the temple-like altarpiece) inside Blessed Sacrament Chapel
5. Much of the marble floor throughout church
6. Bronze canopy over the altar
7. St. Longinus statue (holding a lance) near altar
8. Balconies (above each of the four statues) with corkscrew, Solomonic columns
9. Dove window, bronze sunburst, angels, "Throne," and Church Fathers (in the apse)
10. Tomb of Pope Urban VIII (far end of the apse, right side)
11. Tomb of Pope Alexander VII (between the apse and the left transept, over a doorway, with the gold skeleton smothered in jasper poured like maple syrup). Bizarre...Baroque...Bernini.

Beneath the dove is the centerpiece of this structure, the so-called "Throne of Peter," an oak chair built in medieval times for a king. Subsequently, it was encrusted with tradition and encased in bronze by Bernini as a symbol of papal authority. Statues of four early Church Fathers support the chair, a symbol of how bishops should support the pope in troubled times—times like the Counter-Reformation.

Remember that St. Peter's is a church, not a museum. In the apse, Mass is said daily (Mon–Sat at 17:00, Sun at 17:30) for pilgrims, tourists, and Roman citizens alike. Wooden confessional booths are available for Catholics to tell their sins to a listening ear and receive forgiveness and peace of mind. The faithful renew their faith and the faithless gain inspiration. Sit here, look at the light streaming through the windows, turn and gaze up into the dome, and quietly contemplate your god.

Or...

Contemplate this: the mystery of empty space. The bench you're sitting on and the marble at your feet, solid as they may seem, consist overwhelmingly of open space—99.9999 percent open space. The atoms that form these "solid" benches are themselves mostly open space. If the nucleus of your average atom were as large as the period at the end of this sentence, its electrons would be specks of dust orbiting around it—at the top of Michelangelo's dome. Empty space. Perhaps matter is only an aberration in an empty universe.

• *Like, wow. Stop me before I digress again.*

Now head to the left of the main altar into the south transept. At the far end, find the dark painting of St. Peter crucified upside down.

Left Transept

The painting is at the exact spot (according to tradition) where Peter was killed 1,900 years ago. Peter had come to the world's greatest city to preach Jesus' message of love to the pagan, often hostile Romans.

The Romans were actually quite tolerant of other religions. All they required of their conquered peoples was allegiance to the empire by worshiping the emperor as a god. For most religions, this was no problem, but monotheistic Christians were children of a jealous God who would not allow worship of any others. They refused to worship the emperor even when burned alive, crucified, or thrown to the lions. Their bravery, optimism in suffering, and message of love struck a chord among slaves and members of the lower classes. The religion started by a poor carpenter grew, despite occasional pogroms (persecution of minorities) by fanatical emperors. In three short centuries, Christianity went from a small Jewish sect in Jerusalem to the official religion of the world's greatest empire.

While this is a true painting, nearly all the other "paintings" in the church are actually mosaic copies made from thousands of colored chips the size of your little fingernail. Really. Smoke and humidity would damage real paintings. Around the corner on the right (heading back toward the central nave), pause at the copy of Raphael's huge "painting" (mosaic) of *The Transfiguration*, especially if you won't be seeing the original in the Vatican Museum.

• *Back near the entrance to the church, in the far corner, behind bulletproof glass is...*

The *Pietà*

Michelangelo was 24 years old when he completed this *Pietà* (pee-ay-TAH) of Mary with the dead body of Christ taken from the cross.

Michelangelo, with his total mastery of the real world, captures the sadness of the moment. Mary cradles her crucified son in her lap. Christ's lifeless right arm drooping down lets us know how heavy this corpse is. His smooth skin is accented by the rough folds of Mary's robe. Mary tilts her head downward, looking at her dead son with sad tenderness. Her left hand is upturned as if asking, "How could they do this to you?"

Michelangelo didn't think of sculpting as creating a figure, but as simply freeing the God-made figure from the prison of marble around it. He'd attack a project like this with an inspired passion, chipping away to reveal what God put inside.

Realistic as this work is, its true power lies in the subtle "unreal" features. Look how small and childlike Christ is compared with the massive Mary. Unnoticed at first, this accentuates the subconscious impression of Mary enfolding Jesus in her maternal love. Notice how young Mary is. She's the mother of a 33-year-old man, but here she's portrayed as a teenage girl, showing how Mary was the eternally youthful "handmaiden" of the Lord, always serving Him, even at this moment of supreme sacrifice. She accepts God's will, even if it means giving up her son.

The statue is a solid pyramid of maternal tenderness. Yet within this, Christ's body tilts diagonally down to the right and Mary's hem flows with it. Subconsciously, we feel the weight of this dead God sliding from her lap to the ground.

On Christmas morning, 1972, a madman with a hammer entered St. Peter's and began hacking away at the *Pietà*. The damage was repaired, but that's why there's a shield of bullet-proof glass today.

This is Michelangelo's only signed work. The story goes that he overheard some pilgrims praising his finished *Pietà*, but attributing it to a second-rate sculptor from a lesser city. He was so enraged he grabbed his chisel and chipped "Michelangelo Buonarroti of Florence did this" in the ribbon running down Mary's chest.

On your right (covered in gray concrete with a gold cross) is the inside of the Holy Door. It won't be opened until Christmas Eve, 2024, the dawn of the next Jubilee Year. If there's a prayer inside you, ask that when it's next opened, St. Peter's will no longer need security checks or bulletproof glass.

Up to the Dome (Cupola)

A good way to finish a visit to St. Peter's is to go up to the dome for the best view of Rome anywhere.

There are two levels, the rooftop of the church and the very top of the dome. An elevator (€5) takes you to the first level, on the church roof just above the facade. Even from there, you have a commanding view of St. Peter's Square, the statues on the colonnade, Rome across the Tiber in front of you, and the dome itself—almost terrifying in its nearness—looming behind you.

From here, you can also go inside to the gallery ringing the interior of the dome, where you can look down inside the church. Notice the dusty top of Bernini's seven-story-tall canopy far below. Study the mosaics up close—and those huge letters! It's worth the elevator ride for this view alone.

From this level, if you're energetic, continue all the way up to the top of the dome. The staircase (free at this point) actually winds between the outer shell and the inner one. It's a long, sweaty, stuffy, claustrophobic, 15-minute climb, but worth it. The view from the summit is great, the fresh air even better. Admire the arms of Bernini's colonnade encircling St. Peter's Square. Find the big, white Victor Emmanuel Monument with the two statues on top and the Pantheon with its large, light, shallow dome. The large rectangular building to the left of the obelisk is the Vatican Museum, stuffed with art. Survey the Vatican grounds, with its mini–train system and lush gardens. Look down into the square on the tiny pilgrims buzzing like electrons around the nucleus of Catholicism.

Hours of Dome: Daily May–Sept 8:30–18:00, Oct–April 8:30–17:00. Allow one hour for the full trip up and down, a half hour to go only to the roof and gallery. The entry to the elevator is just outside the basilica, on the porch, on the north side of St. Peter's. Look for signs to the *cupola*.

THE REST OF THE CHURCH

The Crypt: You can go down to the foundations of old St. Peter's, containing tombs of popes and memorial chapels. But you won't see St. Peter's tomb unless you take a tour (€8, call Excavations Office at 06-6988-5318). The staircase entrance varies, but it's usually inside the church near St. Andrew or one of his three fellow statues. Seeing the crypt is free, but the visit takes you back outside the church, a 15-minute detour. (Do it when you're ready to leave.)

The Museum (Museo-Tesoro): If you like old jewels and papal robes, you'll find the treasures and splendors of Roman Christianity a marked contrast to the poverty of early Christians. It's located near (but not in) the left transept, through a gray portal.

Blessed Sacrament Chapel: You're welcome to step through the metalwork gates into this oasis of peace reserved for prayer and meditation. It's located on the right-hand side of the church, about midway to the altar.

ST. PETER-IN-CHAINS
TOUR

San Pietro in Vincoli

Michelangelo—Earth's greatest sculptor—died having failed to complete his greatest work, the tomb of Pope Julius II. Today, you can visit the powerful remains of that unfinished masterpiece, including the famous statue of Moses, housed in a historic church that also contains Peter's chains.

Orientation

Cost: Free.

Dress Code: Modest dress is required.

Hours: Mon–Sat 7:00–12:30 & 15:30–19:00, Sun 7:30–12:30.

Getting There: The church is a 10- to 15-minute walk north of the Colosseum (Metro stop: Colosseo, exit Metro stop to the left and climb the staircase that's roughly 50 meters, or 160 feet, away, then work your way slowly uphill; or get off at Metro: Cavour, exit Metro and go up steep flight of steps, take a right at the top and walk a block).

Length of Our Tour: Thirty minutes.

Cuisine Art: See the recommended eateries listed on page 257.

The Art

• *In the far right corner of the church, you'll find a wall full of marble statues. In the center sits . . .*

Michelangelo's Moses (1515)

Moses has just returned from meeting face to face with God. Now he senses trouble back home. Slowly he turns to see his followers worshiping a golden calf. As his anger builds, he glares at them while tugging obsessively on his beard. His powerful left leg tucks under and tenses, as he's just about to spring up out of his chair and spank the naughty Children of Israel with the Ten Commandments under his arm.

And if he did stand up, this statue would be 4 meters (13 feet) tall, nearly the height of Michelangelo's famous *David*. This Charlton Heston-with-horns is interesting in photographs...and awe-inspiring when confronted face-to-face. His bare, muscular arms emerge from deep-furrowed robes. Michelangelo completed the statue after practicing for four years painting the seated prophets on the Sistine ceiling.

Like other Michelangelo statues, Moses is both at rest (seated) and in motion (his tensed leg, turning head, and nervous fingers). This restlessness may reflect Michelangelo's neo-Platonic belief that the soul is the claustrophobic prisoner of the body. Or it's the statue itself fighting to emerge from the stone around it. A frustrated Michelangelo, working to bring God's statue into existence, reportedly threw his chisel at the thing (some say causing a scar on Moses' right knee), yelling at it: "Speak, dammit, speak!"

The horns are the crowning touch. In medieval times, the Hebrew word for "rays of light" (halo) was mistranslated as "horns." Michelangelo knew better but wanted to give the statue an air of *"terribilità,"* a kind of scary charisma possessed by Moses, Pope Julius II...and Michelangelo. This Moses radiates the smoldering *terribilità* of a borderline-abusive father.

The Tomb Today

In 1542, some of the remnants of the tomb project were brought to St. Peter-in-Chains and pieced together by Michelangelo's assistants. What we see today is a far cry from the original design, which was to have been fully three-dimensional and five times as big. Some of the best statues ended up elsewhere, like the Prisoners in Florence, and the Slaves in the Louvre. Though the assistants had Michelangelo's original instruction manual, they were trying to assemble it with most of the parts missing.

Moses (and the Louvre's Slaves) are the only statues Michelangelo personally completed for the project. Flanking Moses are the Old Testament sister-wives of Jacob, Leah (to our left) and Rachel, both begun by Michelangelo but finished by pupils.

The Tomb of Pope Julius II

Moses sits on the bottom level of a three-story marble wall filled with statues. This is a puny, cobbled-together version of what was to have been a grand tomb for Pope Julius II.

In 1505, Pope Julius II hired young Michelangelo to build his tomb, a huge monument to be placed in the center of St. Peter's Basilica. An excited Michelangelo sketched designs for a three-story, wedding-cake mountain of marble studded with 48 statues and bronze reliefs, and topped with a huge statue of the egomaniacal pope. Moses was to have been placed on an upper level on the right-hand corner, looking away from the monument.

Michelangelo traveled to Carrara, selected 100 tons of marble for the project, and started working. Then Julius changed his mind. He ordered Michelangelo to work, instead, painting the Sistine Chapel. Michelangelo knocked it off in a mere four years so he could return to his true masterwork. Michelangelo would spend 30 years of his life working in fits and starts on the tomb. But when Julius died (1514), the funding for the project petered out, and Michelangelo eventually moved on to other things. Julius was buried in a simple grave in St. Peter's.

On the second story, a Madonna and Child stand above a reclining, thoughtful-looking Pope Julius II on a coffin.

The sheer variety of decoration we see here gives us a glimpse of the tomb's original scope—prophets (Moses) mingle with Roman scholars and pagan sibyls (second story), spiced with spooky ghosts in burial shrouds (bottom level), and laced together with Pompeii-esque garlands and proto-Baroque scrolls.

Michelangelo went to his grave thinking he'd wasted the best years of his life on the tomb. Today, we can only reconstruct it in our minds, imagining a monument intended to exceed "every ancient or imperial tomb ever made."

The Church

Founded in 442, it's one of Rome's oldest, built to house Peter's chains. Though the church was greatly changed in 1475, the 20 Doric columns flanking the wide nave are from the original church.

• *On the altar is a gold-and-glass case, containing what tradition claims are . . .*

Peter's Chains

There are actually two different sets of chains, linked together. One set held Peter (it's said) when he and Paul were in the Mammertine Prison in Rome (near the Forum).

The other dates from when Herod jailed Peter in Jerusalem (Acts 12). During the night, "Peter was sleeping between two soldiers, bound with chains, while sentries were guarding the doors. And behold, an angel of the Lord appeared and a light shone in the cell. The angel struck Peter on the side and woke him, saying, 'Get up quickly.' And the chains fell off his hands." The angel led Peter, who thought he was dreaming, out of the prison to safety. (Raphael depicted this in the Vatican, page 148.)

In the waning days of ancient Rome, the Jerusalem chains ended up here as a gift from the Eastern empress to her son-in-law, the Western emperor. When they arrived and were paired with the Mammertine chains, the two sets—chink!—joined together miraculously.

PILGRIM'S
ROME

Rome is the "capital" of the world's 800 million Catholics. In Rome, you'll rub elbows with religious pilgrims from around the world—Nigerian nuns, Bulgarian theology students, extended Mexican families, and ordinary Catholics returning to their religious roots.

Pilgrims to Rome try to visit four great basilicas: St. Peter's (of course, page 164), Santa Maria Maggiore, San Giovanni in Laterano, and San Paolo Fuori le Mura (St. Paul's Outside the Walls, page 44). For your sightseeing pleasure, we've added a fifth—the fascinating and central San Clemente. And for the best Byzantine-style mosaics in Rome, pilgrims should visit the Church of Santa Prassede.

The pilgrim industry helped shape Rome. Ancient Rome's population peaked at about 1.2 million. When Rome fell in 476, barbarians cut off the water supply by breaking the aqueducts, Romans fled the city, and the Tiber silted up. During the Dark Ages, mosquitoes ruled over a pathetic village of 50,000...bad news for pilgrims, bad news for the Vatican. Back then, the Catholic Church was the Christian Church. Because popes needed a place fit for pilgrimages, the Church revitalized the city. Owners of hotels and restaurants cheered.

In 1587, Pope Sixtus V reconnected aqueducts and built long, straight boulevards connecting the great churches and pilgrimage sites. Obelisks served as markers. As you explore the city, think like a pilgrim. Look down long roads and you'll see either a grand church or an obelisk (from which you'll see a grand church). For example, Via XX Settembre is a montage of pilgrimage churches connecting the Catacombs of St. Agnese (to the east) with the pope's home on the Quirinal (to the west).

Pilgrim's Rome

SAN GIOVANNI IN LATERANO

Imagine the jubilation when this church—the first Christian church in the city of Rome—was opened around A.D. 318. Christians could finally "come out" and worship openly without fear of reprisal. After that glorious beginning, the church has served as the center of Catholicism and the home of the popes up until the Renaissance renovation of St. Peter's. Until 1870, all popes were "crowned" here. Even today, it's the home church of the Bishop of Rome—the pope.

(The church is free and open Mon–Sat 6:15–12:00 & 15:00–18:15, Sun 6:15–12:00 & 15:30–18:45. It's located on Piazza San Giovanni in Laterano, Metro: San Giovanni. From the Metro station, go through the old city walls and look left.)

Exterior

The massive facade is 18th century, with Christ triumphant on the top. The blocky, peach-colored building adjacent on the right is the Lateran Palace, standing on the site of the old Papal Palace—residence of popes until about 1300. Across the street to your right are the pope's private chapel and the Holy Stairs

(Scala Santa), popular with pilgrims. To the left is a well-preserved chunk of the ancient Roman wall.

• *Step inside the portico and look left.*

1. Statue of Constantine (inside the portico, far left end)

It's October 28, A.D. 312, and Constantine—sword tucked under his arm and leaning confidently on a (missing) spear—has conquered Maxentius and liberated Rome. Constantine marched to this spot where his enemy's personal bodyguards lived, trashed their pagan idols, and dedicated the place to the god who gave him his victory—Christ. (In the relief above the statue, see one of Constantine's men straddling and decapitating an enemy.) The holes in Constantine's head once held a golden, halo-like crown for the emperor who legalized Christianity.

2. Central Doorway (in the portico)

These tall green bronze doors, with their floral designs and acorn studs, are the original doors from ancient Rome's Senate House (Curia) in the Forum. The Church moved these here in the 1650s to remind people that from now on, the Church was Europe's lawmaker. The star borders were added to make these big doors bigger.

• *Now go inside the main part of the church.*

3. Giotto Fresco (inside church, second pillar in right aisle)

Pope Boniface VIII proclaims the first (modern) Jubilee Year in 1300, in this fading fresco attributed to the first "modern" painter, Giotto. A servant holds the pope's cue cards.

4. Basilica Floor Plan

San Giovanni was the first public church in Rome and the model for all later churches, including St. Peter's. The floor plan—a large central hall (nave) flanked by two side aisles—was based on the

San Giovanni in Laterano

PIAZZA DI PORTA SAN GIOVANNI

1. STATUE OF CONSTANTINE
2. CENTRAL DOORWAY
3. GIOTTO FRESCO
4. BASILICA FLOOR PLAN
5. BALDACCHINO
6. GOLDEN COLUMNS FROM TEMPLE OF JUPITER
7. BISHOP'S CHAIR
8. MOSAIC

ancient Roman basilica (law courts) floor plan. These buildings were big enough to accommodate the large Christian congregations.

5. Baldacchino (canopy over altar)

In the upper cage are two silver statues of saints Peter (with keys) and Paul (sword), containing their...heads.

The gossip buzzing among Rome's amateur archaeologists is that the Vatican tested DNA from Peter's head (located here) and from his body (located at St. Peter's)...and they didn't match.

6. Golden Columns from Temple of Jupiter
(left transept)

Tradition says that these gilded bronze columns once stood in pagan Rome's holiest spot—the Temple of Jupiter, the King of all Gods, on the summit of Capitol Hill (c. 50 B.C.). Now they support a triangular pediment inhabited by a bearded, Jupiter-like God the Father.

7. Bishop's Chair (in apse)

The chair (or "cathedra") reminds visitors that this is the cathedral of Rome...and the pope himself is the bishop that sits here.

8. Mosaic (in semicircular dome of apse)

The original design dates from about 450. (The mosaic was remodeled with the addition of saints in the 13th century.) Pop in a coin for light. You'll see a cross, animals, plants, and the River Jordan running along the base. Mosaic, of course, was an ancient Roman specialty adapted by medieval Christians. The head of Christ (above the cross) must have been a glorious sight to early worshipers. It was one of the first legal images of Christ ever seen in formerly pagan Rome.

• *Fans of Cosmatesque mosaics (c. 1100–1300) may want to visit the cloister (€2, entrance near left transept).*

The Holy Stairs are outside the church in a building across the street.

Holy Stairs *(Scala Santa)*

In 326, Emperor Constantine's mother (St. Helena) brought home the 28 marble steps of Pilate's residence. Jesus climbed these steps on the day he was sentenced to death. Each day, hundreds of "penitent faithful" climb these steps on their knees (reciting a litany of prayers, available at the desk to the right of the entry). The steps—

covered with walnut wood with small glass-covered holes showing stains from Jesus' blood—lead to the "Holy of Holies" (Sancta Sanctorum), the private chapel of the popes in the Middle Ages. With its world-class relics, this chapel was considered the holiest place on earth. While the relics are now in the Vatican and the chapel is locked up, you can climb the tourist staircases along the sides and look through the grated windows into the chapel.

On September 20, 1870, as nationalist forces unifying Italy took Rome and ended the pope's temporal power, Pope Pius IX left his Quirinal Palace home for the last time. He stopped here to climb the steps, pray in his chapel, and bless his supporters from the top of the steps. Then he fled to the Vatican, where he spent the rest of his days.

SANTA MARIA MAGGIORE

The basilica of Santa Maria celebrates Holy Mary, the mother of Jesus. One of Rome's oldest and best-preserved churches, it was built (A.D. 432) while Rome was falling around it. The city had been sacked by Vandals (410), and the emperors were about to check out (476). Increasingly, popes stepped in to fill the vacuum of leadership. The fifth-century mosaics give the church the feel of the early Christian community.

(The church is free and open daily 7:00–20:00. It's on Piazza Santa Maria Maggiore, Metro: Termini or Vittorio Emanuele. Tel. 06-446-5836.)

Exterior

Mary's column originally stood in the Forum's Basilica of Constantine. The fifth-century church built in her honor proclaims she was indeed the Mother of God—a fact disputed by hair-splitting theologians of the day. When you step inside the church, you'll be exiting Italy and entering the Vatican—the *Maggiore* indicates this church, a Vatican possession, was much more important than other churches dedicated to the Virgin Mary.

Interior

Despite the Renaissance ceiling and Baroque crusting, you still feel like you're walking into an early Christian church. The stately rows of columns, the simple basilica layout, the cheery colors, the

Santa Maria Maggiore

PIAZZA DELL' ESQUILINO

APSE ②

③

① ⑥

PAULINE
CHAPEL ⑦

SIXTUS Ⅴ
CHAPEL ⑤

④

N
A
V
E

20 YARDS
20 m

PORCH

TO STA.
PRASSEDE
(100 M)

DCH

ENTER

PIAZZA SANTA MARIA MAGGIORE

① MANGER FRAGMENTS
② APSE MOSAIC
③ MOSAICS IN CHANCEL ARCH
④ NAVE MOSAICS
⑤ TOMB OF SIXTUS V
⑥ BERNINI'S TOMB
⑦ MADONNA PAINTING AND MIRACLE RELIEF

spacious nave—it's easy to imagine worshipers finding an oasis of peace here as the Roman Empire crashed around them. (The 15th-century coffered ceiling is gilded with gold perhaps brought back from America by Columbus.)

• *In the center of the church is the main altar, under a purple canopy. Underneath the altar, in a lighted niche, are . . .*

1. Manger Fragments

A kneeling pope (Paul IV, a conservative pope during the liberal 1960s) prays before a glass case with an urn that contains several pieces of wood, bound by iron—these pieces are said to be from Jesus' crib. The church, dedicated to Mary's motherhood, displays these relics as physical evidence that Mary was indeed the mother of Christ. (The church is also built on the site of a former pagan temple dedicated to Rome's mother goddess, Juno.) Is the manger the real thing? Look into the eyes of pilgrims who visit.

• *In the apse, topped with a semicircular dome, find . . .*

2. Apse Mosaic

This 13th-century mosaic shows Mary being crowned by Jesus, both on the same throne. They float in a bubble representing heaven, borne aloft by angels. By the Middle Ages, Mary's cult status was secure.

• *Up in the arch that frames the outside of the apse, you'll find some of the church's oldest mosaics.*

3. Mosaics in Chancel Arch

Colorful panels tell Mary's story in fifth-century Roman terms. Mary (top panel on left-hand side) sits on a throne, dressed in gold and crowned like an empress. She's surrounded by haloed senator-saints in white togas. The angel Gabriel swoops down to announce to Mary that she'll conceive Jesus, and the Dove of the Holy Spirit follows. Below (the panel in the bottom left corner) are sheep representing the apostles, entering the city of Jerusalem ("Hiervsalem").

4. Nave Mosaics (right side of nave, starting near altar)

The church contains some of the world's oldest and best-preserved mosaics from Christian Rome. If the floodlights are on (it doesn't hurt to ask someone), those with good eyesight or binoculars will enjoy watching the story of Moses unfold in a series of surprisingly colorful and realistic scenes—more sophisticated than anything that would be seen for a thousand years.

The small, square mosaic panels are above the columns, on

the right-hand side of the nave. Start at the altar and work back toward the entry.

1. It's a later painting, skip it.
2. Pharaoh's daughter (upper left) and her maids take baby Moses from the Nile.
3. Moses (lower half of panel) sees a burning bush that reconnects him with his Hebrew origins.
4. A parade of Israelites (left side) flee Egypt through a path in the Red Sea, while Pharaoh's troops drown.
5. Moses leads them across the Sinai desert (upper half), and God provides for them with a flock of quail (lower half).
6. Moses (upper half) sticks his magic rod in a river to desalinate it.
7. The Israelites battle their enemies while Moses commands from a hillside.
8. Skip it.
9. Moses (upper left) brings the Ten Commandments, then goes with Joshua (upper right) to lie down and die.
10. Joshua crosses the (rather puny) Jordan River...
11. ...attacks Jericho...
12. ...and the walls come a-tumblin' down.

• *Enter the chapel in the right transept. On the right-hand wall is a statue of a praying pope on the...*

5. Tomb of Sixtus V

The Rome we see today is due largely to Pope Sixtus V (or was it Fiftus VI)? This energetic pope (1585–1590) leveled shoddy medieval Rome and erected grand churches connected by long, broad boulevards spiked with obelisks as focal points (such as the obelisk in Piazza dell' Esquilino behind Santa Maria Maggiore). The city of Rome has 13 Egyptian obelisks—all of Egypt has only five. The relief panels (especially the one in the upper right) show some of the obelisks and buildings he commissioned.

• *Between the right transept and the main altar, you'll find on the floor a plaque marking...*

6. Bernini's Tomb

The plaque reads, "Ioannes Laurentivs Bernini—GianLorenzo Bernini (1598–1680)—who brought honor to art and the city, here humbly rests." Next to it is another plaque to the "Familia Bernini." It's a simple memorial for the man who grew up in this neighborhood, then went on to remake Rome in the ornate Baroque style. (For more on Bernini, see page 131.)

• *In the left transept, over the altar, are a...*

7. Madonna Painting and Miracle Relief

The altar, a geologist's delight, is adorned with jasper, agate, amethyst, lapis lazuli, and gold angels. Amid it all is a simple, iconic version of the lady this church is dedicated to: Mary.

Above the painting is a bronze relief panel showing a pope, with amazed bystanders, shoveling snow. One hot August night in the year 432, Mary appeared to Pope Liberius in a dream, telling him: "Build me a church where the snow falls." The next morning, they discovered a small patch of snow here on the Esquiline Hill—on August 5—and this church, dedicated to Santa Maria, was begun.

• *After looking around Santa Maria Maggiore, fans of mosaics, Byzantines, and the offbeat should consider a visit to the nearby church of Santa Prassede, about 100 meters (330 feet) away.*

Exiting Santa Maria Maggiore, walk away from the church, veering along the right side of Mary on her column, down Via Merulana. Immediately turn right down the small street Via S. Giovanni Gualberto.

CHURCH OF SANTA PRASSEDE

The mosaics, from A.D. 822, are the best Byzantine-style mosaics in Rome. The Byzantine Empire, with its capital in Constantinople (modern Istanbul), was the eastern half of the Roman Empire that didn't "fall," remaining Christian, Greek-speaking, and cultured for a thousand years while their distant cousins in Italy were floundering in the Dark Ages. Byzantine craftsmen preserved the techniques of ancient Roman mosaicists (who decorated floors and walls of villas and public buildings), then reinfused this learning during the city's darkest era. Take the time to let your eyes adjust, and appreciate the Byzantine glory glowing out of the dark church.

(The church is free and open daily 7:00–12:00 & 16:00–18:30. Bring €1 coins to buy floodlighting.)

• *The best mosaics are in the apse (behind the main altar) and in the small Chapel of St. Zeno along the right (south) side of the nave.*

Apse Mosaics

On a blue background is Christ, standing in a rainbow-colored river, flanked by saints. Christ has commanded Peter (to our right of Christ, the one with white bushy hair) to spread the Good News to all the world. Peter came here to the world's biggest city to preach love . . . and was met with a hostile environment. He turns his palm up in a plea for help. Persecuted Peter was taken in by a hospitable woman named Pudentia (next to him) and her sister, Praxedes (to the left of Christ, between two other saints), whose house was located on this spot. (The church is named for Praxedes.)

The saint on the far left (to left of Praxedes) is Pope Paschal I, who built the church in the 800s in memory of these early sisters, hiring the best craftsmen in the known world to do the mosaics.

Chapel of St. Zeno

The ceiling is gold, representing the Byzantine heaven. An icon-like Christ emerges from the background, supported by angels. On the walls are saints walking among patches of flowers. In the altar-niche, Mary is flanked by the sisters Praxedes and Pudentia. On the side wall, the woman with the square halo is Theodora, the mom of the pope who built this.

The chapel, covered completely with mosaics, may be under-whelming to our modern eyes, but in the darkness of Rome's medieval era, it was known as the "Garden of Paradise."

SAN CLEMENTE

Here, like nowhere else, you'll enjoy the layers of Rome—a 12th-century basilica sits atop a fourth-century Christian basilica, which sits atop a second-century Mithraic Temple and some even earlier Roman buildings. (The upper church is free, €3 for lower churches, open Mon–Sat 9:00–12:30 & 15:00–18:00, opens Sun at 10:00, on Via di San Giovanni in Laterano, Metro: Colosseo. Tel. 06-7045-1018.)

Upper Church—12th Century

The church (at today's ground level) is dedicated to the fourth pope, Clement, who shepherded the small Christian community when the religion was, at best, tolerated, and at worst, a capital offense. Clement himself was martyred by drowning around A.D. 100—tied to an anchor by angry Romans and tossed overboard. You'll see his symbol, the anchor, around the church. The painting on the ceiling shows Clement being carried aloft to heaven.

Start your visit outside in the courtyard—a kind of defensive atrium common in medieval times. While today's entry is on the side, the original entry was through the courtyard in back. Entering the church from here, notice (on the left) the recon-structions of some ancient fres-coes. You'll see the faded origi-nals in the lower church, but notice the splendid detail of these first. (Note particularly the middle fresco on the top row showing Clement and Sisinnius, discussed below.)

The carved marble choir

enclosure in the middle of the church (Schola Cantorum) was where the cantors sat. About 1,200 years ago, it stood in the old church beneath us, before that church was looted and destroyed by invading Normans.

In the apse, study the fine 12th-century mosaics. The delicate Crucifixion—with Christ sharing the cross with a dozen apostles as doves—is engulfed by a Tree of Life richly inhabited by deer, birds, and saints. Above it all, a triumphant Christ, one hand on the Bible, blesses the congregation.

St. Catherine Chapel

The chapel near the side (tourists') entrance is dedicated to **St. Catherine of Alexandria**, a noblewoman martyred for her defense of persecuted Christians. The fresco on the left wall is by the Florentine master Masolino (1428), perhaps aided by his young assistant, Masaccio. Working from left to right (on the left wall), follow her story:

1. Catherine (lower left panel), in black, confronts an assembly of the pagan Emperor Maxentius and his counselors. She bravely ticks off arguments on her fingers why Christianity should be legalized. Her powerful delivery silences the crowd.

2. Under the rotunda of a pagan temple (upper left panel), Catherine, in blue, points up at a statue and tells a crowd of pagans, "Your gods are puny compared to mine."

3. Catherine, in blue (upper right panel, left side), is thrown in prison, where she's visited by the emperor's wife (in green). Catherine converts her.

4. Emperor Maxentius, enraged, orders his own wife killed. The executioner (upper panel, right side), standing next to the empress' decapitated corpse, impassively sheathes his sword.

5. In the most well known scene (the middle panel on the bottom), Maxentius, in black, looks down from a balcony and condemns Catherine (in black) to be torn apart between two large, spiked wheels turned by executioners. But suddenly, an angel swoops in with a sword to cut her loose.

6. Catherine is eventually martyred (lower right panel). Now dressed in green, she kneels before the executioner, who raises his sword to finish the job.

7. Finally, on the top of holy Mount Sinai (lower right panel, upper right side), two angels bear Catherine's coffin to its final resting place.

Taking a few steps back, look up at the arch that frames the chapel, topped by the delightful Annunciation fresco (top of the arch) by Masolino. Also notice the big St. Christopher, patron saint of travelers (left pillar), with 500-year-old graffiti scratched in by pilgrims.

Lower Church—Fourth Century

Buy a €3 ticket in the bookshop and descend 1700 years to the time when Christians were razzed on their way to church by pagan neighbors. The first room you enter was the original atrium (entry hall)—the nave extends to the right.

Pagan Inscription (in atrium)

This two-sided, marble, recycled burial slab—one side (with leafy decorations) for a Christian, the other for a pagan (you can turn it)—shows how the two Romes lived side by side in the fourth century.

Fresco of St. Clement and Sisinnius
(in nave near altar, on left wall)

Clement (center) holds a secret Mass for early Christians back when it was a capital crime. Theodora, a prominent Roman (in yellow, to the right), is one of the undercover faithful. Her pagan husband, Sisinnius, has come to retrieve and punish her when— zap!—he's struck blind and has to be led away (right side).

But Sisinnius is still unconvinced. When Clement cures his blindness, Sisinnius (lower panel, far right) orders two servants to drag Clement off to the authorities. But the package they carry is not really Clement, who lives to die another day—notice the anchor carved into the church's altar nearby.

• *In the far left corner of the lower church, near the staircase leading down, is the . . .*

Presumed Burial Place of St. Cyril

Cyril, who died in A.D. 869 (see the icon-like mosaic of him), was an inveterate traveler who spread Christianity to the Slavic lands and Russia—today's Russian Orthodox faithful. Along the way, he introduced the Cyrillic alphabet used by Russians and Slavs.

Temple of Mithras *(Mithreum)*—Second Century

Now descend farther to the dark, dank Mithraic Temple (Mithreum). Nowhere in Rome is there a better place to experience this weird cult.

Worship Hall (the barred room to the left)

Worshipers of Mithras—men only—sat on the benches on either side of the room. At the far end is a small statue of the god Mithras, in a billowing cape. In the center sits an altar carved with a relief showing Mithras fighting with a bull that contains all life. A scorpion, a dog, and a snake try to stop Mithras, but he wins, running his sword through the bull. The blood spills out, bringing life to the world.

Mithras' fans gathered here, in this tiny microcosm of the universe (the ceiling was decorated with stars), to celebrate the victory with a ritual meal. Every spring, Mithras brought new life again, and so they ritually kept track of

the seasons—the four square shafts in the corners of the ceiling represent the seasons, the seven round ones were the great constellations. Initiates went through hazing rituals representing the darkness of this world, then emerged into the light-filled world brought by Mithras.

The religion, stressing loyalty and based on the tenuousness of life, was popular among soldiers. It dates back to the time of Alexander the Great, who brought it from Persia. In 67 B.C., soldiers who'd survived the bloody conquest of Asia Minor returned to Rome swearing by Mithras. By imperial times, it was one of several mystery cults from the East (like Christianity) that became popular in Rome. When Christians gained power, they banished it.

Facing the barred room are two Corinthian columns supporting three arches of the temple's entryway, decorated with a fine stucco, coffered ceiling. At the far end of the hallway, another barred door marks the equivalent of a Mithraic Sunday School room. Peeking inside, see a faded fresco of bearded Mithras (right wall) and seven niches carved into the walls representing the seven stages a novice had to go through. Exit signs direct you down several steps into a vast Roman public area. Look down at the stream—part of the aqueduct system that brought fresh drinking water to first-century Rome. Now climb 2,000 years back to today's street level.

OSTIA ANTICA
DAY TRIP

For an exciting day trip, pop down to the Roman port of Ostia, which is similar to Pompeii but a lot closer and, in some ways, more interesting. Because Ostia was a working port town, it shows a more complete and gritty look at Roman life than wealthy Pompeii. Wandering around today, you'll see the remains of the docks, warehouses, apartment flats, mansions, shopping arcades, and baths that served a once-thriving port of 60,000 people.

Orientation

Cost: €5.

Hours: The site is open Tue–Sun 8:30–18:00 in summer, 9:00–16:00 in winter, closed Mon (and May 1, Dec 25, and Jan 1). The museum closes in the afternoon (Tue–Sun 9:00–13:30, closed Mon).

Getting There: From downtown Rome, it's a 45-minute combination Metro/train ride to Ostia Antica. It'll cost you just two Metro tickets one-way (€1.60 total). From Rome, take the Metro (line B) to the Piramide stop. Exit and walk to the left to the Lido trains (2/hr, use a Metro ticket) and ride to Ostia Antica (the stop before Ostia Lido). From the train station, cross the road via the blue skybridge and walk straight down Via della Stazione di Ostia Antica, following signs to *Scavi di Ostia Antica*, about 400 meters (1,300 feet) to the gate.

Tip: To maximize sightseeing efficiency on your Ostia day trip, consider visiting the sights in south Rome—such as St. Paul's Outside the Walls, Montemartini Museum, and Testaccio sights—on your return (see page 44).

Information: Tel. 06-5635-8099.

Tour: The well-done audioguide costs €5.

Length of Our Tour: Allow two hours.

Cuisine Art: A cafeteria is in Ostia's museum.

Ostia Antica

- **1** NECROPOLIS
- **2** PORTA ROMANA
- **3** REPUBLICAN WAREHOUSES
- **4** BATHS OF NEPTUNE
- **5** THEATER
- **6** SQUARE OF THE GUILDS
- **7** MILL
- **8** VIA CASA DI DIANA
- **9** FORUM
- **10** FORUM BATHS
- **11** MUSEUM

History

Located at (and named for) the mouth *(ostium)* of the Tiber, Ostia was founded around 620 B.C. Its main attraction was the salt gleaned from nearby salt flats, which was precious preserver of meat in ancient times. Later, as Rome began expanding (around 400 B.C.), Ostia was conquered, and a fort, or *castrum*, was built here. Ostia—often called Rome's first colony—served as a naval base, protecting Rome from any invasion by river. By A.D. 150, when Rome controlled the Mediterranean, Ostia's importance became commercial rather than military. Rome eventually outgrew the port of Ostia and a vast port was dug nearby (where Rome's airport now stands). But the city remained a key administrative and warehousing center, busy with the big business of keeping over a million Romans fed and in sandals. With the Fall of Rome, the port was abandoned. Over time the harbor silted up and the Tiber retreated about 1.5 kilometers (1 mile) away. The mud, which eventually buried Ostia, actually protected it from the ravages of time—and stone-scavenging medieval peasants.

Overview

Consider your visit a three-part affair: 1.) Follow this tour, which leads you straight down Decumanus Maximus, the town's main drag, with a couple of slight detours, finishing at the forum, the main square. 2.) Pop into the museum and consider a bite to eat at the cafeteria. 3.) Explore the back lanes—going on a visual scavenger hunt—as you wander your way back to the entry point.

THE TOUR

Necropolis

Find the map (30 meters, or 100 feet, inside the gate) for an orientation. Notice how the core of Ostia is a rectangular Roman military camp with two major roads crossing at the forum. One of four city gates lies ahead, and on your left is the necropolis (cemetery). Ancient Romans buried their dead outside the city walls. Detour to find family sepulchres—private open-air rooms lined with niches for ash-filled urns. Until the first century, cremation was common. In the second and third centuries A.D., the Romans here buried their dead in marble and terra-cotta sarcophagi in tombs.

Porta Romana

Ahead (where the road gets narrow) you enter the ancient city of Ostia through the scant remains of the gate Porta Romana. Just as Rome's Porta Ostiense faced Ostia, Ostia's Porta Romana faced Rome. Just inside to the left (under the big tree), you can see on the gate the bits of the Latin inscription that greeted all who entered. It reads: "The Senate and the people of the colony of Ostia constructed the walls." The "colony" reference is a reminder that Ostia was the first bit of the Roman Empire.

From the gate, Ostia's main street (named Decumanus Maximus) leads straight to the forum, where this walk ends. Note that this road was elevated above some buildings' foundations. Over the centuries, Ostia's ground level rose. You can actually identify buildings from the republic (centuries before Christ) and the empire (centuries after Christ) by their level. Anything you walk down into is from the earlier period.

Republican Warehouses *(Magazzini Repubblicani)*
The first century B.C. was busy with activities relating to the river port. Walking along the main street you pass vast warehouses on the right. The goods of the port—such as grain from Sicily, Egypt, and all of North Africa—were processed and stored in warehouses here before being consumed by Rome.

Baths of Neptune *(Terme di Nettuno)*
At the little well in the road, you'll see a viewpoint (with railings, above on right). Climb up for a view of the Baths of Neptune, including a fine mosaic with Neptune riding four horses through the sea. Apart from the cupid riding the dolphin, the sea looks pretty frightening—which it was. The large square to the left of the mosaic would have been busy with people wrestling, stretching, doing jumping jacks, and getting rubdowns. The niches that ring the square housed small businesses.

As you walk into the square, you'll see a path to your left. Follow this path (paralleling the main street), which crosses a typical street lined with apartments *(insulae)*, to the theater.

Theater *(Teatro)*
Up to 4,000 residents could gather here for entertainment. The three rows of marble steps near the orchestra were for big shots. While this theater seems big, it was twice as high in ancient times. (The upper two-thirds of what you see today is reconstructed.) In its day, a wall rose behind the stage, enclosing the theater. Even today, this place—one of the oldest brick theaters anywhere—is used for concerts. Climb to the top of the theater for a fine view.

Square of the Guilds *(Piazzale delle Corporazioni)*
The grand Square of the Guilds (in front of the theater) evolved from a simple place where businessmen would stroll and powwow together to become a monumental square lined with more than 60 offices of shipowners and traders. This was the bustling center of Rome's import/export industry. Along the sidewalk, second-century A.D. mosaics advertise the services offered by the various shops. Walking counterclockwise, circle the square to "read" the mosaics that advertised in Latin and in a sign language for illiterate or non-Latin-reading sailors. The most common symbol—the lighthouse—was the sign of the port of Ostia. Grain containers are reminders that grain was the major import of Ostia. The elephant marking the office of the Sabratans (a place in present-day Libya)

symbolized the sale of ivory or perhaps of exotic animals (great for parties and private spectacles). One shipper advertised dealings with Narbon (Narbonne in present-day France). In the far corner you'll see a mosaic showing porters loading containers from a seagoing ship to a river-going ship and the three-mouthed delta of a river (probably the Nile). Statues of notable local guild members and business leaders decorated the courtyard. The temple in the center was likely related to Ceres, the goddess of harvest and abundance (prosperity from good business).

Mill *(Molino)*

The next intersection is Via dei Molini, which marks the wall of the original military *castrum* (rectangular camp). Before continuing into that oldest part of Ostia, turn right down Via dei Molini and (after nearly 2 blocks), turn left into the mill building, dating from A.D. 120. Before you are several lava millstones that were used to grind grain. Study the workings: a bowl-like lower structure carefully cupped a moving upper section. Grain would be sprinkled in from a sack hanging from the ceiling. Mules or workers would power the grinding by walking in circles, pushing inserted wood poles. Powdery flour (with not much grit) would eventually tumble out of the bottom of the mill, ready to be made into bread. A nearby room contains two ovens. Now, backtrack down Via dei Molini and take the first right onto Via Casa di Diana.

Via Casa di Diana

There are three places of interest along this street—the House of Diana, a tavern, and stairs leading to the second floor of an apartment flat for a commanding view.

The House of Diana is a great example of *insulae* (multistoried tenement complexes where the lower middle class lived). The House of Diana originally had three or four floors (reaching the 20-meter, or 66-foot, maximum height allowed by Ostia's building codes).

Across the street is an inn called the Insula of the Thermopolium. Belly up to this tavern's bar. You'll see display shelves for food and drinks for sale, a small sink, and scant remains of wall paintings.

Across the street, stairs lead to the top floor of the Insula of the Paintings. Climb these for a good view and a chance to imagine life as an apartment dweller in ancient Rome. Now, walk on toward the high red brick temple that marks Ostia's forum.

Forum

Whenever possible, Rome imposed a grid road plan on its conquered cities. After Rome conquered Ostia around 400 B.C., it built a military camp, or *castrum*, a rectangular fort with east, west, north, and south gates and two main roads converging on the forum. Throughout the empire, Romans found comfort in this familiar city plan.

Ostia's main square became a monumental forum in the imperial period. And dominating this square, like most Roman towns, was the **grand temple** (from A.D. 120). The marble veneer was scavenged in the Middle Ages, leaving only the core brick-work. Note the reinforcement arches in the brick. The temple, called the Capitolium after the original atop Capitol Hill in Rome, was dedicated to the pagan trinity of Jupiter, Juno, and Minerva. A forum dominated by a Capitolium temple was a stan-dard feature of colonies throughout the empire. The purpose: to transport the Roman cult of Jupiter, Juno, and Minerva to the newly conquered population.

Opposite the Capitolium is the **Temple of Roma and Augustus**. Its position is powerfully symbolic. The power of the emperor stands equal, facing the power of the Capitolium Triad.

The basilica (from about A.D. 100) lines the side of the forum. This is where legal activities and commercial business took place. Its central nave and two side aisles lead to the "high altar" where the judge sat.

Behind the Capitolium temple, the pink, modern building houses the fine little Ostia Museum. Behind that is a shop and a modern cafeteria (with a tiny Tiber view). And Decumanus Maximus continues through the forum into a vast urban expanse, great for simply wandering (see Archaeological Scavenger Hunt, below), but first make one more stop...

Forum Baths *(Terme del Foro)*

From the forum, a street marked by a grand arch (as you're fac-ing the Temple of Roma and Augustus, it's on your left) leads to Ostia's best and largest baths (entrance on right). As you wander around this huge complex, try to imagine it peopled, steaming, and busy. Government-subsidized baths were a popular social and business meeting place in any Roman city. Roman engineers were experts at radiant heat. A huge furnace heated both the water and air that flowed through pipes under the floors and in the walls. Notice the fine marble steps—great for lounging—that led to the pools. People used olive oil rather than soap to wash, so the water needed to be periodically skimmed by servants. The octagonal room (for sunbathing) leads to the elliptical *laconicum* (sweating room), two *tepidaria* (where Romans were rubbed down by masseuses), and the once-steamy *caldarium* with three pools.

From the baths you can look across the street to the 20-hole

latrine (across from the entry to the baths). You can still see the pivot hole in the floor that once supported its revolving door. The cutout below the seat was to accommodate the washable sponge on a stick used rather than toilet paper. Rushing water (brought in by aqueduct) below each seat did the flushing.

OSTIA MUSEUM

This small museum offers a delightful look at some of Ostia's finest statuary (included in entry fee, Tue–Sun 9:00–13:30, closed Mon). Without worrying too much about exactly what is what, just wander and imagine these fine statues—tangled wrestlers, kissing cupids, playful gods—adorning the courtyards of wealthy Ostia families. Most of the statues are second- and third-century A.D. Roman pieces inspired by rare and famous Greek originals. The portrait busts are of real people—the kind you'd sit next to in the baths (or toilets).

A forte of Roman sculptors was realistic busts. Roman religion revered the man of the house (and his father and grandfather). A statue of daddy and grandpa was common in the corner of any proper house. Also, with the emperor considered a god, you'd find his bust in classrooms, at the post office, and so on.

The sarcophagi (marble coffins) generally show mythological scenes of Dionysus, the Greek god who relates to the afterlife and immortality. A few humble frescoes give a feeling for how living quarters may have been "wallpapered."

Perhaps the most interesting room (to the left as you enter) features statuary from religions of foreign lands. Being a port town, Ostia accommodated people (and their worship needs) from all over the known world. The large statue of a man sacrificing a bull is a Mythraic altarpiece.

The **cafeteria and shop** are in a modern building just behind the museum.

ARCHAEOLOGICAL SCAVENGER HUNT

As you return to the entry gate, get off the main drag and explore Ostia's backstreets. Wandering beyond the forum and then taking the back lanes as you return to the entry, see if you can find:
- Tarp- and sand-protected mosaic flooring.
- White cornerstones put into buildings to fend off wild carts and reflect corners in the dark.

- Fast-food fish joint (on Decumanus Maximus, just beyond the forum)
- Hidden bits of fresco (clue: under hot tin roofs).
- Republican buildings and buildings dating from the empire.
- Stucco roughed up for fresco work (before applying the wet plaster of a fresco, the surface needs to be systematically gouged so the plaster can grip the wall).
- Mill stones for grinding grain (Ostia's big industry).
- Floor patterns made colorful with sliced columns.
- A *domus* (single-family dwellings always faced a fancy central open-air courtyard).

TIVOLI
DAY TRIP

At the edge of the Sabine Hills, 30 kilometers (18 miles) east of Rome, sits the medieval hill town of Tivoli, a popular retreat since ancient times. Today, it's famous for two very different villas: Hadrian's Villa, an emperor's hot and dusty retirement home, and Villa d'Este, the lush and watery residence of a cardinal in exile.

The town of Tivoli, with Villa d'Este in its center, is about four kilometers (2.5 miles) from Hadrian's Villa (Villa Adriana in Italian). The **TI** is on Largo Garibaldi near the garden entry (closed Mon, tel. 0774-334-522).

Note that Hadrian's Villa is open daily and Villa d'Este is closed on Monday.

Getting to Tivoli

Tivoli is famous, but a pain to reach. From Rome, take a Metro/ bus combination. Ride Metro line B to Ponte Mammolo, then take the local LILA/Cotral bus (3/hr, direction: Tivoli) and get off at Via Tiburtina for Hadrian's Villa (500 meters, or 1,600 feet, away from the stop). The same bus continues to the town of Tivoli and Villa d'Este (end of the line).

Villa d'Este

Ippolito d'Este's grandfather was the pope ... probably the only reason Ippolito became a cardinal. Ippolito's claim to fame: his pleasure palace at Tivoli. In the 1550s, Ippolito destroyed a Benedictine monastery to build this fanciful, late-Renaissance palace. Like Hadrian's Villa, it's a large residential villa. But this one features hundreds of Baroque fountains, all gravity– powered. The Aniene River, frazzled into countless threads, weaves its way entertainingly through the villa. At the bottom of the garden, the exhausted little streams once again team up to make a sizable river. Although the fountains seem tired, they have a certain nostalgic charm.

The cardinal had a political falling–out with Rome and was exiled. With this watery wonderland on a cool hill with fine views, he made sure Romans would come to visit. It's symbolic of the luxury and secular interests of the cardinal. Senior travelers—the least able to handle its many stairs—like it best.

Cost and Hours: €6.50, audioguide–€4, Tue–Sun 8:30–18:45, last entry 1 hour before closing, closed Mon (tel. 0774-312-070).

Hadrian's Villa

Built at the peak of the empire by Hadrian (ruled A.D. 125–134), this was the emperor's retreat from the political complexity of court life in Rome. The Spanish–born Hadrian—an architect, lover of Greek culture (nicknamed "the Little Greek"), and great traveler—

created a microcosm of cosmopolitan Rome. In the spirit of Legoland, Disneyworld, and Las Vegas, he re–created famous structures from around the world, making the largest and richest Roman villa anywhere. Today, the ruins of Hadrian's retreat/retirement home sprawl over 300 evocative

acres. Getting here is complicated and time-consuming and the site is hot and comes with lots of unavoidable walking.

Start your visit at the plastic model of the villa. Find the Egyptian Canopus (sanctuary of the god Serapis, a canal lined with statues), the Greek Pecile (from Athens), and the Teatro Marittimo (a circular palace, Hadrian's favorite retreat on an island where he did his serious thinking). This "Versailles of ancient Rome" was plundered by barbarians. The marble was burned to make lime for cement. The art was scavenged and wound up in museums throughout Europe.

Cost and Hours: €6.50, audioguide–€4, daily from 9:00 until 1 hour before sunset, last entry 1 hour before closing (tel. 0774-382-733).

NAPLES AND POMPEII
DAY TRIP

While the eternal city can keep you busy for ages, here are two excuses to leave Rome for a day. The trip south to Naples and Pompeii is demanding (6 hours of train travel), but also rewarding, giving you the chance to wander ancient Rome's most evocative ruins and go on an urban safari in what is perhaps Europe's most intense city.

If you have a week in Rome and are interested in maximum travel thrills, take a day trip to Naples and Pompeii. Note that Naples' Archaeological Museum is closed on Tuesday. Pompeii is open daily.

NAPLES

If you like Italy as far south as Rome, go farther south. It gets better. If Italy is getting on your nerves, don't go farther. Italy intensifies as you plunge deeper. Naples is Italy in the extreme—its best (birthplace of pizza and Sophia Loren) and its worst (home of the Camorra, Naples' "family" of organized crime).

Naples—Italy's third-largest city, with more than two million people—has almost no open spaces or parks, which makes its position as Europe's most densely populated city plenty evident. Watching the police try to enforce traffic sanity is almost comical in Italy's grittiest, most polluted, and most crime-ridden city. But Naples surprises the observant traveler with its impressive knack for living, eating, and raising children in the streets with good humor and decency. Overcome your fear of being run down or ripped off long enough to talk with people—enjoy a few smiles and jokes with the man running the neighborhood tripe shop or the woman taking her day care class on a walk through the traffic. (For a conversation starter, ask a local about the New Year's Eve tradition of tossing chipped dinner plates off of balconies into the streets.)

Twenty-five hundred years ago, Neapolis ("new city") was a thriving Greek commercial center. It remains southern Italy's leading city, offering a fascinating collection of museums, churches, and eclectic architecture.

The pulse of Italy throbs in Naples. Like Cairo or Bombay, it's appalling and captivating at the same time, the closest thing to "reality travel" you'll find in western Europe. But this tangled mess still somehow manages to breathe, laugh, and sing—with a captivating Italian accent.

Planning Your Time

Breakfast on the early Rome–Naples express (7:10–9:00). From Naples, get to Pompeii by either catching a taxi or the Circumvesuviana (commuter train from the central train station basement), tour the excavation (11:00–13:00), then take a taxi or the same train back to Naples. Visit the Archaeological Museum, do the Naples urban jungle walk, have pizza in its birthplace, and ride the late evening train (2 hrs) back to Rome. In the afternoon, Naples' street life slows and many sights close as the temperature soars. The city comes back to life in the early evening.

Arrival in Naples

There are several Naples stations. You want Naples Centrale (facing Piazza Garibaldi), which has a Circumvesuviana stop for commuter trains to Pompeii, baggage check, and a TI (Mon–Sat 9:00–20:00, Sun 9:00–13:00, with your back to the tracks, TI is in the lobby to your left; then, within the lobby, TI is to your right, tel. 081-268-779).

While on the train to Naples, ask the conductor which Naples stations your train stops at. Centrale is ideal (but a dead-end station, so many through trains stop at Piazza Garibaldi, which is actually a subway station just downstairs from Centrale). Get off at the Mergellina station (has a TI) or Campi Flegrei station only if your train does not stop at Centrale or Garibaldi. Campi Flegrei and Mergellina are connected to Centrale by a direct subway route; a railpass or train ticket to Napoli Centrale covers the ride (subway trains depart about every 10 min, less often on Sun).

Continuing to Pompeii: For about €50–60, you can take a **taxi** from Naples to Pompeii; agree on a fixed price without the meter and pay upon arrival.

Naples and Pompeii are on the **commuter train**—the Ferrovia Circumvesuviana—handy for tourists, commuters, and pickpockets (see "Theft Alert," below). Catch it in the basement of Naples' central train station; look for the ticket windows

Naples

marked Circumvesuviana. Schedules are posted on the wall. When you buy your ticket, ask which track your train will depart from ("*Che binario?*"—kay bee-NAH-ree-oh). Don't go through the turnstiles opposite the ticket windows. Instead, continue down the corridor and jog right when it does, down another long corridor that has turnstiles at the end (insert your ticket). The platforms are just beyond. Two trains per hour, marked "Sorrento," get you to Pompeii in 40 minutes (€2.85 one-way, not covered by railpasses; check schedule carefully or confirm with a local before boarding to make sure the train is going to Pompeii). The faster express trains are marked "DD" on the schedule (12/day). When returning to Naples Centrale station on the Circumvesuviana, get off at the second-to-last station, the Collegamento FS or Garibaldi stop (Centrale station is just up the escalator).

Theft Alert: Lately Naples, under a new activist mayor, has been occupied by an army of police and feels much safer. Still, err on the side of caution. Don't venture into neighborhoods that make you uncomfortable. Walk with confidence, as if you know where you're going and what you're doing. Assume able-bodied beggars are thieves. Tighten your money belt and keep it completely hidden. Stick to busy streets and beware of gangs of hoodlums. A third of the city is unemployed, and past local governments set an example the Mafia would be proud of. Assume con artists are more clever than you. Any jostle or commotion is probably a thief team smokescreen. Any bags are probably safest checked at the central train station (€2.60, *deposito bagagli* near track #24).

Perhaps your biggest risk of theft is catching or riding the Circumvesuviana commuter train. Remember, if you're connecting from a major train, you'll be stepping from a relatively secure compartment into a crowded Naples subway filled with thieves hunting disoriented American tourists with luggage. While I ride the Circumvesuviana comfortably and safely, each year I hear of many who get ripped off on this ride. You won't be mugged— just conned or pickpocketed. Con artists may say you need to "transfer" by taxi to catch the Circumvesuviana; you don't. Anyone offering to help you with your bags is likely a thief—there are no porters at the Centrale station or in the basement where the Circumvesuviana station is located. Wear your money belt, hang on to your bag, and don't display any valuables.

Getting around Naples

Naples' subway, the Servizio Metropolitano, runs from the Centrale station through the center of town (direction: Pozzouli), stopping at Piazza Cavour (Archaeological Museum), Piazza Dante, and Montesanto (top of Spanish Quarter and Spaccanapoli). Tickets, which cost €0.75, are good for 90 minutes. All-day tickets cost €2.35. If you can afford a taxi, don't mess with the buses. A short taxi ride costs €3–5 (insist on the meter; supplement charged on Sun).

Getting to the Museum: From the Centrale train station, follow signs to *Metropolitano* (downstairs, buy tickets from window on right, ask which track—"*Binario?*" to Piazza Cavour—it's usually track 4 *[quattro]*, go through a *solo metropolitano* turnstile and ride the subway one stop). As you leave the Metro, take the exit to the right. Walk through the park. At the end of cluttered Piazza Cavour, you'll see several pink buildings ahead. The museum is the pink building on the right side of the street.

Sights—Naples

▲▲▲**Museo Archeologico**—For lovers of antiquity, this museum alone makes Naples a worthwhile stop. It offers the only possible peek into the artistic jewelry boxes of Pompeii and Herculaneum. The actual sights are impressive but barren; the best art and all the artifacts ended up here.

Hours, Cost, and Information: €6.50, Wed–Mon 9:00–20:00, summer Sat until 23:00, closed Tue. Tours in English are offered weekdays at 11:30 and 15:30 (except on Tue when museum is closed) and on Sat and Sun at 10:00, 11:00, 12:00, & 15:30 (€5, 1.5 hrs, depart from entry, confirm tour times by calling 848-800-288). Audioguides cost €4 (at ticket desk, rentable for 3 hrs). Photos are allowed without a flash. The shop sells a worthwhile green guidebook, titled *National Archeological Museum of Naples* (€7.75).

Orientation: Get your €6.50 ticket. At the desk next to the ticket booth, you can sign up for a free 20-minute tour of the Secret Room (containing erotic art from Pompeii and Herculaneum). You'll be given a tour time; meet at the Secret Room *(Gabinetto Segreto)* on the mezzanine near the *Battle of Alexander* mosaic. These short tours, generally offered at the top and bottom of every hour, are usually given in Italian, but English tours are possible—ask.

After passing through the turnstile, follow the corridor around to the staircase. For the Farnese Collection of marble statues, continue straight, then turn right past the staircase. The Pompeii mosaics and the Secret Room are on the small mezzanine level (up the grand staircase and on your left). The huge first floor (top of the grand staircase) contains bronze statues from Herculaneum, frescoes from Pompeii, and vases from Paestum. Stairs behind the grand staircase lead to the basement WCs.

Statues, Frescoes, and Artifacts (top floor): Climb the stairs to the top floor. Before you enter the great hall, look right to locate the entrance to the bronze statues of Herculaneum. This large collection—including a dozen bronze statues, plus busts and marble statues—came from Villa Papiri (Papyrus) in Herculaneum. Look into the lifelike blue eyes of the two intense *atleta* (athletes); they are bent on doing their best.

Step inside the great hall. With your back to the entrance, the rooms on your left feature the Pompeii frescoes, paintings, artifacts, and an interesting model of the town of Pompeii (called *plastico di Pompeii;* near the glass objects). The rooms on your right display ancient Greek art: a model of Paestum and ancient vases discovered on-site. (Paestum, a temple complex south of Naples, was part of a once-thriving region known as Greater Greece; for more info, see "Paestum," below.) If you contrast all of this ancient art with the darkness of medieval Europe, it becomes clear that classical art greatly inspired and enlightened the Renaissance greats.

Mosaics (mezzanine): On the mezzanine floor below (directly under the bronze statues from Herculaneum), you'll find a small, exquisite collection of Pompeian mosaics and the sexy Secret Room. Most of these mosaics were taken from the House of the Faun, which you'll see at Pompeii. Don't miss the house's delightful centerpiece: a bronze statue (a half-meter, or 1.6 feet, high) of the *Dancing Faun*. A highlight of the mosaics is the grand *Battle of Alexander* (a first-century B.C. copy of a fourth-century B.C. Greek original). It decorated a floor in the House of the Faun.

The **Secret Room**, to the left of the *Battle of Alexander* mosaic, contains a small assortment of frescoes, pottery, and statues that once decorated bedrooms, brothels, and even shops at Pompeii and Herculaneum (enter only with a guide, see "Orientation," above). If you didn't bother making an appointment, you can still peek through the iron gate.

When this earthy art was unearthed in the mid-18th century, people were upset to find their view of the Romans as wise administrators and lawmakers upended. Actually, the meaning of an erect penis was more complex back then than today—dealing with abundance and good luck, as well as good sex.

Farnese Collection (ground floor): This floor has enough Egyptian, Greek, Roman, and Etruscan art to put any museum on the map. Its highlight is the Farnese Collection, a giant hall of huge, bright, and wonderfully restored statues excavated from Rome's Baths of Caracalla. The Toro Farnese— a tangled group with a woman being tied to a bull—is the largest intact statue from antiquity. A third-century copy of a Hellenistic original, it was carved out of one piece of marble and restored by Michelangelo and others.

Once upon an ancient Greek time, King Lykos was bewitched by Dirce and abandoned his pregnant wife (standing regally in the background). The single mom gave birth to twin boys (shown here) who grew up to kill their deadbeat dad and tie Dirce to the horns of a bull to be bashed against a mountain.

You can almost hear the bull snorting. Read the worthwhile

descriptions on the walls. At the far end of the hall (opposite the Toro, behind Hercules), a small room contains the sumptuous Farnese Cup, a large ancient cameo made of agates (well-described).

▲▲▲**The Slice-of-Neapolitan-Life Walk**—Walk from the museum through the heart of town and back to the station (allow at least 2 hours plus lunch and sightseeing stops). Sights are listed in the order you'll see them on this walk.

Naples, a living medieval city, is its own best sight. Couples artfully make love on Vespas surrounded by more fights and smiles per cobble here than anywhere else in Italy. Rather than seeing Naples as a list of sights, see the one great museum and then capture its essence by taking this walk through the core of the city. Should you become overwhelmed or lost, step into a store and ask for help: "*Dov'è la stazione centrale?*" (DOH-vay lah staht-zee-OH-nay chen-TRAH-lay?) or point to the next sight in this book.

Via Toledo and the Spanish Quarter (city walk, first half): Leaving the Archaeological Museum at the top of Piazza Cavour (Metro: Piazza Cavour),

cross the street and walk through the ornate galleria (the grand, arched gallery) on your way to Via Pessina to your right. The first part of this walk is a straight 1.5-kilometer (1 mile) ramble down this boulevard to Galleria Umberto I near the Royal Palace.

Busy Via Pessina leads downhill to Piazza Dante—marked by a statue of Dante. Originally, a statue of a Spanish Bourbon king stood here. The grand red-and-gray building is typical of the Bourbon buildings from that period. In 1861, with the unification of Italy, the king—symbolic of Italy's colonial subjugation—was replaced by Dante—considered the father of the Italian language and a strong symbol of Italian nationalism.

Poor old Dante looks out over the urban chaos with a hopeless gesture. The Alba Gate, part of Naples' old wall and the entrance to a small street often lined with street-side book vendors, is to Dante's left. Via Pessina, the long, straight road we're walking, originated as a military road built by Spain around 1600. It skirted the old town wall to connect the Spanish military headquarters (now the museum) with the royal palace (down by the bay).

A new subway station has recently been built here on Piazza Dante. Construction was slowed by the city's rich underground

Naples Walk

history: four meters (13 feet) down—Roman ruins, seven meters (23 feet) down—Greek ruins.

Continue walking downhill, remembering that here in Naples red lights are considered "decorations." Try to cross with a local. The people here are survivors; a long history of corrupt and greedy colonial overlords has taught Neapolitans to deal with authority creatively. Many credit this aspect of Naples' past for the advent of organized crime here.

Via Pessina becomes Via Toledo, Naples' principal shopping street. In 1860, from the white marble balcony (on the neoclassical building) overlooking Piazza Sette Settembre, the famous revolutionary Garibaldi declared Italy united and Victor Emmanuel its first king. A year later, the dream of Italian unity was actually realized.

Continue straight on Via Toledo (even though the arterial jogs left). About five blocks below Piazza Dante, at Via Maddaloni, you cross the long, straight street called **Spaccanapoli** (literally, "split Naples"). Look left. Look right. Since ancient times, this thin street (which changes names several times) has bisected the city. (We'll be returning to this street later. If you want to abbreviate this walk, turn left here and skip down to the Spaccanapoli section.)

Via Toledo runs through Piazza Carita (also known by its new name, Piazza Salvo D'Acquisto), with fascist architecture (from 1938, sternly straight and obedient lines) overlooking the square. Wander down Via Toledo a few blocks, past more fascist architecture—the two banks on the left. Try robbing the second one (Banco di Napoli, Via Toledo 178).

Up the hill to your right is the **Spanish Quarter**, Naples at its rawest, poorest, and most historic. Thril-seekers (or someone in need of a prostitute) can take a stroll up one of these streets and loop back to Via Toledo.

The only thing predictable about this Neapolitan tide pool is the ancient grid plan of its streets (which survives from Greek times), the friendliness of its shopkeepers, and the boldness of its mopeds. Concerned locals will tug on their lower eyelids, warning you to be wary. Pop into a grocery shop and ask the man to make you his best ham and mozzarella sandwich. Trust him on the price—it should be around €3.

Continue down Via Toledo to Piazza Plebiscito. From here, you'll see the Church of San Francesco di Paola with its Pantheon-inspired dome and broad, arcing colonnades. (A TI is in the colonnade, to the right, Mon–Fri 9:00–19:00, Sat 9:00–14:00, closed Sun.) Opposite is the **Royal Palace**, which has housed Spanish, French, and even Italian royalty. The lavish interior is open for tours (€4, Thu–Tue 9:00–20:00, closed Wed, shorter hours off-season). Next door, peek inside the neoclassical Teatro San Carlo, Italy's second-most-respected opera house (after Milan's La Scala). The huge castle on the harborfront just beyond the palace houses government bureaucrats and is closed to tourists.

Under the Victorian iron and glass of the 100-year-old **Galleria Umberto I**, enjoy a coffee break or sample a unique Neapolitan pastry called *sfogliatella* (crispy scallop shell–shaped pastry filled with sweet ricotta cheese). Go through the tall yellow arch at the end of Via Toledo or across from the opera house. Gawk up.

Spaccanapoli back to the station (city walk, second half): To continue your walk, double back up Via Toledo to Piazza Carita. From there, take Via Morgantini to the straight-as-a-

Greek-arrow street, Spaccanapoli. Formerly the main thoroughfare of the Greek city of Neapolis, it starts up the hill near the Montesanto funicular.

The rest of this walk is basically a straight line down the series of streets locals have nicknamed Spaccanapoli. Where Via Morgantini hits Spaccanapoli—at Piazza Gesu

Nuovo—you'll see two bulky old churches. The square is also marked by a towering monument to the Counter-Reformation (Baroque, early 18th century). With its Spanish heritage, Jesuits were powerful in Naples. But locals never attacked Protestants with the full fury of the Spanish Inquisition.

Check out the austere, fortresslike church of **Gesu Nuovo.** The unique pyramid grill facade was from a fortress (1470), which predated the church (1600s). Step inside for a brilliant Baroque interior. The second chapel on the right features a much-kissed statue of Giuseppe Moscati, a Christian doctor famous for helping the poor. Moscati was made a saint in 1987. Continue on to the third chapel and enter the Sale Moscati for a huge room filled with Ex Voto—tiny red-and-silver plaques of thanksgiving for miracles attributed to Saint Moscati. Each has a relief symbolic of the ailment cured. Naples' practice of "Ex Voto," while incorporated into its Catholic rituals, goes back to its pagan Greek roots. A glass case displays possessions and photos of the great doctor. As you leave, notice the big bomb casing hanging in the corner. It fell through the church's dome in 1943 but never exploded . . . yet another miracle.

Across the street, the simpler Gothic church of **Santa Chiara** dates from a period of French Angevin rule (14th century). Notice the stark Gothic/Baroque contrast between this church and the Gesu Nuovo. The faded Trinity (from the school of Giotto, left of entry) is an example of the fine frescoes that once covered the walls (most removed during Baroque times). The altar is adorned with the finely carved Gothic tomb of an Angevin king (both churches free, Mon–Sat 8:30–13:00 & 15:30–18:30, Sun 8:30–13:00).

Continue straight down traffic-free Via B. Croce. Since this is a university district, you'll see lots of students and bookstores. This neighborhood is also extremely superstitious. You may see incense-burning women with carts of good-luck charms for sale. At Via Santa Chiara, a detour left leads to shops of antique musical instruments.

The next square is Piazza S. Domenico Maggiore—marked by an ornate 17th-century plague monument. The venerable **Scaturchio Pasticceria** is another good place to try Naples' *sfogliatella* pastry (€1 to go, costs double at a table).

From this square, detour left (along the right side of the castle-like church, then follow yellow signs and take first right) to **Cappella Sansevero** (€5, Mon and Wed–Sat 10:00–19:00, Nov–April 10:00–17:00, Sun year-round 10:00–13:30, closed Tue, Via de Sanctis 19). No photos are allowed in the chapel (postcards available in gift shop).

This small chapel is a Baroque explosion mourning the body of Christ, who lies on a soft pillow under an incredibly realistic veil. It's also the personal chapel of Raimondo de Sangro, an eccentric Freemason. The monuments to his relatives have a second purpose: To share the Freemason philosophy of freedom through enlightenment. For example, the statue of *Despair* struggling with a marble rope net (carved out of a single piece of marble) shows how knowledge—in the guise of an angel— frees the human mind.

Study the incredible *Veiled Christ* in the center. It's all carved out of marble and is like no other statue I've seen (by Giuseppe "howdeedoodat" Sammartino, 1753). The Christian message (Jesus died for our salvation) is accompanied by a Freemason message. (The veil represents how the body and ego are an obstacle to real spiritual freedom.) As you walk from Christ's feet to his head, notice how the expression of Jesus' face goes rom suffering to peace. When you stand directly behind Him, the veil over the face and knees disappears.

Raimondo de Sangro, an inventor, created the deep green pigment used on the ceiling fresco. De Sangro is even credited with a crude 18th-century version of Gore-Tex.

To the right of *Despair* and the net, an inlaid Escher-esque maze on the floor leads to de Sangro's tomb. The maze is another Freemason reminder of the importance of how the quest for knowledge gets you out of the maze of life. Your Sansevero finale is downstairs: two mysterious ... skeletons. Perhaps another of the mad inventor's fancies: Injecting a corpse with a fluid to fossilize the veins so they'll survive the body's decomposition.

Return to Via B. Croce, turn left, and continue your Spaccanapoli cultural scavenger hunt. At the intersection of Via Nilo, find the statue of *The Body of Naples*, with the abundant cornucopia symbolizing the abundance of Naples. (I asked a Neapolitan man to describe the local women, who are famous for their beauty. He replied simply, "Abundant.") This intersection is considered the center of old Naples.

At Via San Gregorio Armeno, a left leads you into a very colorful district (kitschy Baroque church on left with a Vesuvius lava shrine in its portico, lots of shops selling tiny components of fantastic manger scenes).

As Via B. Croce becomes Via S. Biagio dei Librai, notice the gold and silver shops. Some say stolen jewelry ends up here, is melted down immediately, and appears in a salable form as soon as it cools. The wonderful Sr. Grassi runs the Ospedale delle Bambole (doll hospital) at #81.

Cross busy Via Duomo. The street and side-street scenes along Via Vicaria intensify. Paint a picture with these thoughts: Naples has the most intact street plan of any ancient Roman city. Imagine this city then (retain these images as you visit Pompeii), with street-side shop-fronts that close up after dark to form private homes. Today it's just one more page in a 2,000-year-old story of a city: all kinds of meetings, beatings, and cheatings; kisses, near misses, and little-boy pisses.

You name it, it occurs right on the streets today, as it has since ancient times. People ooze from crusty corners. Black-and-white death announcements add to the clutter on the walls. Widows sell cigarettes from buckets. For a peek

behind the scenes in the shade of wet laundry, venture down a few side streets. Buy two carrots as a gift for the woman on the fifth floor if she'll lower her bucket to pick them up. The neighborhood action seems best around 18:00.

At the tiny fenced-in triangular park, veer right onto Via Forcella. Turning right on busy Via Pietro Colletta, walk 50 meters (165 feet) and step into the North Pole. Reward yourself for surviving this safari with a stop at the **Polo Nord Gelateria**

Pizza in Naples

Drop by one of the two most traditional pizzerias. Naples, baking just the right combination of fresh dough, mozzarella, and tomatoes in traditional wood-burning ovens, is the birthplace of pizza. **Antica Pizzeria da Michele**, a few blocks from the train station, is for purists (Mon–Sat 11:00–23:00, closed Sun, cheap, filled with locals, 50 meters, or 165 feet, off Corso Umberto on Via Cesare Sersale, look for the vertical red "Antica Pizzeria" sign, tel. 081-553-9204). It serves two kinds: *margherita* (tomato sauce and mozzarella) or *marinara* (tomato sauce, oregano, and garlic, no cheese). A pizza with beer costs €5. Some locals prefer **Pizzeria Trianon** across the street. Da Michele's archrival offers more choices, higher prices, air-conditioning, and a cozier atmosphere (daily 10:00–15:30 & 18:30–23:00, Via Pietro Colletta 42, tel. 081-553-9426).

(Via Pietro Colletta 41, sample their *bacio* or "kiss" flavor before ordering). Via Pietro Colletta leads past Napoli's two most competitive **pizzerias** (see "Eating," below) to Corso Umberto.

Turn left on the grand-boulevardian Corso Umberto. From here to the station, it's a 10-minute walk (if you're tired, hop on a bus; they all go to the station). To finish the walk, continue on Corso Umberto—past a gauntlet of purse/CD/sunglasses salesmen and shady characters hawking stolen camcorders—to the vast, ugly Piazza Garibaldi. On the far side is the Centrale station.

Markets—Naples' **fish market** is fun for photos, with sawed-off swordfish, wriggly eels in pans, and mussels taking a shower. It's at Piazza Nolana, a few blocks southwest of the train station (at the piazza, follow your nose and go through the old gate; market spills down small street, Vico Sopramuro). A bigger **general market** starts at the far corner of Piazza Capuana (several blocks northwest of the train station), filling the street Via Sant' Antonio Abate with a mix of clothes, olives, bags of gnocchi, hanging hams, shoes, produce, umbrellas, and shoppers on foot or on Vespas (both markets open Mon–Sat 7:00–16:00, Sun 8:00–13:00).

POMPEII

▲▲▲**Pompeii**—Stopped in its tracks by the eruption of Mount Vesuvius in A.D. 79, Pompeii offers the best look anywhere at what life in Rome must have been like 2,000 years ago. An entire city of well-preserved ruins is yours to explore. Once a thriving commercial port of 20,000, Pompeii grew from Greek and Etruscan roots

Pompeii

- ■ - KEY RUINS
- ⬚ - OTHER RUINS

200 YARDS
200 METERS

PORTO ERCOLANO

HOUSE OF VETTI

VIA VESUVIO

VIC. VESUVIO

VIA DI VETTI

VIC. MERCURIO

TO VILLA DEI MISTERI

HOUSE OF FAUN

VIA CONSOLARE

VIA FORTUNA

VIA STABIANA

VIA ABBONDANZA

UNEXCA-VATED AREA

TO ❿

TO VILLA DEI MISTERI

VIA FORO

VIA

VIALE DELLE GINESTRA

TO NAPLES

PORTO MARINA MAIN ENTRANCE

FORUM

CIRCUM-VESUVIANA TRAIN STN.

FROM AUTOSTRADA EXIT

TO SORRENTO

PIAZZA ESEDRA

TO POMPEI TOWN

PATH

① FORUM
② TERME DEL FORO & CAFE
③ HOUSE OF FAUN
④ HOUSE OF VETTI
⑤ BAKERY & MILL
⑥ TABERNA HEDONES
⑦ BROTHEL (LUPANARE)
⑧ TEMPLE OF ISIS
⑨ THEATER
❿ TO AMPHITHEATER

to become an important Roman city. Then, it was buried under nine meters (30 feet) of hot mud and volcanic ash. For archaeologists, this was a shake-and-bake windfall, teaching them almost all they know about daily Roman life. Pompeii was rediscovered in the 1600s; excavations began in 1748.

Cost, Hours, Information: €10, or €13.50 combo-ticket includes Herculaneum and three lesser sites (valid 3 days), April–Oct daily 8:30–19:30, Nov–March daily 8:30–17:00. The ticket office closes 1.5 hours before closing time. A good map is included with admission (for more information, check www.pompeiisites.org). A free baggage check is near the ticket window.

Stop by the bookshop. A guidebook on Pompeii makes this site more meaningful. (Books are also on sale in Sorrento.) The small Pompeii and Herculaneum "Past and Present" book has a helpful text and allows you to re-create the ruins with plastic overlays—with the "present" actually being 1964 (available for €9.50 in bookstore unless they're "finished"; if you buy from a street vendor, pay no more than €9.50). Audioguides cost €4. Guides cluster near the ticket booth. If you gather 10 people, the price is reasonable when split (around €10 apiece, total cost about €100, 2 hrs). For a local guide, consider Gaetano Manfredi (tel. 081-863-9816, cellular 33-033-7567).

Background: Pompeii was a booming Roman trading city. Most streets would have been lined with stalls and jammed with customers from sunup to sundown. Chariots vied with shoppers for street space, and many streets were off-limits to chariots during shopping hours (you'll still see street signs with pictures of men carrying vases—this meant pedestrians only).

Fountains overflowed into the streets, flushing the gutters into the sea (thereby cleaning the streets). The stones you see at intersections allowed pedestrians to cross the constantly gushing streets. A single stone designated a one-way street (just enough room for one chariot, stone straddled by its two oxen), and two stones meant a two-way chariot street. There were no posh neighborhoods. Rich and poor mixed it up, as elegant homes existed side by side with simple homes throughout Pompeii. While nearby Herculaneum would have been a classier place to live (traffic-free streets, more elegant homes, far better drainage), Pompeii was the place for action and shopping. It served its estimated 20,000 residents with more than 40 bakeries, 30 brothels, and 130 bars, restaurants, and hotels. Rome controlled the entire Mediterranean 2,000 years ago—making it a kind of free-trade zone—and Pompeii was a central and booming port town. With most buildings covered by brilliant, white ground-marble stucco, Pompeii in A.D. 79 was an impressive town. Remember, Pompeii's best art is in the Naples Archaeological Museum, described above.

Tour of Pompeii: Allow at least three hours to tour the site. Consider the following route, starting at the Porta Marina (town gate) after the ticket booth. Before Vesuvius blew, the sea came nearly to this gate. As you approach the Porta Marina, notice the two openings—big for chariots, small for pedestrians.

From the Porta Marina, Via Marina leads straight to Pompeii's main square, the forum.

The **forum** *(foro)*, Pompeii's commercial, religious, and political center, stands at the intersection of the city's two main streets. While the most ruined part of Pompeii, it's grand nonetheless—

with temples, lots of pedestals that once sported statues (now in the museum in Naples), and the basilica (Pompeii's largest building, the ancient equivalent of law courts and stock market—on the right as you enter). The Curia (home of the government) stands at the end of the forum. It's built of brick and mortar, a Roman invention. While brick now, it was once faced with marble. Note that while Pompeii was destroyed by the eruption of A.D. 79, it was also devastated by an earthquake in A.D. 62. It's safe to assume any brick you see dates from between A.D. 62 and A.D. 79—restoration work done by Pompeians after the quake.

Walk (away from the Curia) along the fenced, roofed area that runs alongside the forum. Behind the iron fence are piles of pottery and, at the end, some eerie casts of volcano victims. With the unification of Italy in the 1860s, national spirit fueled efforts to excavate Pompeii. During this period, archaeologists made these molds (detecting hollows underfoot—left by decomposed bodies—as they dug, they'd pour liquid plaster into them, let dry, and dig up).

Such a busy square needed a public toilet. Just past the warehouse, turn left into an ancient public WC. Notice the ditch that led to the sewer (marked by an arch in the corner). The stone supports once held wooden benches with the appropriate holes. Even back then, this area had pay toilets.

Continue on, leaving the forum through the gate at the end. Take an immediate right, then a left. You're on Via del Foro, passing a convenient 21st-century cafeteria (decent value, gelato, books, WCs upstairs; a fancier restaurant in a more elegant ancient gymnasium setting is adjacent).

Head down Via del Foro and enter the impressive baths, **Terme del Foro** (on the left, past the cafeteria). You'll enter through the gymnasium. After working out, clients would find four rooms: a waiting room, warm bath *(tepidarium)*, hot bath *(caldarium)*, and cold-plunge bath *(frigidarium)*.

The *tepidarium* is ringed by mini-statues or *telamones* (male caryatids, figures used as supporting pillars), which divided clients' lockers. They'd undress and warm up here, perhaps stretching out on one of the benches near the bronze heater for a massage. Notice the ceiling: half crushed by the eruption and half surviving with its fine blue-and-white stuccowork.

Next, in the *caldarium*, you'd get hot. Notice the engineering. The double floor was heated from below—so nice with bare feet (look into the grate to see the brick support towers). The double walls with brown terra-cotta tiles held the heat. Romans soaked in the big tub, which was filled with hot water. To keep condensation from dripping annoyingly from the ceiling, the fluting (ribbing) was added to carry the drips down the walls.

Next came the cold plunge in the *frigidarium*—a circular marble basin with the spout spewing frigid water, opposite the entry.

Exit the baths. Notice the oxcart wheel grooves and stepping stones in the street. In ancient times, rainstorms would turn the streets into filthy rivers. Do as the ancient Romans did. Keep your feet dry by using the stepping stones to cross the street. Directly in front of you is an ancient fast-food stand (notice the holes in the counters for pots). To your left, a few doors down, is the **House of the Tragic Poet** (Casa de Poeta Tragico), with its famous "Beware of Dog" *(Cave Canum)* mosaic in the entryway. On either side, grooves in the doorway indicate a shop with sliding doors.

Face the House of the Tragic Poet, then walk to your right two blocks to the House of the Faun (Casa del Fauno, Danzante). Notice the holes drilled into the curbs—to hitch your animal or perhaps to support an awning from your storefront.

Pompeii's largest home (with 40 rooms), the **House of the Faun,** provided Naples' Archaeological Museum with many of its top treasures, including the original dancing faun (you'll see a copy here) and the famous mosaic of the "Battle of Alexander." Wander past the welcome mosaic (*HAVE* or "hail to you") and through its courtyards. The back courtyard leads to the exit. It's lined by pillars rebuilt after the A.D. 62 earthquake. Take a close look at the brick, mortar, and fake marble stucco veneer.

Back on the street, turn right and look for the exposed 2,000-year-old lead pipes in the wire cage (ahead and down on the ground to your right). The lead was imported from Roman Britannia. A huge water tank—fed by an aqueduct—stood at the high end of town. Three independent pipe systems supplied water to the city from here: one each for baths, private homes, and public water fountains. In the case of a water shortage, supply could be limited. Democratic priorities prevailed: first the baths were cut, then the private homes. The last water to be cut was that which fed the public fountains (where the people got their water for drinking and cooking).

Take your first left on Vicolo dei Vetti. Enter Pompeii's best-preserved home, the House of the Vetti (Casa dei Vetti).

The **House of the Vetti**, which has retained its mosaics and frescoes, was the bachelor pad of two wealthy merchant brothers. In the entryway, see if you can spot the erection. This is not pornography. There's a meaning here: The penis and the sack of money balance each other on the goldsmith scale above a fine bowl of fruit. The meaning: Only with a balance of fertility and money can you have abundance.

Step into the atrium with its open sky to collect light and rainwater. The pool, while decorative, was a functional water-supply tank. It's flanked by large money boxes anchored to the floor. They were certainly successful merchants, and possibly money-lenders, too.

Exit on the right, passing the tight servant quarters, and go into the kitchen, with its bronze cooking pots (and a touchable lead pipe on the back wall). The passage dead-ends in the little Venus Room with its erotic frescoes behind glass.

Return to the atrium and pass into the big colonnaded garden. It was planted according to the plan indicated by traces of roots excavated in the volcanic ash. This courtyard is ringed by richly frescoed entertainment rooms. Circle counterclockwise. The dining room is finely decorated in "Pompeian red" (from iron rust) and black. Study the detail. Notice the lead humidity seal between the wall and the floor designed to keep the wet-sensitive frescoes dry. (Had Leonardo taken this clever step, his *Last Supper* in Milan might be in better shape today.) Continuing around, notice the square white stones inlaid in the floor. Imagine them reflecting like cat eyes as the brothers and their friends wandered around by oil lamp late at night. Frescoes in the Yellow Room (near the exit) show off the ancient mastery of perspective, which was not matched elsewhere in Europe for nearly 1,500 years.

Leaving the House of the Vetti, go left past the pipes again. Then turn right, following Vicolo dei Vetti to Via della Fortuna, where you'll see a public fountain. Intersections like this were busy neighborhood centers, where the rent was highest and people gathered.

Turn left on Via della Fortuna and take a quick right on Vicolo Storto, which leads down a curving street to the **bakery and mill** *(forno e mulini)*. The ovens look like a modern-day pizza oven. And the stubby stone towers are flour grinders: After grain was poured into the top, donkeys pushed wooden bars that turned the stones, and eventually powdered grain dropped out the bottom as flour—flavored with tiny bits of rock.

Take the first left after the bakery onto Via degli Augustali, and check out the mosaics on the left at the Taberna Hedones. This must be the tavern of hedonism—see the cute welcome mosaic reading *HAVE* ("hail to you"), with the bear licking his wounds.

Next turn right, over the street dam, and follow the signs to the **brothel** *(lupanare)*, at #18. Prostitutes were nicknamed *lupas* (she-wolves). Wander into the brothel, a simple place with stone beds and pillows. The ancient graffiti includes stroke tallies and exotic names of the girls, indicating they came from all corners of the Mediterranean. The faded frescoes above the cells may have served as a kind of menu for services offered. Note the idealized portrayal of women (white, considered beautiful) and men (dark, considered horny). Outside at #17 is a laundry—likely to boil the sheets (thought to guard against venereal disease).

Leaving the brothel, go down the hill to Pompeii's main drag, Via Abbondanza. The forum (and exit) is to the right. (The huge amphitheater—which you can skip—is 10 min to your left.) Go straight down Via dei Teatri, then left before the columns, downhill to the **Temple of Isis** (on the right). This Egyptian temple served Pompeii's Egyptian community. The little shrine with the plastic roof housed holy water from the Nile. Pompeii must have had a synagogue, but it has yet to be excavated.

Immediately upon leaving, follow the lane at #17 to our last stop, the **theater**. Originally a Greek theater (Greeks built theirs with the help of a hillside), this marks the spot of the birthplace of the Greek port here in 470 B.C. During Roman times, it sat 5,000 in three price ranges: the five marble terraces up close (filled with romantic wooden seats for two), the main section, and the cheap nosebleed section (surviving only on the right). The square stones above the cheap seats used to support a canvas rooftop. Notice the high-profile boxes, flanking the stage, for guests of honor. From this perch, you can see the gladiator barracks—the colonnaded courtyard beyond the theater. They lived in tiny rooms, trained in the courtyard, and fought in the nearby amphitheater.

There's much more to see; 75 percent of Pompeii's 164 acres has been excavated. But this tour's over. *Ciao!*

Getting to Pompeii: Pompeii is 40 minutes from Naples by direct Circumvesuviana train (€2.85 one-way, not covered by railpasses, 2/hr). Make sure you're on the Naples-Sorrento train line. Get off at the "Pompei Scavi, Villa dei Misteri" stop. You can check your bag at the train station (at the bar) for €0.75, or, better yet, at the Pompeii site for free. From the train station, turn right and walk down the road about a block to the entrance (first left turn). The TI is farther down the street, but not a necessary stop for your visit.

SLEEPING

For hassle-free efficiency, we favor hotels and restaurants handy to your sightseeing activities. Rather than listing hotels scattered throughout Rome, we describe our favorite neighborhoods and recommend the best accommodations values in each, from $15 bunks to plush, with-all-the-comforts $250 doubles.

Sleeping in Rome is expensive. Cheap big-city hotels can be depressing. Tourist-information services cannot give opinions on quality. A major feature of this book is its extensive listing of good-value rooms. We like places that are clean, small, central, quiet at night, traditional, inexpensive, and friendly, with firm beds—and those not listed in other guidebooks. (In Rome, for us, 6 out of 9 attributes means it's a keeper.)

Many prices here are promised only to people who show this book and reserve directly, without using a room-finding service. And many places prefer hard cash.

Hotels

Double rooms listed in this book will range from about €60 (very simple, toilet and shower down the hall) to €260 (maximum plumbing and more), with most clustering around €120 (with private bathrooms). A nicer hotel (around €130 with a bathroom and air-conditioning) provides an oasis and refuge, making it easier to enjoy this intense and grinding city.

Three or four people economize by sharing larger rooms. Solo travelers find that the cost of a *camera singola* is often only 25 percent less than a *camera doppia*. Most listed hotels have rooms for anywhere from one to five people. If there's room for an extra cot, they'll cram it in for you. English works in all but the cheapest places.

You normally get close to what you pay for. Prices are fairly standard. Shopping around earns you a better location and more character, but rarely a cheaper price.

However, prices at nearly any hotel can get soft if you do any of the following: arrive direct (without using a pricey middleman like the TI), offer to pay cash, stay at least three nights, or visit off-season July–Aug, Nov–mid-March). Room rates are lowest in sweltering August.

Breakfasts are legally optional (though some hotels insist they're not). Initial prices quoted often include breakfast and a private bathroom. Offer to skip breakfast for a better price.

You'll save €10 to €20 if you ask for a room without a shower and just use the shower down the hall. Generally rooms with a bath or shower also have a toilet and a bidet (which Italians use for quick sponge baths). Tubs usually come with a frustrating "telephone shower" (handheld nozzle). If a shower has no curtain, the entire bathroom showers with you. The cord that dangles over the tub or shower is not a clothesline. You pull it when you've fallen and can't get up.

Double beds are called *matrimoniale*, even though hotels aren't interested in your marital status. Twins are *due letti singoli*.

Many hotel rooms have a TV and phone. Rooms in fancier hotels usually come with air-conditioning (sometimes you pay an extra per-day charge for this), a small safe, and a small stocked fridge called a *frigo bar* (FREE-goh).

When you check in, the receptionist will normally ask for your passport and keep it for a couple of hours. Hotels are legally required to register each guest with the local police. Relax. Americans are notorious for making this chore more difficult than it needs to be.

The hotel breakfast, while convenient, is often a bad value— €9 for a roll, jelly, and usually unlimited *caffè latte*. You can request cheese or salami (€3 extra). To save money, consider taking breakfast at the corner café. It's OK to supplement what you order with a few picnic goodies.

Rooms are safe. Still, zip cameras and keep money out of sight. More pillows and blankets are usually in the closet or available on request. In Italy, towels and linen aren't always replaced every day. Hang your towel up to dry.

Your hotel can point you to the nearest **laundrette** (usually open daily 8:00–22:00, about €6 to wash and dry a 15-pound load). The Bolle Blu chain comes with Internet access (€4.25/hr, near train station at Via Milazzo 20, Via Palestro 59, and Via Principe Amedeo 116, tel. 06-446-5804).

Most hotels are eager to connect you with a shuttle service to the airport. It's reasonable and easy for leaving, but upon arrival, I think it's easiest to simply catch a cab or the shuttle train.

Almost no hotels have parking, but nearly all have a line on spots in a nearby garage (about €21/day).

To avoid the time-wasting crowd at the reception desk in the morning, settle up your bill the evening before you leave.

Country Code and Exchange Rate

To phone Italy, you'll need to know its country code: 39.
To call Italy from the United States. or Canada, dial 011-39-local number. If calling Italy from another European country, dial 00-39-local number.

The exchange rate: 1 euro (€) = about $1.

Making Reservations

Reserve your room with a phone call, fax, or e-mail as soon as you can commit to a date. It's possible to visit Rome without booking ahead, but given the high stakes and the quality of the gems we've found for this city guide, we would highly recommend making reservations. Easter, September, and Christmas are the most crowded and expensive. On Easter (April 20 in 2003), April 25, and May 1, the entire city gets booked up.

Traffic in Rome roars. With the recent arrival of double-paned windows and air-conditioning, night noise is not the problem it was. Even so, light sleepers should always ask for a *tranquillo* room.

To reserve from home, telephone first to confirm availability, then fax or e-mail your formal request. It's easy to reserve by phone (follow the dialing instructions above). Most hotels listed are accustomed to English-only speakers. Fax costs are reasonable, e-mail's a steal, and simple English is usually fine. To fax, use the handy form in the appendix; for e-mailers, the form's online at www.ricksteves.com/reservation. If you don't get an answer to your fax request, consider that a "no." (Many smaller places get 20 faxes a day after they're full and can't afford to respond.)

A two-night stay in August would be "2 nights, 16/8/03 to 18/8/03" (Europeans write the date day/month/year and hotel jargon uses your day of departure). You'll often receive a response back requesting one night's deposit. If your credit-card number is accepted as the deposit (which is usually the case), you can pay with your card or cash when you arrive; if you don't show up, you'll be billed for one night. Always reconfirm your reservations a day in advance by phone. (Don't needlessly reconfirm rooms through the tourist office; they'll take a commission.)

Honor (or cancel by phone) your reservations. Long distance is cheap from public phone booths. Don't let these people down—we promised you'd call and cancel if for some reason you can't show up.

Sleep Code

To help you easily sort through these listings, I've divided the rooms into three categories based on the price for a standard double room with bath:

Higher Priced—Most rooms more than €180.
Moderately Priced—Most rooms €180 or less.
Lower Priced—Most rooms €115 or less.

To give maximum information in a minimum of space, I use the following code to describe the accommodations listed in this book. Prices listed are per room, not per person.

S = Single room (or price for one person in a double).

D = Double or Twin room. "Double beds" are often two twins sheeted together and are usually big enough for nonromantic couples.

T = Triple (generally a double bed with a single).

Q = Quad (usually two double beds).

b = Private bathroom with toilet and shower or tub.

s = Private shower or tub only (the toilet is down the hall).

CC = Accepts credit cards (Visa and MasterCard, rarely American Express).

no CC = Doesn't accept credit cards; pay in local cash.

SE = Speaks English. This code is used only when it seems predictable that you'll encounter English-speaking staff.

NSE = Does not speak English. Used only when it's unlikely you'll encounter English-speaking staff.

According to this code, a couple staying at a "Db-€140, CC, SE" hotel would pay a total of €140 (about $140) for a double room with a private bathroom. The hotel accepts credit cards or Italian cash (euros). The staff speaks English.

Sleeping on Via Firenze (zip code: 00184)

I generally stay on Via Firenze because it's safe, handy, central, and relatively quiet. It's a 10-minute walk from the central train station and airport shuttle, and two blocks beyond Piazza della Repubblica and the TI. The Defense Ministry is nearby, and you've got heavily armed guards watching over you all night. Virtually all the city buses that rumble down Via Nazionale (#64, #70, #115, #640, and the #40 express) take you to Piazza

Hotels in East Rome

1. Hotel Oceania & Nardizzi
2. Hotel Aberdeen
3. Residence Adler & Residenza Cellini
4. Hotel Rex
5. Hotel Britannia
6. Hotel Sonya
7. Hotel Pensione Italia
8. Hotel Cortina
9. YWCA Casa per Studentesse
10. Suore di Santa Elisabetta
11. Hotel Montreal
12. Hotel Fenicia & Magic
13. Albergo Sileo
14. Hotel Duca d'Alba
15. Hotel Grifo
16. Pensione per Pelligrini
17. Hotel Paba
18. Hotel Lancelot
19. Casa Olmata Hostel
20. The Beehive Hostel
21. Gulliver's House Rome
22. Hotel Le Petit
23. Pharmacy

Venezia (Forum) and Largo Argentina (Pantheon). From Largo
Argentina, electric trolley #8 goes to Trastevere (first stop after
crossing the river) and #64 (jammed with people and thieves)
and the #40 express continue to St. Peter's. Farmacia Piram
is the neighborhood 24-hour pharmacy (Via Nazionale 228,
tel. 06-488-4437).

HIGHER PRICED

Residenza Cellini is a gorgeous new place with six rooms. It
offers "ortho/anti-allergy beds" and four-star comforts and service
(Db-€165, larger Db-€185, €30 discount in off-season—Aug
plus mid-Nov–mid-March, these prices with this book and payment in cash through 2003, elevator, air-con, Via Modena 5,
tel. 06-4782-5204, fax 06-4788-1806, www.residenzacellini.it,
e-mail: residenzacellini@tin.it, SE).

MODERATELY PRICED

Hotel Oceania is a peaceful slice of air-conditioned heaven.
This 16-room, manor house–type hotel is spacious and quiet,
with spotless rooms, run by a pleasant father-and-son team (Sb-
€105, Db-€135, Tb-€165, Qb-€192, these prices through 2003
with this book only, additional 25 percent off in Aug and winter,
large roof terrace, TV room, CC, Via Firenze 38, 3rd floor, tel.
06-482-4696, fax 06-488-5586, www.hoteloceania.it, e-mail:
hoceania@tin.it, son Stefano SE, dad Armando serves world-
famous coffee).

 Hotel Aberdeen, while a more formal place, offers the same
great value, with minibars, phones, and showers in its 36 modern,
air-conditioned, and smoke-free rooms. It's warmly run by Anna-
maria, with support from her cousins Sabrina, Laura, and Cinzia
(Sb-€102, Db-€139, Tb-€164, Qb-€190, prices through 2003
with this book only, €30 less per room in Aug and winter, CC,
free Internet access, nearby parking—€21/day, Via Firenze 48, tel.
06-482-3920, fax 06-482-1092, check for deals online at www
.travel.it/roma/aberdeen, e-mail: hotel.aberdeen@travel.it, SE).

 Hotel Seiler is a last resort, with 33 sleepable rooms and
too much chipped plaster (Sb-€83, Db-€119, Tb-€145, Qb-
€165, these discounted prices good only with this book, CC,
fans, elevator, Via Firenze 48, tel. 06-485-550, fax 06-488-0204,
e-mail: acropoli@rdn.it, Silvio and Alessia SE).

LOWER PRICED

Residence Adler offers breakfast on a garden patio, wide halls,
and eight quiet, elegant, and air-conditioned rooms in a great
location. A good deal, it's run the old-fashioned way by a charming

family (Db-€115, Tb-€150, Qb-€180, Quint/b-€195, prices through 2003 with this book only, CC, additional 5 percent off with cash, 15 percent off in Aug, Jan, and Feb; elevator, Via Modena 5, 2nd floor, tel. 06-484-466, fax 06-488-0940, www.hoteladler-roma.com, e-mail: info@hoteladler-roma.com, gracious Sr. Brando Massini NSE but tries).

Hotel Nardizzi Americana, with 18 simple, pleasant, air-conditioned rooms and a delightful rooftop terrace, is loosely run (Sb-€90, Db-€110, Tb-€135, Qb-€150, prices through 2003 with this book only, discounts for off-season and long stays, air-con, CC, additional 10 percent off with cash, elevator, Via Firenze 38, 4th floor, tel. 06-488-0368, fax 06-488-0035, SE).

Hotel Texas Seven Hills, a stark, institutional throwback to the 1960s, rents 18 dreary rooms (D-€83, Db-€93, often soft prices, CC, single-paned windows, Via Firenze 47, 1st elevator on the right to 3rd floor, tel. 06-481-4082, fax 06-481-4079, www.yellowpage.it/hoteltexas, e-mail: reserva@texas7hills.com, SE).

Sleeping between Via Nazionale and Basilica Santa Maria Maggiore
(zip code: 00184 unless otherwise noted)

HIGHER PRICED
Hotel Britannia stands like a marble fruitcake, offering all the comforts in tight quarters. Lushly renovated with over-the-top classical motifs, its 33 air-conditioned rooms are small but comfortable with bright, modern bathrooms (Sb-€210, Db-€245, cheaper in Aug and off-season, CC, free parking, Via Napoli 64, tel. 06-488-3153, fax 06-488-2343, www.hotelbritannia.it, e-mail: info@hotelbritannia.it).

Hotel Rex is a business-class, modern fortress—a quiet, plain, and stately four-star place with 50 rooms and all the comforts (Sb-€206, Db-€258, Tb-€299, 25 percent less Aug and winter, CC, elevator, air-con, Via Torino 149, tel. 06-482-4828, fax 06-488-2743, e-mail: rex@hotelrex.net, SE).

MODERATELY PRICED
Hotel Le Petit has 11 colorful, cozy rooms with a modern flair (Sb-€80, Db-€135, Tb-€155, 20 percent off in low season, CC, air-con, Via Torino 122, tel. 06-4890-7085, fax 06-474-4645, www.hotel-le-petit.com, e-mail: lepetit@venere.it, SE).

Hotel Sonya is a small, family-run, but impersonal place with 23 comfortable, well-equipped rooms, a great location, and decent prices (Db-€119, Tb-€134, Qb-€155, Quint/b-€170, CC, air-con, elevator, facing the opera at Via Viminale 58, tel. 06-481-9911, fax 06-488-5678, e-mail: hotelsonyaroma @katamail.com, Francesca SE).

Hotel Cortina rents 14 modern, air-conditioned rooms on a busy street. Ask for a quieter room on the courtyard or side street (Db-€140 in 2003 with this book, CC, Via Nazionale 18, tel. 06-481-9794, fax 06-481-9220, www.travel.it/roma/hotelcortina, e-mail: hotelcortina@pronet.it, John Carlo and Angelo SE).

LOWER PRICED

Hotel Pensione Italia, in a busy, interesting, and handy locale, is placed safely on a quiet street next to the Ministry of the Interior. Thoughtfully run by Andrea, Isabelle, and Alberico, it has 31 comfortable, airy, clean, and bright rooms (Sb-€75, Db-€100, Tb-€145, Qb-€165, air-con for €8 extra, prices through 2003 with this book and cash only, all rooms 20 percent off mid-July–Aug and winter, elevator, Via Venezia 18, just off Via Nazionale, tel. 06-482-8355, fax 06-474-5550, www.hotelitaliaroma.com, e-mail: hitalia@nettuno.it, SE). Most rooms have a fan. Their fine singles are all on the quiet courtyard and they have eight decent annex rooms across the street.

Hotel Montreal, run with care, is a bright, solid, business-class place on a big street a block southeast of Santa Maria Maggiore (Db-€115 but €90 in July–Aug, Tb-€140 but €120 in July–Aug, mention this book, CC, air-con, elevator, good security, 1 block from Metro: Vittorio, 3 blocks west of train station, Via Carlo Alberto 4, 00185 Roma, tel. 06-445-7797, fax 06-446-5522, www.hotelmontrealroma.com, e-mail: info @hotelmontrealroma.com, SE).

Clarin Hotel, a plain slumbermill with 21 rooms, is quiet, safe, and run-down (Db-€88, Tb-€109, Qb-€129, prices good with this book and cash, 3 percent extra with CC, Via Palermo 36, tel. 06-4782-5170, fax 06-4788-1393, e-mail: clarinhotel@hotmail.com, Renaldo, Franco, and Marco SE).

YWCA and Convents

YWCA Casa Per Studentesse accepts men and women. It's an institutional place, filled with white-uniformed maids, colorful Third-World travelers, and 75 single beds (€26 per person in 3- and 4-bed rooms, S-€31, Sb-€37, D-€62, Db-€74, includes breakfast except on Sun, elevator, Via C. Albo 4, tel. 06-488-0460, fax 06-487-1028). The YWCA faces a great little street market.

Suore di Santa Elisabetta is a heavenly Polish-run convent. While often booked long in advance and a challenge in communication, it's an incredible value (S-€31, Sb-€38, D-€51, Db-€66, Tb-€85, Qb-€103, CC, 23:00 curfew, elevator, fine view roof terrace, a block southwest of Basilica Santa Maria Maggiore at Via dell' Omata 9, tel. 06-488-8271, fax 06-488-4066, a little English spoken).

Pensione Per Pelligrini is another nun-run place with 39 big, simple rooms and lots of twin beds. There's a language barrier, but the price is right (S-€34, Sb-€41, D-€67, Db-€82, Tb-€93, breakfast-€4.25, closed Aug, peaceful garden, elevator, just off Piazza Vittorio Emmanuel II, Istituto Buon Salvatore, Via Leopardi 17, no sign, from station take bus #714, #649, or #360 or Metro: Vittorio, tel. 06-446-7147 or 06-446-7225, fax 06-446-1382, Sister Anna Maria SE).

Sleeping Cheap, Northeast of the Train Station (zip code: 00185)

The cheapest hotels in town are northeast of the station. Some travelers feel this area is weird and spooky after dark, but these hotels feel plenty safe. With your back to the train tracks, turn right and walk two blocks out of the station. The first two hotels are located in the same building.

LOWER PRICED

Hotel Fenicia rents 13 comfortable, well-equipped rooms at a fine price. The bigger rooms upstairs are quieter, but there's no elevator (Sb-€53, Db-€80, Tb-€103, bigger and fancier Db-€93, prices through 2003 with this book only, air-con-€10.50/day, breakfast-€5.25; they say they take CC but—according to readers—sometimes they don't; Via Milazzo 20, tel. & fax 06-490-342, www.hotelfenicia .it, e-mail: info@hotelfenicia.it, Georgio and Anna SE).

Hotel Magic has 10 clean, marbled rooms, high enough off the road to escape the traffic noise. It's family-run, though not with much warmth (Sb-€52, Db-€77, Tb-€103, Qb-€114, air-con-€10.50/day, breakfast-€3.75, prices through 2003 with this book only, confirm rates, cheaper in Aug and winter, CC, thin walls, midnight curfew, Via Milazzo 20, 3rd floor, tel. & fax 06-495-9880, www.hotelmagicaroma.com, Carmela, Rosanna, and Caesarina NSE).

Albergo Sileo is a shiny-chandeliered, 10-room place. It has a contract to house train conductors who work the night shift, so most of the simple, pleasant rooms are rented from 19:00 to 9:00 only. If you can handle this, it's a great value. During the day, they store your luggage, and though you won't have access to a room, you're welcome to hang out in their lobby or bar (D-€39, Db-€47, Tb-€62, Db for 24 hours-€62—a steal, CC, elevator, Via Magenta 39, tel. & fax 06-445-0246, www.hotelsileo.com, friendly Alessandro and Maria Savioli NSE, daughter Anna SE).

Sleeping near the Colosseum (zip code: 00184)

These places are buried in a Roman world of exhaust-stained, medieval ambience. Take the subway one stop from the train station to the Cavour Metro stop. The *electrico* bus line #117 (San Giovanni in Laterano, Colosseo, Trevi Fountain, Piazza di Spagna, and Piazza del Popolo) connects you with the sights.

HIGHER PRICED

Hotel Duca d'Alba, a tight and modern pastel/marble/hardwood place, is more professional than homey (Sb-€134, Db-€201, much cheaper July–Aug and winter, extra bed-€21, CC, air-con, safes, phones, TV, elevator, Via Leonina 14, tel. 06-484-471, fax 06-488-4840, check Web site for deals, www.hotelducadalba.com, Angelo SE).

MODERATELY PRICED

Hotel Paba is a little six-room place, chocolate box–tidy and lovingly cared for by Alberta and Pasquale Castelli. While over-looking busy Via Cavour just two blocks from the Colosseum, it's quiet enough (Db-€124, extra bed-€21, CC, show this book for 5 percent discount, breakfast served in room, air-con, elevator, Via Cavour 266, tel. 06-4782-4902, fax 06-4788-1225, www.hotelpaba.com, e-mail: info@hotelpaba.com, SE).

Hotel Grifo has a homey, tangled floor plan with 20 dimly lit modern rooms and a roof terrace. The double-paned windows almost keep out the Vespa noise (Db-€119, €109 July–Aug, CC, elevator, air-con, some rooms have terraces, 2 blocks off Via Cavour at Via del Boschetto 144, tel. 06-487-1395, fax 06-474-2323, e-mail: hotelgrifo@hotmail.com, Alessandro SE).

Hotel Lancelot, a favorite among United Nations workers, is big, with 60 rooms, a shady courtyard, rooftop terrace, bar, and restaurant. It's quiet, safe, well-run by Faris and Lubna Khan, and popular with returning guests (Sb-€93–108, Db-€144, Tb-€168, Qb-€183, add €10 for balcony, CC, air-con, elevator, parking-€11/day, behind Colosseum near San Clemente Church at Via Capo D'Africa 47, tel. 06-7045-0615, fax 06-7045-0640, www.lancelothotel.com, e-mail: info@lancelothotel.com, SE).

Near the Palatine

LOWER PRICED

Hotel Casa Kolbe, located in a former monastery, rents out 63 monkish, spartan rooms with no fans or air-conditioning. With vast public spaces and a peaceful garden, it's popular with groups. But the location is great: it's on the river side of the Palatine ruins,

on a quiet side street about a block from a little-used entrance
to the Forum (Sb-€62, Db-€78, Tb-€98, Qb-€109, breakfast-
€5.25, CC, elevator, garden, courtyard, not handy to public transit
so taxi from the station, Via S. Teodoro 44, tel. 06-679-4974 or
06-679-8866, fax 06-6994-1550, Maurizio and Antonio SE).

Sleeping near Campo de' Fiori (zip code: 00186)

You pay a premium to stay in the old center, but each of these
places is romantically set deep in the tangled backstreets near the
idyllic Campo de' Fiori and, for many, worth the extra money.

MODERATELY PRICED

Casa di Santa Brigida overlooks the elegant Piazza Farnese.
With soft-spoken sisters gliding down polished hallways, and
pearly gates instead of doors, this lavish 23-room convent makes
exhaust-stained Roman tourists feel like they've died and gone to
heaven. If you're unsure of your destiny (and don't need a double
bed), this is worth the splurge (Sb-€85, Db-€150, 3 percent extra
with CC, great €16 dinners, roof garden, plush library, air-con,
physical address: Monserrato 54, mailing address: Piazza Farnese
96, 00186 Roma, tel. 06-6889-2596, fax 06-6889-1573, www
.brigidine.org/italia_roma, e-mail: hesselblad@tiscalinet.it, many
of the sisters are from India and speak English). If you get no
response to your fax or e-mail within three days, consider that
a "no." Groups are very welcome here.

LOWER PRICED

Hotel Smeraldo, with 50 rooms, is well-run, clean, air-conditioned, and a great deal (Sb-€73, D-€73, Db-€114, Tb-€130,
roof terrace, CC, Civolo dei Chiodaroli 9, midway between
Campo de' Fiori and Largo Argentina, tel. 06-687-5929,
fax 06-6880-5495, www.hotelsmeraldoroma.com, e-mail:
albergosmeraldoroma@tin.it, SE).

   Hotel Arenula, the only hotel in Rome's old Jewish quarter,
or ghetto, is a fine place in the thick of old Rome with 50 comfy
rooms (Sb-€88, Db-€114, Tb-€134; €26 less in July, Aug, and
winter; air-con-€10.50/day, no elevator, CC, just off Via Arenula at
Via Santa Maria de' Calderari 47, tel. 06-687-9454, fax 06-689-6188,
www.hotelarenula.com, e-mail: hotel.arenula@flashnet.it, SE).

Sleeping near the Pantheon (zip code: 00186)

These four places are buried in the pedestrian-friendly heart of
ancient Rome, each within a four-minute walk of the Pantheon.
You'll pay more here—but you'll save time and money by being
exactly where you want to be for your early and late wandering.

Sleeping in the Heart of Rome

❶ Casa di Santa Brigida
❷ Hotel Smeraldo
❸ To Hotel Arenula
❹ Hotel Due Torri
❺ Hotel Navona
❻ Residenza Zanardelli
❼ Hotel Nazionale
❽ To Residenza Frattina
❾ Hotel Giardino

HIGHER PRICED

Hotel Nazionale, a four-star landmark, is a 16th-century palace sharing a well-policed square with the national Parliament. Its 90 rooms are served by lush public spaces, fancy bars, and a uniformed staff. It's a big hotel with a revolving front door, but it's a worthy splurge if you want security, comfort, and the heart of old Rome at your doorstep (Sb-€186, Db-€289, extra person-€62, suite-€439, less in Aug and winter, CC, air-con, elevator, Piazza Montecitorio 131, tel. 06-695-001, fax 06-678-6677, see Web site for discounts in summer and weekends, www.nazionaleroma.it, e-mail: hotel@nazionaleroma.it, SE).

MODERATELY PRICED

Hotel Due Torri hides out on a tiny, quiet street. It feels professional yet homey, with an accommodating staff, generous public spaces, and 26 comfortable-if-small rooms—four with balconies (Sb-€108, Db-€176, family apartment-€232 for 3 and €258 for 4, CC, air-con, Vicolo del Leonetto 23, a block off Via della Scrofa, tel. 06-6880-6956, fax 06-686-5442, www.hotelduetorriroma.com, e-mail: hotelduetorri@interfree.it, SE).

Residenza Zanardelli, a sumptuous little place with six classy and quiet rooms, is two blocks north of Piazza Navona (Db-€135, air-con-€10.50/day, no CC; on busy street but double-paned windows minimize noise; Via G. Zanardelli 7, tiny name next to doorbell, tel. 06-6821-1392 or 06-6880-9760, fax 06-6880-3802).

LOWER PRICED

Hotel Navona is a fine value, offering 41 basic rooms in an ancient building (with a perfect locale) a block off Piazza Navona. Top-floor rooms come with wood-beamed character and more stairs (D-€100, Db-€110, air-con-€16/day, family rooms, no CC, Via dei Sediari 8, tel. 06-686-4203, fax 06-6880-3802, www.hotelnavona.com, e-mail: info@hotelnavona.com; run by a friendly Australian named Corry, his Italian wife Patricia, and her dad Pino, SE).

Sleeping near the Spanish Steps
(zip code: 00187)

MODERATELY PRICED

Residenza Frattina is a pink palace in a posh locale. It has an old-fashioned feel and an unbeatable location on a main pedestrian shopping drag near Piazza di Spagna (Db-€180, Tb-€200, prices are soft, CC, air-con, Via Frattina 23, tel. & fax 06-679-5509, www.residenzafrattinacorso.com, e-mail: residenza.frattina @flashnet.it, SE).

Sleeping near Piazza Venezia (zip code: 00187)

MODERATELY PRICED

Hotel Giardino, run by Englishwoman Kate, offers 11 pleasant rooms in a central location three blocks northeast of Piazza Venezia (Sb-€80, Db-€120, these discounted prices good with this book, air-con-€7/night, CC, double-paned windows, busy street off Piazza di Quirinale, Via XXIV Maggio 51, tel. 06-679-4584, fax 06-679-5155, www.hotel-giardino-roma.com, e-mail: hotel_giardino@libero.it).

Sleeping in Trastevere (zip code: 00153)
To locate hotel, see map on page 43.

MODERATELY PRICED
Hotel Santa Maria sits like a lazy hacienda in the midst of Trastevere. Surrounded by a medieval skyline, you'll feel as if you're on some romantic stage set. Its 18 small but well-equipped, air-conditioned rooms—former cells in a cloister—are all ground floor, circling a gravelly courtyard of orange trees and stay-awhile patio furniture. Because this is the only hotel in Trastevere, you'll pay about 25 percent more—but for poets, it's a deal (Db-€155, Tb-€191, Qb-€217, for this 20–25 percent discount it's cash only and a 3-night minimum, good with this book through 2003, smaller discounts also available with this book for shorter stays and credit cards and during off-season, a block north of Piazza Maria Trastevere at Vicolo del Piede 2, tel. 06-589-4626, fax 06-589-4815, www.htlsantamaria .com, e-mail: hotelsantamaria@libero.it, Stefano SE).

Sleeping "Three Stars" near the Vatican Museum (zip code: 00192)
To locate hotels, see map on page 39.

HIGHER PRICED
Hotel Sant' Anna is pricey, but located on a charming-for-Rome pedestrian street that fills up with restaurant tables at dinnertime. Its 20 rooms are overly decorated with classical themes, though the furnishings are comfy (Sb-€145, Db-€190, Db-€145 July–Aug and winter, CC, air-con, elevator, courtyard, Borgo Pio 133, near intersection with Mascherino, a couple blocks from entrance to St. Peter's, tel. 06-6880-1602, fax 06-6830-8717, www.travel.it/roma/santanna, Viscardo SE).

  Hotel Bramante sits like a grand medieval lodge in the shadow of the fortified escape wall that runs from the Vatican to Castel Sant' Angelo. The public spaces and the 16 rooms are generously sized, with rough wood beams and high ceilings (Sb-€142, Db-€210, Tb-€239, Qb-€250, 8 percent discount with this book, CC, air-con, no elevator, Vicolo delle Palline 24, tel. 06-6880-6426, fax 06-687-9881, www.hotelbramante.com, e-mail: bramante@excalhq.it, Maurizio and Loredana SE).

MODERATELY PRICED

Hotel Alimandi is a good value, run by the friendly and entrepreneurial Alimandi brothers—Paolo, Enrico, and Luigi—and the next generation, Marta and Germano. Their 35 rooms are air-conditioned, modern, and marbled in white (Sb-€90, Db-€150, Tb-€175, 5 percent discount with this book and cash, CC, closed Jan–mid Feb, elevator, grand buffet breakfast served in great roof garden, small gym, Internet access, pool table, piano lounge, free parking, down stairs directly in front of Vatican Museum, Via Tunisi 8, near Metro: Cipro-Musei Vaticani, reserve by phone, no reply to fax means they are full, tel. 06-3972-6300, toll-free in Italy tel. 800-122-121, fax 06-3972-3943, www.alimandi.org, e-mail: alimandi@tin.it, SE). They offer free airport pickup and drop-off, though you must reserve when you book your room and wait for a scheduled shuttle (every 2 hrs, see their Web site). Marta Alimandi rents out three rooms in her apartment, a 20-minute bus ride from the Vatican (Db-€83, see www.alimandi.org).

Hotel Spring House, with a hotelesque feel, offers 51 attractive rooms—some with balconies or terraces (Db-€135, Tb-€155, Qb-€175, mention this book to get a 15 percent discount July–Aug and Jan–Feb, CC, Internet access, air-con, elevator, free loaner bikes, Metro: Cipro-Musei Vaticani, Via Mocenigo 7, 2 blocks from Vatican Museum, tel. 06-3972-0948, fax 06-3972-1047, www.hotelspringhouse.com, Stefano Gabbani SE).

Hotel Gerber is modern and air-conditioned, with 27 businesslike rooms, set in a quiet residential area (2 S without air-con-€57, Sb-€100, Db-€130, Tb-€150, Qb-€170, 10 percent discount with this book in high season, 15 percent discount in low season, CC, Via degli Scipioni 241, a block from Metro: Lepanto, at intersection with Ezio, tel. 06-321-6485, fax 06-321-7048, www.hotelgerber.it, e-mail: info@hotelgerber.it, friendly pup Kira, Peter and Simonetta SE).

Hotel Emmaus offers 30 basic rooms on the south side of St. Peter's, just a communion-wafer's toss from the square (Sb-€105, Db-€150, Tb-€160, Qb-€180, CC, air-con, elevator, Via delle Fornaci 23, tel. & fax 06-635-658, www.emmaushotel.it, e-mail: emmaus@flashnet.it, SE).

Sleeping in Hostels and Dorms (zip code: 00184)

For easy communication with young, friendly entrepreneurs, cheap dorm beds, and the very cheapest doubles in town—within a 10-minute hike of the train station—consider the following places:

Casa Olmata is a laid-back backpackers' place midway between the Termini train station and Colosseum (dorm beds €17–18, S-€35, bunk bed D-€44, one queen-size D-€55, lots of stairs, laundry service, free Internet access, video rentals, games, rooftop terrace with views, communal kitchen, dinners twice weekly, a block southwest of Basilica Santa Maria Maggiore, Via dell' Omata 36, 3rd floor, tel. 06-483-019, fax 06-474-2854, www.casaolmata.com, e-mail: casaolmata30@hotmail.com, Mirella and Marco).

The Beehive is especially good for older vagabonds. This tidy little place has dorms (€18 beds) and double rooms that are a great value (D-€60, Db-€80, T-€90, Tb-€120, Q-€120, Qb-€160, no CC, no curfew or lock-out). It's thoughtfully run by a friendly young American couple, Steve and Linda (2 blocks south of Basilica Santa Maria Maggiore at Via Giovanni Lanza 99, tel. 06-474-0719. They hope to move by 2003 to a new location; check their Web site—www.the-behive.com—to find their new address.). They also run a B&B booking service (fine private rooms in the old center, offering comparable quality for €65–95— about half the cost of a hotel, www.cross-pollinate.com).

Gulliver's House Rome is a fun little hostel in a safe and handy locale, run by helpful Simon and Sara. Its 24 beds in cramped quarters work fine for backpackers (€18 per bunk bed in 8-bed dorm, one D-€57, no CC, closed 12:00–16:00, 1:00 curfew, small kitchen, Via Palermo 36, tel. 06-481-7680, www.gullivershouse.com, e-mail: info@gullivershouse.com).

EATING

The Italians are masters of the art of fine living. That means eating...long and well. Lengthy, multicourse lunches and dinners and endless hours sitting in outdoor cafés are the norm. Americans eat on their way to an evening event and complain if the check is slow in coming. For Italians, the meal is an end in itself, and only rude waiters rush you. When you want the bill, mime-scribble on your raised palm or ask for it: "*Il conto?*"

Even those of us who liked dorm food will find that the local cafés, cuisine, and wines become a highlight of our Italian adventure. Trust us, this is sightseeing for your palate, and even if the rest of you is sleeping in cheap hotels, your taste buds will relish an occasional first-class splurge. You can eat well without going broke. But be careful; you're just as likely to blow a small fortune on a disappointing meal as you are to dine wonderfully for $20.

TYPES OF EATERIES

Restaurants

When restaurant-hunting, choose places filled with locals, not the place with the big neon signs boasting, "We speak English and accept credit cards." Restaurants parked on famous squares generally serve bad food at high prices to tourists. Locals eat better at lower-rent locales. Family-run places operate without hired help and can offer cheaper meals.

The word *osteria* (normally a simple, local-style restaurant) makes us salivate. For unexciting but basic values, look for a *menù turistico*, a three- or four-course, set-price menu. Galloping gourmets order à la carte with the help of a menu translator. (The *Marling Italian Menu Master* is excellent. *Rick Steves' Italian Phrase Book* has enough phrases for intermediate eaters.)

Tipping

Tipping is an issue only at restaurants that have waiters and waitresses. If you order your food at a counter, don't tip.

If the menu states that service is included *(servizio incluso)*, there's no need to tip beyond that, but if you like to tip and you're pleased with the service, throw in ¤1–2 euros per person.

If service is not included, tip 5 to 10 percent by rounding up or leaving the change from your bill. Leave the tip on the table or hand it to your server. It's best to tip in cash even if you pay with your credit card; otherwise the tip may never reach your waiter.

A full meal consists of an appetizer *(antipasto,* €3-6), a first course *(primo piatto,* pasta or soup, €4.50-7.50), and a second course *(secondo piatto,* expensive meat and fish dishes, €5.50-11). Vegetables *(contorni, verdure)* may come with the *secondo* or cost extra (€3.50) as a side dish. The euros can add up in a hurry. Light and budget eaters get a *primo piatto* each and share an *antipasto.* Italians admit that the *secondo* is the least-interesting aspect of the local cuisine.

Restaurants normally pad the bill with a cover charge *(pane e coperto*—"bread and cover charge," around €1) and a service charge *(servizio,* 15 percent, see Tipping, above); these charges are listed on the menu.

Wine Bars

An *enoteca* (wine bar) is a popular, fast, and inexpensive option for lunch. Surrounded by the local office crowd, you can get a fancy salad, plate of meats and cheeses, and a great glass of wine (see blackboards for the day's selection and price per glass). The area around the Parliament (popular with that crowd) has plenty of *enoteche* handy for your sightseeing lunch break (see page 255).

Bars/Cafés

Italian "bars" are not taverns but cafés. These local hangouts serve coffee, mini-pizzas, sandwiches, and cartons of milk from the cooler. Many dish up plates of fried cheese and vegetables from under the glass counter, ready to reheat. This is my budget choice, the Italian equivalent of English pub grub.

For quick meals, bars usually have trays of cheap, ready-made sandwiches *(panini* or *tramezzini)*—some kinds are delightful grilled. To save time for sightseeing and room for dinner, my favorite lunch is a ham and cheese *panini* at a bar (called *tost*, grilled twice to get really hot). To get food "to go," say, "*Da portar via*" (for the road). All bars have a WC (*toilette, bagno*) in the back, and the public is entitled to use it.

Coffee: Coffee is as important as wine in Rome, and Italian coffee is some of the world's best. If you ask for "*un caffè*," you'll get espresso. Cappuccino is served to locals before noon and tourists any time of day. (To an Italian, cappuccino is a breakfast drink and a travesty after anything with tomatoes.) Italians like it only warm. To get it hot, request "*Molto caldo*" (very hot) or "*Più caldo, per favore*" (hotter, please; pronounced pew KAHL-doh, pehr fah-VOH-ray).

Experiment with a few of the options:

- *cappuccino*: espresso with foamed milk on top
- *caffè latte*: tall glass with espresso and hot milk mixed
- *caffè hag*: espresso decaf (decaf is easily available for any coffee drink)
- *macchiato*: espresso with only a little milk
- *caffè Americano*: espresso diluted with water
- *caffè corretto*: espresso with a shot of liqueur

Juice: *Spremuta* means freshly squeezed as far as *succa* (fruit juice) is concerned.

Beer: Beer on tap is *alla spina*. Get it *piccola* (33 cl, 11 oz), *media* (50 cl, 17 oz), or *grande* (a liter, 34 oz).

Wine: To order a glass (*bicchiere*; bee-kee-AY-ree) of red (*rosso*) or white (*bianco*) wine, say, "*Un bicchiere di vino rosso/bianco.*" *Corposo* means full-bodied. House wine often comes in a quarter-liter carafe (*un quarto*). For more on wine, see below.

Other drinks: A common *digestivo* in Rome is an **Amaro**, which means bitter. These alcoholic brews are often homemade by restaurants from a secret combination of herbs to aid digestion. Popular commercial brands are **Fernet Branca** and **Montenegro**. If your tastes run sweeter, try an anise-flavored liqueur called **Sambuca**, served *alla moscha* (with three "flies"—coffee beans).

Prices: You'll notice a two-tiered price system. Drinking a cup of coffee while standing at the bar is cheaper than drinking it at a table. If you're on a budget, don't sit without first checking out the financial consequences.

If the bar isn't busy, you'll often just order and then pay when you leave. Otherwise: 1) decide what you want; 2) find out the price by checking the price list on the wall, the prices posted near the food, or by asking the barman; 3) pay the cashier; and 4) give the receipt to the barman (whose clean fingers handle no dirty euros) and tell him what you want.

Ordering Food at Tavola Caldas

plate of mixed veggies	*piatto misto di verdure*	pee-AH-toh MEES-toh dee vehr-DOO-ray
"Heated, please."	*"Scaldare, per favore."*	skahl-DAH-ray, pehr fah-VOH-ray
"A taste, please."	*"Un assaggio, per favore"*	oon ah-SAH-joh, pehr fah-VOH-ray
artichoke	*carciofo*	kar-CHOH-foh
asparagus	*asparagi*	ah-spah-RAH-jee
beans	*fagioli*	fah-JOH-lee
green beans	*fagiolini*	fah-joh-LEE-nee
broccoli	*broccoli*	BROK-oh-lee
canteloupe	*melone*	May–LOH-nay
carrots	*carote*	kah-ROT-ay
ham	*prosciutto*	proh-SHOO-toh
mushrooms	*funghi*	FOONG-ghee
potatoes	*patate*	pah-TAH-tay
rice	*riso*	REE-zoh
spinach	*spinaci*	speen-AH-chee
tomatoes	*pomodori*	poh-moh-DOH-ree
zucchini	*zucchine*	zoo-KEE-nay
breadsticks	*grissini*	gree-SEE-nee

(Excerpted from *Rick Steves' Italian Phrase Book*)

Delis, Cafeterias, Pizza Shops, and *Tavola Calda* (Hot Table) Bars

Rome offers many cheap alternatives to restaurants. Stop by a *rosticcería* for great cooked deli food; a self-service cafeteria (called "free flow" in Italian) that feeds you without the add-ons; a *tavola calda* bar for an assortment of veggies; or a Pizza Rustica shop for stand-up or take-out pizza.

Pizza is cheap and everywhere. Key pizza vocabulary: *capricciosa* (generally ham, mushrooms, olives, and artichokes), *funghi* (mushrooms), *marinara* (tomato sauce, oregano, garlic, no cheese), *quattro formaggi* (4 different cheeses), and *quattro stagioni* (different toppings on each of the 4 quarters for those who can't choose just 1 menu item). If you ask for *peperoni* on your pizza, you'll get green or red peppers, not sausage (*diavola* is the closest thing in Italy to American "pepperoni"). At Pizza Rustica take-out shops, slices are sold by weight (100 grams, or *un etto*, is a hot and cheap snack; 200 grams, or *due etti*, makes a light meal).

For a fast, cheap, and healthy lunch, find a *tavola calda* bar with a buffet spread of meat and vegetables, and ask for a mixed plate of vegetables with a hunk of mozzarella *(piatto misto di verdure con mozzarella)*. Don't be limited by what you can see. If you'd like a salad with a slice of cantaloupe and a hunk of cheese, they'll whip that up for you in a snap. Belly up to the bar and, with a pointing finger and key words in the chart in this chapter, you can get a fine mixed plate of vegetables. If something's a mystery, ask for *un assaggio* (a little taste).

Picnics

In Rome, picnicking saves lots of euros and is a great way to sample local specialties. For a colorful experience, gather your ingredients in the morning at one of Rome's open-air produce markets (see page tk); you'll probably visit several small stores or market stalls to put together a complete meal. A local *alimentari* is your one-stop corner grocery store (most will slice and stuff your sandwich for you if you buy the ingredients there). A *supermercato* gives you more efficiency with less color for less cost.

Juice-lovers can get a liter (34 ounces) of O.J. for the price of a Coke or coffee. Look for "100% *succo*" (juice) on the label. Hang onto the half-liter mineral-water bottles (sold everywhere for about €0.50). Buy juice in cheap liter boxes, then drink some and store the extra in your water bottle. Tap water—*acqua del rubinetto*— is fine; I drink water from the public taps found all over the city.

Picnics can be an adventure in high cuisine. Be daring. Try the fresh mozzarella, *presto* pesto, shriveled olives, and any UFOs the locals are excited about. Shopkeepers are happy to sell small quantities of produce. But in a busy market, a merchant may not want to weigh and sell three-carrot-type quantities. In this case, estimate generously what you think it should cost, and hold out the coins in one hand and the produce in the other. Wear a smile that says, "If you take the money, I'll go." He'll grab the money. A typical picnic for two might be fresh rolls, 100 grams of cheese, 100 grams of meat (100 grams = about a quarter pound, called *un etto* in Italy), two tomatoes, three carrots, two apples, yogurt, and a liter box of juice. Total cost—about $10.

ROMAN CUISINE

In ancient times, the dinner party was the center of Roman social life. It was a luxurious affair, set in the *triclinium* (formal dining room). Guest lists were small (3–9 people) and the select few reclined on couches during the exotic multicourse meal. Today the couches

Eating with the Seasons

Italian cooks love to serve you fresh produce and seafood at its tastiest. If you must have porcini mushrooms outside of October and November, they'll be frozen. To get the freshest veggies at a fine restaurant, request *"Il piatto del la stagioni, per favore."* (A plate of what's seasonal, please).

Here are a few examples of what's fresh when:

April–May:	Calamari, squid, green beans, and zucchini flowers
April, May, Sept, Oct:	Black truffles
May–June:	Mussels, asparagus, zucchini, cantaloupe, and strawberries
May–Aug:	Eggplant
Oct–Nov:	Mushrooms and white truffles
Fresh year-round:	Clams, meats, and cheese

are gone and the fare may not include jellyfish, boiled tree fungi, and flamingo, but the *cucina romanesca* influence remains.

Roman meals are still lengthy social occasions. Simple, fresh, seasonal ingredients dominate the dishes. The *cucina* is robust, strongly flavored, and unpretentious—much like the people who created it over the centuries. It is said that Roman cooking didn't come out of emperors' or popes' kitchens but from the *cucina povera*—the home cooking of the common people. This may explain the fondness Romans have for meats known as the *quinto quarto* (fifth quarter) such as tripe, tail, brain, and pigs' feet, as well as their interest in natural preservatives like chili peppers and garlic. Rome belongs to the warm, southern region of Lazio, which produces a rich variety of flavorful vegetables and fruit that are the envy of American supermarkets. Rome's proximity to the Mediterranean Sea also allows for a great variety of seafood (especially on Fridays) that can be pricey if you're dining out. Beware: Seafood and steak are often priced by the *etto* (100 gram unit, about a quarter of a pound) rather than the portion.

To eat like a Roman today means to stop at the local bar each morning for a pastry and coffee (usually cappuccino or espresso). Lunch is usually around 13:00 to 15:00 and is traditionally the largest meal of the day, although work habits have changed this for many people who don't want to spend time commuting. Instead they grab a quick meal in a *tavola calda* (cafeteria) buffet, or a *panino* or *tramezzino* (sandwich). Dinnertime is generally 20:00 to 22:00 and in restaurants is a multicourse affair.

For a snack, try a *suppli* (pron. SOO-plee), a deep-fried rice ball filled with mozzarella cheese. When it's hot outside, a *granita* at a *grattachecce* (pron. grah-tah-KAY-chay) cools you down fast. These little booths scrape shavings off ice blocks, then flavor them with syrups. Try the combo-flavors such as *lemoncocco*—lemon and coconut syrups with fresh chunks of coconut.

ROMAN SPECIALTIES
Local specialties you may find on a menu include:

Antipasto (appetizer)
Antipasto misto: A plate of marinated or grilled vegetables (eggplant, artichokes, peppers, mushrooms), cured meats, or seafood (anchovies, octopus).

Primi Piatti (first course)
Spaghetti alla carbonara: Any type of pasta with a sauce made from beaten eggs, fried *pancetta* (bacon) or *guaniciale* (cured pork cheek), cheese (pecorino romano or parmigiano reggiano), and black pepper.

Bucatini amatriciana: Thin pasta tubes with a sauce of tomatoes, onion, pork, and pecorino cheese on top.

Gnocchi alla romana: Small dumpling-like disks made from semolina instead of potato and baked with butter and cheese.

Penne all' arrabbiata: Literally, "angry quills"—quill-shaped pasta topped with a spicy tomato sauce of chili peppers *(pepperocini)*, garlic, and bacon or pork.

Rigatoni con la pajata: Medium-size wide pasta tubes topped with a stew of milk-fed calf intestines.

Stacciatella alla romana: Meat broth with eggs, semolina, and parmesan cheese.

Spaghetti alla vongole veraci: Small clams in the shell sautéed with white wine and herbs, served over pasta.

Secondi Piatti (second course)
Saltimbocca alla romana: Literally "jump-in-the-mouth"—thinly sliced veal layered with prosciutto and sage, then lightly fried.

Abbacchio alla scottadito: Baby lamb chops grilled and eaten as finger food.

Trippa alla romana: Tripe braised with onions, carrots, and mint.

Coda alla vaccinara: Oxtail braised with garlic, wine, tomato, and celery.

Involtini al sugo: Veal cutlets rolled with prosciutto, celery, and cheese in a tomato sauce.

Anguillette in umido: Stewed baby eels from nearby Lake Bracciano.
Filletti di baccalà: Dried cod fried in a batter.

Contorni (side dishes)

Sometimes the second course is not served with a vegetable and
you may want to order a side dish separately. If you get a salad,
note that olive oil and wine vinegar are the only dressings.
Carciofi alla giudia: Small artichokes flattened and fried.
Fiori di zucca fritti: Squash blossoms battered and fried.
Fave al guanciale: Fava beans simmered with *guanciale* (cured
pork cheek) and onion.
Misticanza: Mixed green salad of arugula *(rughetta)* and curly
endive *(puntarelle)* with anchovies.

Dolci (desserts)

Dessert can be a seasonal fruit such as *fragole* (strawberries) or
pesche (peaches), or even cheese, such as *pecorino romano* (ewe's
cheese) or *caciotta romana* (combination of ewe's and cow's cheese).
Crostata di ricotta: A cheesecake-like dessert with ricotta,
Marsala, cinnamon, and bits of chocolate.
Bignè: Profiterole-like pastries filled with *zabaione* (egg yolks,
sugar, and Marsala wine).
Tartufo: Rich dark chocolate gelato. *Con panna* gets you
whipped cream on top.
Gelato: For Rome's best gelato, see "Eating near the
Pantheon," below.

Vini (wine)

No large meal in Italy would be complete without wine. Although
Lazio is not the most notable wine region in Italy, it produces
several pleasant white wines and a few reds.

Frascati, probably the best-known wine of the region, is an
inexpensive dry white made from Trebbiano and Malvasia grapes.
Castelli Romani, from the hills just south of Rome, is also from
the Trebbiano grape and is similar to *Marino*, *Colli Albani*, and
Velletri, all light and fairly dry. *Torre Ercolana* is known as
Lazio's finest red. This dense wine is made from the local
Cesanese grape as well as Cabernet and Merlot. Produced in
small quantities, it must be aged for at least five years.

RESTAURANTS IN ROME

Although I've listed a number of restaurants, I recommend that
you just head for a scenic area and explore. Piazza Navona, the
Pantheon area, Campo de' Fiori, and Trastevere are neighborhoods packed with characteristic eateries. Sitting with tourists

on a famous square enjoying the scene works fine. But for places
more out of the way, consider my recommendations.

Eating in Trastevere

Colorful Trastevere is also now pretty touristy. Still, Romans join
the tourists to eat on the rustic side of the Tiber River. Start at the
central square (Piazza Santa Maria in Trastevere). Then choose:
Eat with tourists enjoying the ambience of the famous square, or
wander the backstreets in search of a mom-and-pop place with
barely a menu. Consider these places before making a choice
(all are in the tangle of lanes between Ponte Sisto and the Piazza
Santa Maria in Trastevere—see map on page 43):

At **Taverna del Moro da Tony**, Tony scrambles—with a
great antipasti table—to keep his happy eaters (mostly tourists)
well-fed and returning. Until we start telling him to "hold the
mayo," his *bruschetta* will come buried in it (Tue–Sun 12:00–
24:00, closed Mon, CC, off Via del Moro at Vicolo del Cinque 36,
tel. 06-580-9165, SE).

For good home cooking Roman-style, consider these two
fun little places (within a block of each other): **Trattoria da Lucia**
(closed Mon, indoor or outdoor seating, Vicolo del Mattonato 2,
tel. 06-580-3601, NSE) and the homey **Trattoria de Olindo**
(closed Sun, Vicolo della Scala 8, tel. 06-581-8835, NSE).

Osteria Ponte Sisto, a rough-and-tumble little place, specializes in traditional Roman cuisine with a menu that changes often.
Since it's just outside of the tourist zone, it offers the best value
and caters mostly to Romans. It's also easiest to find: As you
approach Trastevere, crossing Ponte Sisto (pedestrian bridge),
continue across the little square (Piazza Trilussa) and you'll find
it on the right (daily 12:30–15:30 & 19:30–24:00, CC, Via Ponte
Sisto 80, tel. 06-588-3411, SE).

The fine little **Gelateria alla Scala** (across from the church on
Piazza della Scala) dishes up oh-wow pistachio (daily 12:30–24:00).

Eating on and near Campo de' Fiori

While it is touristy, Campo de' Fiori offers a classic and romantic
square setting. And, since it is so close to the collective heart of
Rome, it remains popular with locals. For greater atmosphere than
food value, circle the square, considering each place. Bars and pizzerias seem to overwhelm the square. The **Taverna** and **Vineria** at
numbers 16 and 15 offer good perches from which to people-watch
and nurse a glass of wine. The only real restaurant is **La Carbonara**.
While famous and atmospheric, it gets mixed reviews (closed Tue,
Campo de' Fiori 23, CC, tel. 06-686-4783). Meals on small nearby
streets are a better value, but lack that Campo de' Fiori magic.

Restaurants in the Heart of Rome

1. Taverna, Vineria, & La Carbonara Rist.
2. Ostaria da Giovanni ar Galletto
3. Osteria Enoteca al Bric
4. Filetti de Baccala & Trattoria der Pallaro
5. Rist. Grotte del Teatro di Pompeo
6. Cul de Sac bar & L'Insalata Ricca Rist.
7. Brek Rist.
8. Il Delfino Rist. & Frullati di Frutta
9. Osteria da Mario Rist.
10. Rist. Myosotis di Marsili
11. Enoteca Spiriti
12. To Rist. alla Rampa, & Rist. Il Gabriello, Gusto
13. Rist. La Taverna degli Amici
14. Rist. Pizzeria Sacro e Profano
15. Trinity College
16. Giolitti Gelateria
17. Gelateria della Palma
18. Gelateria San Crispino
19. Non Solo Bevi (2 locations)

Nearby, on the more elegant and peaceful Piazza Farnese, **Ostaria da Giovanni ar Galletto** has a dressier local crowd, great outdoor seating, and moderate prices. Giovanni and his son Angelo serve fine food, but sometimes they turn single diners away (closed Sun, tucked in corner of Piazza Farnese at #102, CC, tel. 06-686-1714). Of all my listings, Giovanni offers perhaps the best alfresco dining experience.

Osteria Enoteca al Bric is a mod Italian/French bistro-type place run by a man who loves to cook and serves good wine. Wine-case lids decorate the wall like happy memories. With candlelit elegance and no tourists, it's perfect for the wine snob in the mood for pasta and fine cheese. Choose your bottle (or half bottle) from the huge selection lining the walls as you enter (open from 19:30, closed Mon, CC, 100 meters, or 330 feet, off Campo de' Fiori at Via del Pellegrino 51, tel. 06-687-9533).

Filetti de Baccala is a tradition for many Romans. Basic-ally a fish bar with paper tablecloths and cheap prices, it has grease-stained, hurried waiters, who serve old-time favorites—fried cod fillets, a strange bitter *puntarelle* salad, and delightful anchovies with butter—to nostalgic locals (Mon–Sat 17:30–23:00, closed Sun, a block east of Campo de' Fiori tumbling onto a tiny and atmospheric square, Largo dei Librari 88, no CC, tel. 06-686-4018).

Trattoria der Pallaro has no menu but plenty of return eaters. Paola Fazi—with a towel wrapped around her head turban-style—and her family serve up a five-course festival of typically Roman food for €18, including wine, coffee, and a wonderful mandarin liqueur. Their slogan: "Here, you'll eat what we want to feed you." Make like Oliver Twist asking for more soup and get seconds on the mandarin liqueur (Tue–Sun 12:00–15:00 & 19:00–24:00, closed Mon, indoor/outdoor seating on quiet square, a block south of Corso Vittorio Emmanuele, down Largo del Chiavari to Largo del Pallaro 15, tel. 06-6880-1488).

Ristorante Grotte del Teatro di Pompeo, sitting atop an ancient theater, serves good food at fair prices (closed Mon, Via del Biscione 73, tel. 06-6880-3686). This is great if you want to dine on a characteristic street busy with strolling people.

Between Campo de' Fiori and Piazza Navona: For interest-ing bar munchies, try **Cul de Sac** on Piazza Pasquino (often crowded, daily 12:00–18:00 & 19:00–24:00, a block southwest of Piazza Navona). **L'Insalata Ricca**, next door, is a popular chain that specializes in hearty and healthy salads (daily 12:00–15:45 & 18:45–22:00, Piazza Pasquino 72, tel. 06-6830-7881). Another branch is nearby with more spacious outdoor seating (just off Corso Vittorio Emmanuele on Largo del Chiavari).

Eating near the Pantheon

You'll find a mix of cafeterias, groceries, restaurants, wine bars, and gelato shops.

Cafeterias: **Brek**, on Largo Argentina just south of the Pantheon, is an appealing, self-service restaurant with a modern, efficient atmosphere and really cheap prices (daily 12:00–15:30 & 18:30–23:00, skip the sandwiches and pizza slices downstairs and go to the "free flow" cafeteria upstairs, northwest corner of square, Largo Argentina 1, tel. 06-6821-0353).

Il Delfino, also on Largo Argentina, is a tired but handy self-service cafeteria that serves throughout the day (daily 7:00–21:00, not cheap but fast). Across the side street, **Frullati di Frutta** sells refreshing fruity frappés.

Grocery: The *alimentari* on the Pantheon square will make you a sandwich for a temple-porch picnic. Sit at the base of a column in the shade and munch lunch.

Restaurants: **Osteria da Mario**, a great little mom-and-pop joint with a no-stress menu, serves delicious traditional favorites. You'll feel right at home with locals who know a good value. The pop (Mario), who passed away—you'll see his photo on the wall— would be happy with the way his wife and kids are carrying on (Mon–Sat 13:00–15:00 & 19:30–23:00, closed Sun, 2 blocks in front of Pantheon and to the left at Piazza delle Coppelle 51, tel. 06-6880-6349).

Ristorante Myosotis di Marsili, a dressy place with black-tie waiters and a coat check, is popular with local politicians and diners classy enough to look into the fish locker and make a knowledgeable choice. It has a traditional-yet-imaginative menu with a good wine list. Everything here is homemade (Mon–Sat 12:30–15:30 & 19:30–23:30, closed Sun, reservations smart, near Osteria da Mario, 2 blocks in front of Pantheon at Vicolo Della Vaccarella 3, tel. 06-686-5554).

Wine Bars: **Enoteca Spiriti**, a wine bar two blocks from the Pantheon, is run by Raffaele, son Matteo, and daughter Daria. They serve great wine (*"corposo"* means full-bodied) by the glass and light meals with integrity. Raffaele and I have designed a treat for travelers with this book: "A Taste of Italy for Two" includes two glasses of fine Amarone wine (or the equivalent in value), fresh bread, and a plate decorated with a tasty variety of Italian cheeses and meats for a total of €20. Choose: cool jazz interior or classic Roman sidewalk exterior (open at 12:30, very busy with local office workers at 13:30, dinner from 19:30, facing Pantheon walk around to the right and take 2 rights to Via S. Eustachio 5, no CC, no phone).

On Piazza de Pietra between the Pantheon and Via del

Corso, classy **Osteria dell' Ingegno** (tel. 06-678-0662) and the simpler **Non Solo Bevi** offer hearty salads and good indoor/outdoor seating (daily 12:00–15:00, tel. 06-679-4519). Another Non Solo Bevi *enoteca* is several blocks north, tucked into a distant corner of the pedestrian square Piazza San Lorenzo. At this uncharacteristically friendly place, Francesco and Lamberto (Beppo) serve fine wine and delightful toothpick munchies free with a glass. Their coffee *bomba* is memorable (Lucina 15, tel. 06-687-1683).

Gelato: Two of Rome's top ice-cream joints are a minute's walk in front of the Pantheon. The venerable **Giolitti's** is good, with cheap take-away prices and elegant Old World seating (just off Piazza Colonna and Piazza Monte Citorio at Via Uffici del Vicario 40, tel. 06-699-1243). But **Gelateria della Palma** is the new king of gelato—fresher, tastier, and with more options, including sugar-free and frozen-yogurt varieties (100 flavors, 2 blocks in front of Pantheon at Via della Maddalena 20, tel. 06-6880-6752).

Eating near the Spanish Steps

Ristorante alla Rampa is a classic old restaurant tucked away just around the corner from the touristy crush of the Spanish Steps. You'll get quality Roman cooking here, with great indoor/outdoor ambience, for a moderate price. They take no reservations, so arrive by 19:30 or be prepared to wait (closed Sun, 100 meters, or 330 feet, east of Spanish Steps at Piazza Mignanelli 18, tel. 06-678-2621).

Ristorante Il Gabriello is inviting and small, offering a peaceful and local-feeling respite from all the top-end fashion shops in the area. Claudio serves while his brother cooks traditional Roman cuisine using fresh, organic products from their sister's farm (reasonable prices, dinner only, Mon–Sat 19:00–24:00, closed Sun, air-con, reservations smart, CC, Via Vittoria 51, 3 blocks from Spanish Steps, tel. 06-6994-0810).

Gusto is *the* trendy place in Rome today with a restaurant, pizzeria, and wine bar. The only reason to eat here is to be surrounded by Rome's young and hip—which is not a bad thing (dinner from 19:45, reservations recommended, Piazza Augusto Imperatore 9, tel. 06-322-6273).

Eating near Piazza Venezia

Ristorante La Taverna degli Amici is a dressy yet friendly, candlelit place draped in ivy and tucked away on a sleepy square two blocks toward the Pantheon from the Victor Emmanuel Monument. This is a great and peaceful spot for a break before or after your Capitol Hill sightseeing. The waiters are friendly and the clientele is local and upscale (reserve for dinner to avoid the basement, Tue–Sun 12:30–15:00 & 19:30–24:00, closed Mon, CC, Piazza Margana 36, tel. 06-6920-0493).

For a woody English pub lunch break, **Trinity College** is a fine if smoky place serving creative salads and thriving with locals (just off Via del Corso, 3 blocks from Piazza Venezia at Via del Collegio Romano 6, tel. 06-678-6472).

Eating near the Trevi Fountain

Ristorante Pizzeria Sacro e Profano fills an old church with spicy south Italian (Calabrian) cuisine and some pricey exotic dishes. Run by Pasquale and friends, this is just far enough away from the Trevi mobs. To avoid a shock when the bill comes, note that seafood is sold here by the *etto* (100 gram unit), not the portion—allow €25–45 per person depending on wine (a block off Via del Tritone at Via dei Maroniti 29, tel. 06-6791-836).

Romans in the know flock to **Gelateria San Crispino** for gelato made from ingredients such as balsamic vinegar, pear, and cinnamon. They serve only in cups because cones degrade the taste (Via della Panetteria 42, tel. 06-679-3924).

Eating between the Colosseum and St. Peter-in-Chains Church

You'll find good views but poor value in the restaurants directly behind the Colosseum. To get your money's worth, eat a block away from the Colosseum. There are two handy eateries at the top of Terme Di Tito, a block uphill from the Colosseum, near St. Peter-in-Chains church (of Michelangelo's Moses fame).

For a real restaurant meal, try **Ostaria da Nerone**. The Santis family serves traditional Roman cuisine in a homey indoor or outdoor setting (Mon–Sat 12:00–15:00 & 19:00–23:00, closed Sun, Via delle Terme di Tito 96, tel. 06-481-7952). Next door at **Caffè dello Studente**, Pina and Mauro serve typical "bar gastronomia" fare (pizza, toasted sandwiches, various drinks). Stand up at the crowded bar, take away, or enjoy the outdoor tables (Mon–Sat 7:30–21:30, closed Sun, tel. 06-488-3240).

Eating near Via Firenze and Via Nazionale Hotels

Snack Bar Gastronomia is a great local hole-in-the-wall for lunch or dinner (daily 7:00–24:00; fresh meat or veggie sandwiches, fresh-squeezed juices, and Greek-style yogurt—yummy with fruit; ask the price first; Via Firenze 34). There's a classic old-fashioned *alimentari* (grocery) across the street (7:00–19:30).

Popular for its top-quality Sicilian specialties, especially pastries and ice cream, **Pasticceria Dagnino** is frequented by people

Eating in East Rome

To VILLA BORGHESE

T – TAXI STAND
M – METRO STN

1/4 MILE
400 METERS

U.S. EMB.
SANTA MARIA VITTORIA
To SPANISH STEPS
VENETO
CAPPUCCIN CRYPT
VIA BARBERINI
PIAZZA BARB.
SANTA SUSANNA
QUATTRO
QUIRNALE PALACE
SAN CARLINO
GUIRNALE
VIA
To TREVI FOUNTAIN PANTHEON
FONTANE
FORI IMPERIALI
FORUM
ARCH OF CONSTANTINE
To CIRCUS MAXIMUS

SETTEMBRE
PARIGI
S. MARIA D. ANGELI (BATHS OF DIO.)
PIAZZA INDEP.
PIAZZA REP.
DE NICOLA
PIAZZA CINQUE-CENTO
MARSALA
TERMINI STATION
GIOL.
NATIONAL MUSEUM (PALAZZO MASSIMO)
PANISPERNA
S. PRASSEDE
SANTA MARIA MAGGIORE
VIA LANZA
CAVOUR
SERPENTI
MERULANA
St PETER IN CHAINS
NERO'S GOLDEN HOUSE
VIA LABICANA
SAN CLEM.
HOLY STAIRS
COLOSSEUM
SAN GIOVANNI IN LATERANO

1 Snack Bar Gastronomia
2 Pasticceria Dagnino
3 Hostaria Romana
4 Ristorante Giovanni
5 Restaurant Target
6 Rist. Cinese Int'l.

7 Monte D.O.C. Vineria
8 Nerone & Caffe dello Studente
9 Cafeteria Nazionale
10 Flann O'Brien

who work at my recommended hotels (daily 7:00–22:00, in Galleria Esedra off Via Torino, tel. 06-481-8660). Their *arancino*— a rice, cheese, and ham ball—is a greasy Sicilian favorite, and their cannoli is sweet. Direct the construction of your meal at the bar, pay for your trayful at the cashier, and climb upstairs where you'll find the dancing Sicilian girls (free).

Hostaria Romana is a great place for traditional Roman cuisine. For an air-conditioned, classy, local favorite, eat here (closed Sun, midway between Trevi Fountain and Piazza Barberini, Via del Boccaccio 1, at intersection with Via Rasella, no reservations needed before 20:00, tel. 06-474-5284). Go ahead and visit the antipasto bar in person to assemble your plate. They're happy to serve an *antipasti misto della casa* and pasta dinner. Take a hard look at their *Specialita Romane* list.

Ristorante da Giovanni is a serviceable, hardworking place feeding locals and tired travelers now for 50 years (tired €12 menu, Mon–Sat 12:00–15:00 & 19:00–22:30, closed Sun and in Aug, CC, just off Via XX Settembre at Via Antonio Salandra 1, tel. 06-485-950).

Cafeteria Nazionale, with woody elegance, offers light lunches—including salads—at reasonable prices (Mon–Sat 7:00–20:00, closed Sun, CC, Via Nazionale 26-27, at intersection with Via Agostino de Pretis, tel. 06-4899-1716). Their lunch buffet is a delight (€7.50, 12:30–15:00).

Ristorante Cinese Internazionale is your best neighborhood bet for Chinese (daily 12:00–15:00 & 18:00–23:00, inexpensive, no pasta, just off Via Nazionale behind Hotel Luxor at Via Agostino de Pretis 98, tel. 06-474-4064).

Restaurant Target is a soulless, modern, but handy place serving decent pizza and pasta near recommended hotels (open daily, indoor and outdoor seating, don't expect great service, Via Torino 33, tel. 06-474-0066).

The **McDonald's** restaurants on Piazza della Repubblica (free piazza seating outside), Piazza Barberini, and Via Firenze offer air-conditioned interiors and salad bars.

Flann O'Brien Irish Pub is an entertaining place for a light meal (of pasta or something *other* than pasta, served early or late when other places are closed), fine Irish beer, live sporting events on TV, and perhaps the most Italian crowd of all (daily 7:30–13:00, Via Nazionale 17, at intersection with Via Napoli, tel. 06-488-0418).

Eating near Santa Maria Maggiore

For a classy taste of Tuscany in a woody wine bar filled with local office workers, drop by **Monti D.O.C. Vineria Wine Bar** for lunch (chalkboard shows daily specials, daily 10:00–24:00, 2 blocks from basilica next to recommended Beehive hostel at Via Giovanni Lanza 93, tel. 06-487-2696).

Eating near the Vatican Museum and St. Peter's

Avoid the restaurant pushers handing out fliers near the Vatican: bad food, expensive menu tricks. Try any of these instead.

Antonio's Hostaria dei Bastioni is tasty and friendly. It's conveniently located midway on your hike from St. Peters' to the Vatican Museum, with noisy street-side seating and a quiet interior (Mon–Sat 12:00–15:00 & 19:00–23:30, closed Sun, €5.25–6.25 pastas, €7.75 *secondi*, no cover charge, at corner of Vatican wall, Via Leone IV 29, CC, tel. 06-3972-3034). Antonio is your gracious host.

La Rustichella serves a sprawling antipasti buffet (€7.75 for a meal-sized plate). Arrive when they open at 19:30 to avoid a line and have the pristine buffet to yourself (Tue–Sun 12:30–15:00 & 19:30–23:00, closed Mon, near Metro: Cipro-Musei Vaticani, opposite church at end of Via Candia, Via Angelo Emo 1, CC, tel. 06-3972-0649). Consider the fun and fruity **Gelateria Millennium** next door.

Viale Giulio Cesare is lined with cheap **Pizza Rustica** shops and fun eateries, such as **Cipriani Self-Service Rosticcería** (Tue–Sun 10:00–22:00, closed Mon, pleasant outdoor seating, near Ottaviano subway stop, Viale Guilio Cesare 195). Restaurants such as **Tre Pupazzi**, which line the pedestrian-only Borgo Pio—a block from Piazza San Pietro—are worth a look.

Turn your nose loose in the wonderful **Via Andrea Doria** open-air market, three blocks north of the Vatican Museum (Mon–Sat roughly 7:00–13:30, until 16:30 Tue and Fri except summer, corner of Via Tunisi and Via Andrea Doria). If the market is closed, try the nearby **IN's supermarket** (Mon–Sat 8:30–13:30 & 16:00–20:00, closed Thu eve, a half block straight out from Via Tunisi entrance of open-air market, Via Francesco 18).

ROME WITH
CHILDREN

Sorry, but Rome is not a great place for little kids. Parks are rare. Kid-friendly parks are more rare. Most of the museums are low-tech and lack hands-on fun.

The good news for kids? Pizza and gelato. Any person under a meter (39 inches) tall travels free on the public transit. And Italians are openly fond of kids, so you'll probably get lots of friendly attention from locals.

Here are some tips:

- Take advantage of local information. *Roma c'è*, the periodical entertainment guide (sold at newsstands), has a children's section in English. Ask at Rome's TIs about kid-friendly activities. TIs often have a helpful "kid's pack."
- Don't overdo it. Tackle only one or two key sights a day (Vatican Museum, or Colosseum and Forum) and mix with a healthy dose of fun activities.
- Rome's hotels often give price breaks for kids. (Air-conditioning can be worth the splurge.)
- Eat dinner early (around 19:00) and you'll miss the romantic crowd. Skip the famous places. Look instead for self-serve cafeterias, bars (kids are welcome), or even fast-food restaurants where kids can move around without bothering others. Picnic lunches and dinners work well. For ready-made picnics that can please adults and kids, try the *rosticceríe* (delis). Pizza Rustica shops sell cheap take-out pizza; kids like *margherita* (tomato and cheese) and *diavola* (similar to pepperoni).
- Public WCs are hard to find: Try museums, bars, gelato shops, and fast-food restaurants.
- Follow this book's crowd-beating tips to a tee. Kids don't like standing in a long line for a museum (which they might not even want to see).

Sights to Consider

Rome's many squares are traffic-free, with plenty of space to run and pigeons to feed while Mom and Dad enjoy a coffee at an outdoor table.

Explora, the new children's museum in Rome, is a hands-on wonderland for kids 12 and under. The exhibits are in Italian, but kids probably won't care (€6-kids, €5-adults, parents must accompany children, 4 sessions/day, Tue–Fri 9:30, 11:30, 15:00, & 17:00; Sat 10:00, 12:00, 15:30, & 17:30, closed Sun & Mon, Via Flaminia 80, Metro: Flaminia, 10-min walk from Piazza del Popolo, tel. 06-361-3776, www.mdbr.it, helpful staff SE).

When visiting the ancient sites, have some fun with *Ancient Rome—Then and Now*, a fun book for kids, with plastic overlays showing how the ruins used to look. It's available at stalls near the entrance of ancient sites.

The **Vatican Museum** comes with mummies and fun statues of animals. There's an entire hall of statues with their penises broken off that my kids found entertaining. Nearby, **Castel Sant' Angelo**—with Vatican views and weapon displays—appeals to young knights.

Villa Borghese is Rome's sprawling central park. The best kids' zones are near Porta Pinciana where you'll find rental bikes, pony rides, and other amusements. Rome's **zoo**, Bioparco, in the northeast section of the park, houses about 900 animals—including the endangered black lemur, pygmy hippopotamus, Gila monster, and painted hunting dog (kids under 4-free, €5-kids 5 and older, €7-adults, daily Nov–March 9:30–17:00, April–Oct 9:30–18:00, last entry 1 hour before closing, café and picnic areas, Piazzale del Giardino Zoologico 1, tel. 06-360-8211, www.bioparco.it).

The ghoulish **Cappuccin Crypt** (decorated with skeletons) and the **Catacombs** tunnels are goblin pleasers. (For Crypt, see page 38; for Catacombs, page 48.) The **Church of St. Ignazio**, with its false dome, fascinates kids and adults (see page 98).

Your children can visit Egypt—without the diarrhea— by visiting Rome's funky little **pyramid** (free and always viewable, Metro: Piramide, page 46).

Bocca di Verità, the legendary Mouth of Truth, draws a young crowd and parents with cameras. Stick your hand in the mouth of the gaping stone face on the wall. As the legend goes, if you're a liar, your hand will be gobbled up. (The mouth is free and always open, on the porch of the Church of Santa Maria in Cosmedin, on Piazza Bocca della Verità, near the north end of Circus Maximus.)

Budding **soccer** stars could enjoy a trip to the Flaminio or Olympic Stadiums to take in a local match.

Rome feels safe at night, and you can easily take your kids on the **walks** suggested in this book such as the Dolce Vita Stroll on page tk. ★ On the Night Walk Across Rome (page 52), children like slurping up chocolatey *tartufo* at the Tre Scalini café (Piazza Navona) and tossing coins in the Trevi Fountain.

The **Luna Park** at E.U.R. is a tired, old amusement park (Metro to Magliana, then bus to Via delle Tre Fontana, tel. 06-592-5933). Rome also has a big water park called **Hydromania** (€11.50, daily 9:30–18:30, Vicolo Casal Lumbroso 200, tel. 06-6618-3183).

Older children might like exploring **Pompeii** (see page 221). For a long day trip, consider a train ride to **Pisa** (3 hours one-way) to visit its famous tipsy tower. It's now open for climbing, but you need to reserve a time slot when you buy your ticket—and you might have to wait a few hours. Online booking is in the works; check www.duomo.pisa.it or call 050-560-547 for the latest (tower climb-€15, Mon–Sat 8:00–17:20, Sun 9:00–17:00).

SHOPPING

Shops are open from 9:00 to 13:00 and from 16:00 to 19:00.
They're often closed on summer Saturday afternoons and
winter Monday mornings.

If all you need are souvenirs, a surgical strike at any souvenir
shop will do. Otherwise, try...

Department Stores

Large department stores offer relatively painless one-stop shop-
ping. A good upscale department store is **La Rinascente**. Its
main branch is on Piazza Fiume, and there's a smaller store on
Piazza Colonna. **COIN**, near Piazza Fiume, is also fashionable
(like an Italian Macy's or Bon Marché). **UPIM** is the Roman
Kmart (many branches, including Via Nazionale 111, Piazza
Santa Maria Maggiore, and Via del Tritone 172). **Cinecitta
Due** is the nearest shopping mall (Via P. Togliatti 2, Metro:
Subaugusta, tel. 06-722-0902).

Boutiques

For top fashion, stroll the streets around the Spanish Steps,
including **Via Condotti**, **Via Borgognona** (for the big-name
shops), and **Via del Babuino** (trendy design shops and galleries).
For antiques, stroll **Via de Coronari** (between Piazza Navona
and the bend in the river), **Via Giulia** (between Campo de' Fiori
and the river), and **Via Margutta** (classier, with art galleries too,
from Spanish Steps to Piazza del Popolo).

Open-Air Produce Markets

Rome's outdoor markets provide a fun and colorful dimension
of the city that even the most avid museum-goer should not miss.
Wander through the easygoing neighborhood produce markets,

Getting a VAT Refund

Wrapped into the purchase price of your Roman souvenirs is a Value Added Tax (VAT) that's generally about 17 percent. If you purchase more than €155 worth of goods at a store that participates in the VAT refund scheme, you're entitled to get most of that tax back. Personally I've never felt that VAT refunds are worth the hassle, but if you do, here's the scoop.

If you're lucky, the merchant will subtract the tax when you make your purchase (this is more likely to occur if the store ships the goods to your home). Otherwise, you'll need to:

Get the paperwork. Have the merchant completely fill out the necessary refund document, called a "cheque." You'll have to present your passport.

Get your stamp at the border. Process your cheque(s) at your last stop in the EU with the customs agent who deals with VAT refunds. It's best to keep your purchases in your carry-on for viewing, but if they're too large or dangerous (such as knives) to carry on, then track down the proper customs agent to inspect them before you check your bag. You're not supposed to use your purchased goods before you leave. If you show up at customs wearing your new shoes, officials might look the other way—or deny you a refund.

Collect your refund. You'll need to return your stamped document to the retailer or its representative. Many merchants work with a service, such as Global Refund or Cashback, which have offices at major airports, ports, or border crossings. These services, which extract a 4 percent fee, can refund your money immediately in your currency of choice or credit your card (within two billing cycles). If you have to deal directly with the retailer, mail the store your stamped documents and then wait. It could take months.

which clog certain streets and squares every morning (7:00–13:00) except Sunday. Consider the huge **Mercato Andrea Doria** (3 blocks in front of Vatican Museum at Via Andrea Doria). Smaller but equally charming slices of everyday Roman life are at markets on these streets and squares: **Piazza delle Coppelle** (near Pantheon), **Via Balbo** (near recommended hotels off Via Nazionale near Termini station), **Piazza Vittorio** (near Termini train station), and **Via della Pace** (near Piazza Navona). The covered **Mercato di Testaccio** is mostly produce and a hit with photographers and people-watchers (Piazza Testaccio, near Metro: Piramide). And **Campo de' Fiori,** while newly renovated to fit European Union standards, is still a fun scene.

Flea Markets

For antiques and fleas, the granddaddy of markets is the **Porta Portese** *mercato delle pulci*—flea market. This Sunday-morning market is long and spindly, running between the actual Porta Portese (a gate in the old town wall) and the Trastevere train station. Starting at Porta Portese, walk through the long, tacky parade of stalls selling cheap bras and shoes. Along the way, check out the con artists with the shell games. Each has shills in the crowd "winning big money" to get suckers involved. Hang on to your wallet—literally in your front pocket. This is a den of thieves. The heart of the market for real flea-market junk (hiding a few little antique treasures) is the area from Piazza Ippolito Nievo to the Trastevere station (6:30–13:00 Sun only, on Via Portuense and Via Ippolito Nievo; to get to the market, catch bus #75 from Termini station or tram #3 from Largo Argentina; get off the bus or tram on Viale Trastevere and walk toward the river—and the noise).

At the **Via Sannio** market, you'll find clothing and some handicrafts (Mon–Sat 8:00–13:00, a couple of blocks south of San Giovanni in Laterano, Metro: San Giovanni).

Airport Souvenirs

Leonardo da Vinci Airport ("Fiumicino") sells Italian specialty foods vacuum-packed to clear U.S. customs. Most shops are near the departure gates (after you check your bags and pass through security). Try Parmigiano-Reggiano cheese, dried porcini mushrooms or peppers, and better olive oil than you can buy at home.

NIGHTLIFE

Romans get dressed up and eat out in casual surroundings for their evening entertainment. For most visitors, the best after-dark entertainment is simply to stroll the medieval lanes that connect the romantic, floodlit squares and fountains. Head for Piazza Navona, the Pantheon, Campo de' Fiori, Trevi Fountain, Spanish Steps, Via del Corso, Trastevere, or Monte Testaccio. (⭑ See "Night Walk Across Rome," page tk and "Dolce Vita Stroll," below.)

Get a copy of either of the entertainment guides, *Roma c'è* (sold at newsstands, €1) or *L'Evento* (free at TI). Look at the current listings of concerts, operas (the opera house is at Via Firenze 72, near recommended Via Nazionale hotels, tel. 06-481-601), dance, and films. Classical music-lovers will seek out the new Rome Auditorium (Parco della Musica), a mega-music complex with three concert halls (Via Vittorio Veneto 96, bus #23, #53, #217, #910, or Metro to Flaminio and then tram #2, tel. 06-487-2310, fax 06-482-0781, www.musicaperroma.it, e-mail: info@musicaperroma.it). Posters around town also advertise upcoming events.

At **Pasquino**, Rome's English movie theater, you'll find movies daily in English (3 screens, in Trastevere at Piazza S. Egidio 9, catch tram #8 from Largo Argentina, tel. 06-580-3622). **Warner Village Moderno** shows some films in English (usually Wed–Thu, Piazza Repubblica, near train station and recommended hotels, tel. 06-477-791). Some theaters around town run movies in their original language (look for "V.O."—*versione originale*).

An interesting place for club-hopping is **Monte Testaccio**. After 21:00, ride the Metro to Piramide and follow the noise. Monte Testaccio, once an ancient trash heap, is now a small hill whose cool caves house funky restaurants and trendy clubs. (It stands amid a pretty rough neighborhood, though.)

Pub Crawls, offered year-round, attract a boisterous crowd. Show up at 20:00 at the Colosseum Metro stop and finish at a disco six pubs later around midnight. I've never seen 50 young, drunk people having so much fun (€18, €3 discount if you wear a toga, no need to reserve, cellular 333-470-5773, www.walksofeurope.com).

Some **museums** have late opening hours (especially on Sat in summer), offering a good chance to see art in a cooler, less crowded environment. Ask at any TI which museums are currently open late on Saturdays (possibly Castel Sant' Angelo, Capitol Hill Museum, and Borghese Gallery—reservations required only for Borghese).

The Dolce Vita Stroll down Via del Corso

This is the city's chic stroll, from Piazza del Popolo (Metro: Flaminio) down a wonderfully traffic-free section of Via del Corso, and up Via Condotti to the Spanish Steps each evening around 18:00 (Sat and Sun are best). Shoppers, people-watchers, and flirts on the prowl fill this neighborhood of Rome's most fashionable stores (open after siesta 16:30–19:30).

Throughout Italy, early evening is time to stroll. While elsewhere in Italy this is called the *passeggiata*, in Rome it's a cruder, big-city version called the *struscio*. (*Struscio* means "to rub.") Unemployment among Italy's youth is very high; many stay with their parents even into their 30s. They spend a lot of time being trendy and hanging out. Hard-core cruisers from the suburbs, which lack pleasant public spaces, congregate on Via del Corso to make the scene. The hot *vroom vroom* motorscooter is their symbol; haircuts and fashion are follow-the-leader. They are the *coatto*. In a more genteel small town, the *passeggiata* comes with sweet whispers of "*bella*" and "*bello*" ("pretty" and "handsome"). In Rome, the admiration is stronger, oriented toward consumption— they say "*buona*" and "*buono*"—meaning "good" (terms used to describe food). But despite how lusty this all sounds, you'll see as many chunky, middle-aged Italians on this walk as hormone-charged youth on the prowl.

Start on **Piazza Popolo**. The delightfully car-free square is marked by an obelisk that was brought to Rome by Augustus after he conquered Egypt. (It used to stand in the Circus Maximus.) In medieval times, this area was just inside Rome's main entry.

The Baroque church of **Santa Maria del Popolo**, on the square, contains Raphael's Chigi Chapel (pron. kee-gee, third chapel on left) and two Caravaggio paintings (the side paintings in chapel left of altar). The church is open daily (Mon–Sat 7:00–12:00 & 16:00–19:00, Sun 8:00–13:30 & 16:30–19:30, next to gate in the old wall, on far side of Piazza del Popolo, to the right as you face gate).

From Piazza del Popolo, shop your way down **Via del Corso**.

Dolce Vita Stroll

If you need a rest or a viewpoint, join the locals sitting on the steps of various churches along the street.

At Via Pontefici, historians turn right and walk a block to see the massive, rotting, round-brick **Mausoleum of Augustus**, topped with overgrown cypress trees. Beyond it, next to the river, is Augustus' Ara Pacis, or Altar of Peace (due to reopen in 2005 after renovation).

From the mausoleum, return to Via del Corso and the 21st century, continuing straight until **Via Condotti**. Shoppers should take a left to join the parade to the **Spanish Steps**. The streets that parallel Via Condotti to the south (Borgognona and Frattini) are just as popular. You can catch a taxi home at the taxi stand a block south of the Spanish Steps (at Piazza Mignonelli, near American Express and McDonald's).

Historians: Ignore Via Condotti. Continue a kilometer (0.6 mile) down Via del Corso—straight since Roman times— to the Victor Emmanuel Monument. Climb Michelangelo's stairway to his glorious (especially when floodlit) square atop Capitol Hill. From the balconies at either side of the mayor's palace, catch the lovely views of the Forum as the horizon reddens and cats prowl the unclaimed rubble of ancient Rome.

TRANSPORTATION
CONNECTIONS

ROME'S TRAIN STATIONS

Rome's main train station, **Termini**, is a minefield of tourist services: a TI (daily 8:00–21:00, off-season 9:00–20:00), train info office (daily 7:00–21:45), ATMs, late-hours banks, 24-hour thievery, luggage lockers (near track 24), the main city-bus hub (in front of train station), a subway stop, and the handy, cheery Ciao Self-Service Ristorante (daily 11:00–22:30, WC at entrance, near east end of station; although there are several Ciao bars scattered throughout the station, the most comfortable is this sit-down Ristorante). In the modern mall downstairs, under the station, you'll find a grocery (oddly named "Drug Store," daily 7:00–24:00), pharmacy (daily 7:30–22:00), public showers, and Internet access at Thenetgate (daily 6:00–23:30, near Dunkin' Donuts, cheapest to buy a €4 60-minute card). The station has some sleazy sharks with official-looking cards. In general, avoid anybody selling anything at the station if you can.

Long-distance buses (e.g., from Siena and Assisi) arrive at Rome's small **Tiburtina** station, which is on Metro line B, with easy connections to the main train station (a straight shot 4 stops away) and the entire Metro system.

Most of my hotel listings are easily accessible by foot (those near the Termini train station) or by Metro (those in the Colosseum and Vatican neighborhoods). The train station has its own Metro stop (Termini).

Types of Trains

You'll encounter several types of trains in Italy. Along with the various milk-run trains, there are the slow IR (Interregional) and *directo* trains, the medium *expresso*, the fast IC (Intercity), and the bullet-train T.A.V.—Treno Alta Velocita (supplement costs €16 even with train pass). Fast trains, even with supplements, are affordable

Italy's Public Transportation

KEY: — RAIL --- BUS ···· SHIP
NOT TO SCALE ● GOOD OVERNIGHT STOPS

(e.g., a second-class Rome–Venice ticket costs about $50 with
an express supplement). Buying supplements on the train comes
with a nasty penalty. Buying them at the station can be a time-waster.
Try to buy them at travel agencies (CIT or AmEx) in towns. The
cost is the same, the lines and language barrier are smaller, and
you'll save time.

Schedules

Newsstands sell up-to-date regional and all-Italy timetables
(€3.75, ask for the *orario ferroviaro*). There is a single all-Italy
telephone number for train information—848-888-088 (daily
7:00–21:00, automated Italian recording, have an Italian-speaker
listen for you). On the Web, check http://bahn.hafas.de/bin
/query.exe/en or www.fs-on-line.com.

Strikes are common. They generally last a day, and train
employees will simply say "*sciopero*" (strike). Still, sporadic trains—
following no particular schedule—lumber down the tracks during
most strikes.

By train from Rome to: Venice (6/day, 5–8 hrs), **Florence**
(12/day, 2 hrs, most stop at Orvieto en route), **Pisa** (8/day, 3–4
hrs), **Genova** (7/day, 6 hrs, overnight possible), **Milan** (12/day,
5 hrs, overnight possible), **Naples** (6/day, 2 hrs), **Brindisi** (2/day,
9 hrs), **Amsterdam** (2/day, 20 hrs), **Bern** (5/day, 10 hrs), **Frank-
furt** (4/day, 14 hrs), **Munich** (5/day, 12 hrs), **Nice** (2/day, 10 hrs),
Paris (5/day, 16 hrs), **Vienna** (3/day, 13–15 hrs).

ROME'S AIRPORTS

Rome's two airports—Fiumicino (a.k.a. Leonardo da Vinci) and
the small Ciampino—share the same Web site (www.adr.it).

Fiumicino Airport: Rome's major airport has a TI (Mon–Sat
8:00–19:00, closed Sun, tel. 06-6595-4471), ATMs, banks, luggage
storage, shops, and bars.

A slick, direct **train** connects the airport and Rome's central
Termini train station in 30 minutes. Trains run twice hourly in
both directions from roughly 7:30 to 22:00. From the airport,
trains depart at :07 and :37 past the hour. From the airport's
arrival gate, follow signs to "Stazione/Railway Station." Buy your
ticket from a machine or the Biglietteria office (€9, CC). Make
sure the train you board is going to "Roma Termini," not "Roma
Orte" or others.

Going from the Termini train station to the airport, trains
depart at :21 and :51 past the hour, usually from track 25 or 26;
to reach these tracks, take a 10-minute walk along track 24 to the
end of the station (moving walkways are inside the building to
the right on the lower level). Check the departure boards for
"Fiumicino Aeroporto"—the local name for the airport—and
confirm with an official or a local on the platform that the train
is indeed going to the airport (€10.30, buy ticket from computer-
ized yellow ticket machines, any *tabacchi* shop in station, or at
the desk near entrance to track 26). Read your ticket: If it requires validation, stamp it in a yellow machine near the platform before boarding.

Your hotel can arrange a **taxi** to the airport at any hour for about €40. To get from the airport into town cheaply by taxi, try teaming up with any tourist also just arriving (most are heading for hotels near yours in the center). Splitting a taxi and hopping out once downtown at a taxi stand to take another to your hotel will save you about €15. Avoid unmarked, unmetered taxis.

For **airport information**, call 06-65951. To inquire about flights, call 06-6595-3640 (Alitalia: tel. 06-65643, British Air: toll-free tel. 848-812-266, Delta: toll-free tel. 800-864-114, KLM/Northwest: tel. 06-6501-1441, Lufthansa: tel. 06-6568-4004, SAS: tel. 06-6501-0771, Swiss Air: tel. 06-847-0555, United: tel. 0266-7481).

Ciampino Airport: Rome's smaller airport (tel. 06-794-941) handles budget and charter flights. To get to downtown Rome from the airport, take the LILA/Cotral bus (2/hr) to the Anagnina Metro stop, where you can connect by Metro to the stop nearest your hotel.

DRIVING IN ROME

Greater Rome is circled by the Grande Raccordo Anulare. This ring road has spokes that lead you into the center. Entering from the north, leave the autostrada at the Settebagni exit. Following the ancient Via Salaria (and the black-and-white *Centro* signs), work your way doggedly into the Roman thick of things. This will take you along the Villa Borghese park and dump you right on Via Veneto (where there's an Avis office). Avoid rush hour and drive defensively: Roman cars stay in their lanes like rocks in an avalanche. Parking in Rome is dangerous. Park near a police station or get advice at your hotel. The Villa Borghese underground garage is handy (€18/day, Metro: Spagna).

Consider this: Your car is a worthless headache in Rome. Avoid a pile of stress and save money by parking at the huge, easy, and relatively safe lot behind the Orvieto station (follow P signs from autostrada) and catching the train to Rome (every 2 hrs, 75 min).

ROMAN
HISTORY

THREE MILLENNIA IN FIVE PAGES

History in a Hurry

Ancient Rome lasted a thousand years (500 B.C.–A.D. 500), half as an expanding republic, half as a dominating empire. When Rome fell to invaders, all Europe suffered a thousand years of poverty and ignorance (A.D. 500–1500), though Rome's influence could still be felt in the Catholic Church. Popes rebuilt Rome for pilgrims, in Renaissance then Baroque and neoclassical styles (1500–1800). As capital of a newly united Italy, Rome followed Fascist Mussolini into World War II (and lost) but rebounded in Italy's postwar economic boom.

Want more?

Legendary Birth (1200–500 B.C.)

Aeneas flees burning Troy (1200 B.C.), wanders like Odysseus, and finally finds a home along the Tiber. His descendants, Romulus and Remus—orphaned at birth, suckled by a she-wolf, raised by shepherds—grow up to steal wives and build a wall, founding Rome (753 B.C.).

Closer to fact, the local agrarian tribes were dominated by more sophisticated neighbors to the north (Etruscans) and south (Greek colonists). Their convenient location on the Tiber was perfect for a future power.

Sights
- Romulus' "hut" and wall (Palatine Hill)
- She-Wolf statue (Capitol Hill Museum)
- Frescoes of Aeneas and Romulus (National Museum of Rome)
- Bernini's Aeneas statue (Borghese Gallery)
- Etruscan wing (Vatican Museum)
- Etruscan Museum (in Villa Borghese gardens)
- Etruscan legacy (the original Circus Maximus, the drained Forum)

The Republic (509–27 B.C.)

The city expands throughout the Italian peninsula (500–300 B.C.), then defeats Hannibal's North African Carthaginians (the Punic Wars, 264–146 B.C.) and Greece (168 B.C.). Rome is master of the Mediterranean, and booty and captured slaves pour in. Romans bicker among themselves over their slice of the pie, pitting the wealthy landowners (the ruling Senate) against the working class (plebs) and the rebellious slaves (Spartacus' revolt, 73 B.C.). In the chaos, charismatic generals like Julius Caesar, who can provide wealth and security, become dictators. Change is necessary...and coming.

Sights

- Forum's Curia, Temple of Saturn, Temple of Castor and Pollux, Rostrum, Basilica Aemilia, Temple of Julius Caesar, and Basilica Julia (all rebuilt later)
- Appian Way built, lined with tombs
- Aqueducts, which carry water to a growing city
- Portrait busts of citizens (National Museum of Rome)
- The republic's "S.P.Q.R." belief and motto, seen today on statues, buildings, and even manhole covers: the **S**enatus and **P**ublicus **Q** (which constitute) **R**omanus. (Some northern Italians, who feel the south is dragging them down, translate S.P.Q.R. as Sono Porci Questi Romani—These Romans Are Pigs.)

The Empire—The "Roman Peace," or Pax Romana (A.D. 1–200)

After Julius Caesar was killed by disgruntled Republicans, his adopted son Augustus took undisputed control, ended the civil wars, declared himself emperor, and established his family to succeed him, setting the pattern of rule for the next 500 years.

Rome ruled an empire of 54 million people, stretching from Scotland to Africa, from Spain to Turkey. The city, with over a million inhabitants, was decorated with Greek-style statues and monumental structures faced with marble...it was the marvel of the known world. The empire prospered on a (false) economy of booty, slaves, and trade, surviving the often turbulent and naughty behavior of emperors like Caligula and Nero.

Sights

- Colosseum
- Forum
- Palatine Hill palaces
- Poems by Virgil, Catullus, Horace, and Ovid (from time of Augustus)
- Augustus' house (Casa di Livia) on Palatine Hill
- Pantheon
- Trajan's Column and Forum
- Greek and Greek-style statues and emperor's busts (National Museum of Rome, Vatican Museum, Capitol Hill Museum)
- Piazza Navona (former stadium)
- Hadrian's Villa (Tivoli) and tomb (now Castel Sant' Angelo)

Rome Falls (200–476)

Corruption, disease, and the constant pressure of barbarians pecking away at the borders slowly drained the unwieldy empire. Despite Diocletian's division of the empire and Constantine's legalizing Christianity (313), the city was sacked (410) and the last emperor checked out (476). Rome fell like a huge column, kicking up dust that would plunge Europe into a thousand years of darkness.

Sights

- Arch of Constantine
- The Forum's Basilica of Constantine
- Baths of Diocletian
- Old Roman Wall (gates at Via Veneto or Piramide)

Medieval Rome (500–1500)

The once-great city of a million people dwindled to a rough village of 10,000, with a corrupt pope, forgotten ruins, and malaria-carrying mosquitoes. Cows grazed in the ruined Forum and wolves prowled the Vatican at night. During the 1300s, even the popes left Rome to live in France. What little glory Rome retained was in the pomp, knowledge, and wealth of the Catholic Church.

Sights
- The damage done to ancient Roman monuments caused by disuse, barbarian looting, and pillaging for precut stones
- Early Christian churches built before Rome fell (Santa Maria Maggiore, San Giovanni in Laterano, and San Clemente)
- Churches of Santa Maria sopra Minerva and Santa Maria in Trastevere
- Castel Sant' Angelo

Renaissance and Baroque Rome (1500–1800)

As Europe's economy recovered, energetic popes rebuilt Rome to attract pilgrims. The best artists decorated palaces and churches, carved statues, and built fountains. The city was not a great political force, but, as the center of Catholicism during the struggle against Protestants (c. 1520–1648), it was an influential religious and cultural capital.

Renaissance Sights
- Michelangelo's Sistine Chapel (Vatican Museum), dome of St. Peter's, *Pietà* (St. Peter's), Moses (St. Peter–in–Chains church), Christ statue (Santa Maria sopra Minerva), Capitol Hill Square, Santa Maria degli Angeli church (in former Baths of Diocletian)

- Raphael's *School of Athens* and *Transfiguration* (Vatican Museum)
- Paintings by Raphael, Titian, and others (Borghese Gallery)

Baroque Sights
- St. Peter's Square and interior (largely by Bernini)

- Bernini statues (at Borghese Gallery; also *St. Teresa in Ecstasy* at Santa Maria della Vittoria church) and fountains (Piazza Navona, Piazza Barberini)
- Ancient obelisks erected in squares (Piazza del Popolo, Piazza Navona)
- Trevi Fountain and Spanish Steps
- Gesu and St. Ignazio churches
- Caravaggio's *Calling of St. Matthew* (San Luigi dei Francesi church) and other paintings (Borghese Gallery and Vatican Museum)
- Baroque paintings (Borghese Gallery)
- Borromini's facade of Santa Agnese church (Piazza Navona)

Modern Rome (1800–present)

Rome becomes the capital of a newly reunited Italy (1870), is modernized by Fascist Mussolini, and survives the destruction of World War II. Italy's postwar "economic miracle" makes Rome a world-class city of cinema, banking, and tourism.

Sights

- Victor Emmanuel II Monument, which honors modern Italy's first (democratic) king
- Mussolini: The balcony he spoke from (at Palazzo Venezia, on Piazza Venezia), his planned city (E.U.R.), grand boulevards (Via dei Fori Imperiali, Via Conciliazione), and Olympic Stadium
- Cinecitta film studios and Via Veneto nightlife, which have faint echoes of Fellini's "La Dolce Vita" Rome
- Subway system, broad boulevards, smog

Rome Today

After surviving the government-a-year turbulence and Mafia-tainted corruption of the postwar years, Rome is stabilizing. Today, the average Roman makes more money than the average Englishman. The city is less polluted and more organized. Several years ago, in celebration of the millennium, this eternal city gave its monuments a facelift. Rome is ready for pilgrims, travelers, and you to come and make more history.

APPENDIX

Let's Talk Telephones

Here's a primer on making phone calls. For information specific to Italy, see "Telephones" in the Introduction.

Making Calls within a European Country: About half of all European countries use area codes; the other half use a direct-dial system without area codes.

To make calls within a country that uses a direct-dial telephone system (Italy, Belgium, the Czech Republic, Denmark, France, Portugal, Norway, Spain, and Switzerland), you dial the same number whether you're calling across the country or across the street.

In countries that use area codes (such as Austria, Britain, Finland, Germany, Ireland, the Netherlands, and Sweden), you dial the local number when calling within a city, and you add the area code if calling long distance within the country.

Making International Calls: You always start with the international access code (011 if you're calling from the U.S. or Canada, or 00 from Europe), then dial the country code of the country you're calling (see chart below).

What you dial next depends on the phone system of the country you're calling. If the country uses area codes (and remember that some do not), drop the initial zero of the area code, then dial the rest of the number.

Countries that use direct-dial systems (no area codes) vary in how they're accessed internationally by phone. For instance, if you're making an international call to Italy, the Czech Republic, Denmark, Norway, Portugal, or Spain, simply dial the international access code, country code, and phone number. But if you're calling Belgium, France, or Switzerland, drop the initial zero of the phone number.

International Access Codes

When dialing direct, first dial the international access code (00 if calling from Europe, 011 if calling from the U.S. or Canada). Virtually all European countries—including Italy—use "00" as their international access code; the only exceptions are Finland (990) and Lithuania (810).

Country Codes

After you've dialed the international access code, dial the code of the country you're calling.

Austria—43	Ireland—353
Belgium—32	Italy—39
Britain—44	Morocco—212
Canada—1	Netherlands—31
Czech Rep.—420	Norway—47
Denmark—45	Portugal—351
Estonia—372	Spain—34
Finland—358	Sweden—46
France—33	Switzerland—41
Germany—49	Turkey—90
Gibraltar—350	United States—1
Greece—30	

Useful Italian Phone Numbers

Emergency (English-speaking police help): 113
Emergency (military police): 112
Road Service: 116
Directory Assistance (for €0.50, an Italian-speaking robot gives the number twice, very clearly): 12
Telephone help (in English; free directory assistance): 170

Numbers and Stumblers

- Europeans write a few of their numbers differently than we do. 1 = 1 , 4 = 4 , 7 = 7 . Learn the difference or miss your train.
- In Europe, dates appear as day/month/year, so Christmas is 25/12/03.
- Commas are decimal points and decimals commas. A dollar and a half is 1,50, and there are 5.280 feet in a mile.
- When pointing, use your whole hand, palm down.
- When counting with fingers, start with your thumb. If you hold up your first finger to request one item, you'll probably get two.
- What Americans call the second floor of a building is the first floor in Europe.
- Europeans keep the left "lane" open for passing on escalators and moving sidewalks. Keep to the right.

European Calling Chart

Just smile and dial, using this key:
AC = Area Code, LN = Local Number.

European Country	Calling long distance within...	Calling from the U.S.A./ Canada to...	Calling from another European country to...
Austria	AC (Area Code) + LN (Local Number)	011 + 43 + AC (without the initial zero) + LN	00 + 43 + AC (without the initial zero) + LN
Belgium	LN	011 + 32 + LN (without initial zero)	00 + 32 + LN (without initial zero)
Britain	AC + LN	011 + 44 + AC (without initial zero) + LN	00 + 44 + AC . (without initial zero) + LN
Czech Republic	LN	011 + 420 + LN	00 + 420 + LN
Denmark	LN	011 + 45 + LN	00 + 45 + LN
Estonia	LN	011 + 372 + LN	00 + 372 + LN
Finland	AC + LN	011 + 358 + AC (without initial zero) + LN	00 + 358 + AC (without initial zero) + LN
France	LN	011 + 33 + LN (without initial zero)	00 + 33 + LN (without initial zero)
Germany	AC + LN	011 + 49 + AC (without initial zero) + LN	00 + 49 + AC (without initial zero) + LN
Gibraltar	LN	011 + 350 + LN	00 + 350 + LN From Spain: 9567 + LN
Greece	LN	011 + 30 + LN	00 + 30 + LN

European Country	Calling long distance within...	Calling from the U.S.A./ Canada to...	Calling from another European country to...
Ireland	AC + LN	011 + 353 + AC (without initial zero) + LN	00 + 353 + AC (without initial zero) + LN
Italy	LN	011 + 39 + LN	00 + 39 + LN
Morocco	LN	011 + 212 + LN (without initial zero)	00 + 212 + LN (without initial zero)
Nether-lands	AC + LN	011 + 31 + AC (without initial zero) + LN	00 + 31 + AC (without initial zero) + LN
Norway	LN	011 + 47 + LN	00 + 47 + LN
Portugal	LN	011 + 351 + LN	00 + 351 + LN
Spain	LN	011 + 34 + LN	00 + 34 + LN
Sweden	AC + LN	011 + 46 + AC (without initial zero) + LN	00 + 46 + AC (without initial zero) + LN
Switzer-land	LN	011 + 41 + LN (without initial zero)	00 + 41 + LN (without initial zero)
Turkey	AC (if no initial zero is included, add one) + LN	011 + 90 + AC (without initial zero) + LN	00 + 90 + AC (without initial zero) + LN

The instructions above apply whether you're calling a fixed phone or cell phone.

- The international access codes (the first numbers you dial when making an international call) are 011 if you're calling from the U.S.A./Canada, or 00 if you're calling from virtually anywhere in Europe. Finland and Lithuania are the only exceptions. If calling from either of these countries, replace the 00 with 990 in Finland and 810 in Lithuania.
- To call the U.S.A. or Canada from Europe, dial 00 (unless you're calling from Finland or Lithuania), then 1 (the country code for the U.S.A. and Canada), then the area code and number. In short, 00 + 1 + AC + LN = Hi, mom!

2003

JANUARY						
S	M	T	W	T	F	S
			1	2	3	4
5	6	7	8	9	10	11
12	13	14	15	16	17	18
19	20	21	22	23	24	25
26	27	28	29	30	31	

FEBRUARY						
S	M	T	W	T	F	S
						1
2	3	4	5	6	7	8
9	10	11	12	13	14	15
16	17	18	19	20	21	22
23	24	25	26	27	28	

MARCH						
S	M	T	W	T	F	S
						1
2	3	4	5	6	7	8
9	10	11	12	13	14	15
16	17	18	19	20	21	22
23/30	24/31	25	26	27	28	29

APRIL						
S	M	T	W	T	F	S
		1	2	3	4	5
6	7	8	9	10	11	12
13	14	15	16	17	18	19
20	21	22	23	24	25	26
27	28	29	30			

MAY						
S	M	T	W	T	F	S
				1	2	3
4	5	6	7	8	9	10
11	12	13	14	15	16	17
18	19	20	21	22	23	24
25	26	27	28	29	30	31

JUNE						
S	M	T	W	T	F	S
1	2	3	4	5	6	7
8	9	10	11	12	13	14
15	16	17	18	19	20	21
22	23	24	25	26	27	28
29	30					

JULY						
S	M	T	W	T	F	S
		1	2	3	4	5
6	7	8	9	10	11	12
13	14	15	16	17	18	19
20	21	22	23	24	25	26
27	28	29	30	31		

AUGUST						
S	M	T	W	T	F	S
					1	2
3	4	5	6	7	8	9
10	11	12	13	14	15	16
17	18	19	20	21	22	23
24/31	25	26	27	28	29	30

SEPTEMBER						
S	M	T	W	T	F	S
	1	2	3	4	5	6
7	8	9	10	11	12	13
14	15	16	17	18	19	20
21	22	23	24	25	26	27
28	29	30				

OCTOBER						
S	M	T	W	T	F	S
			1	2	3	4
5	6	7	8	9	10	11
12	13	14	15	16	17	18
19	20	21	22	23	24	25
26	27	28	29	30	31	

NOVEMBER						
S	M	T	W	T	F	S
						1
2	3	4	5	6	7	8
9	10	11	12	13	14	15
16	17	18	19	20	21	22
23/30	24	25	26	27	28	29

DECEMBER						
S	M	T	W	T	F	S
	1	2	3	4	5	6
7	8	9	10	11	12	13
14	15	16	17	18	19	20
21	22	23	24	25	26	27
28	29	30	31			

Public Holidays and Festivals

Italy has more than its share of holidays. Each town has a local festival honoring its patron saint. Italy (including most major sights) closes down on these national holidays: January 1, January 6 (Epiphany), Easter Sunday and Monday (April 20 and 21 in 2003), April 25 (Liberation Day), May 1 (Labor Day), Ascension Day, August 15 (Assumption of Mary), November 1 (All Saints' Day), December 8 (Immaculate Conception of Mary), and December 25 and 26. In addition, June 29 (Saints Peter and Paul Day) is a Roman holiday. This isn't a complete list. Holidays strike without warning.

Metric Conversion (approximate)

1 inch = 25 millimeters	32 degrees F = 0 degrees C
1 foot = 0.3 meter	82 degrees F = about 28 degrees C
1 yard = 0.9 meter	1 ounce = 28 grams
1 mile = 1.6 kilometers	1 kilogram = 2.2 pounds
1 centimeter = 0.4 inch	1 quart = 0.95 liter
1 meter = 39.4 inches	1 square yard = 0.8 square meter
1 kilometer = .62 mile	1 acre = 0.4 hectare

Rome's Climate

First line—average daily low; second line—average daily high; third line—days of no rain.

J	F	M	A	M	J	J	A	S	O	N	D
40°	42°	45°	50°	56°	63°	67°	67°	62°	55°	49°	44°
52°	55°	59°	66°	74°	82°	87°	86°	79°	71°	61°	55°
13	19	23	24	26	26	30	29	25	23	19	21

Basic Italian Survival Phrases

English	Italian	Pronunciation
Good day.	Buon giorno.	bwohn **jor**-noh
Do you speak English?	Parla inglese?	**par**-lah een-**glay**-zay
Yes. / No.	Sì. / No.	see / noh
I (don't) understand.	(Non) capito.	(nohn) kah-**pee**-toh
Please.	Per favore.	pehr fah-**voh**-ray
Thank you.	Grazie.	**graht**-seeay
I'm sorry.	Mi dispiace.	mee dee-speeah-chay
Excuse me.	Mi scusi.	mee **skoo**-zee
(No) problem.	(Non) c'è un problema.	(nohn) cheh oon proh-**blay**-mah
Good.	Va bene.	vah **behn**-ay
Goodbye.	Arrivederci.	ah-ree-vay-**dehr**-chee
one / two	uno / due	**oo**-noh / **doo**-ay
three / four	tre / quattro	tray / **kwah**-troh
five / six	cinque / sei	**cheeng**-kway / **sehee**
seven / eight	sette / otto	**seht**-tay / **ot**-toh
nine / ten	nove / dieci	**nov**-ay / **deeay**-chee
How much is it?	Quanto costa?	**kwahn**-toh **kos**-tah
Write it?	Me lo scrive?	may loh **skree**-vay
Is it free?	È gratis?	eh **grah**-tees
Included?	È incluso?	eh een-**kloo**-zoh
Where can I buy / find...?	Dove posso comprare / trovare...?	**doh**-vay **pos**-soh kohm-**prah**-ray / troh-**vah**-ray
I'd like / We'd like...	Vorrei / Vorremo...	vor-**rehee** / vor-**ray**-moh
...a room.	...una camera.	**oo**-nah **kah**-meh-rah
...the bill.	...il conto.	eel **kohn**-toh
...a ticket to ___.	...un biglietto per ___.	oon beel-**yeht**-toh per
Is it possible?	È possibile?	eh poh-**see**-bee-lay
Where is...?	Dov'è...?	**doh**-veh
...the train station	...la stazione	lah staht-seeoh-nay
...the bus station	...la stazione degli autobus	lah staht-seeoh-nay **dayl**-yee **ow**-toh-boos
...tourist information	...informazioni per turisti	een-for-maht-seeoh-nee pehr too-**ree**-stee
...toilet	...la toilette	lah twah-**leht**-tay
men	uomini, signori	**woh**-mee-nee, seen-**yoh**-ree
women	donne, signore	**don**-nay, seen-**yoh**-ray
left / right	sinistra / destra	see-**nee**-strah / **dehs**-trah
straight	sempre diritto	**sehm**-pray dee-**ree**-toh
When do you open / close?	A che ora aprite / chiudete?	ah kay oh-rah ah-**pree**-tay / keeoo-**day**-tay
At what time?	A che ora?	ah kay oh-rah
Just a moment.	Un momento.	oon moh-**mayn**-toh
now / soon / later	adesso / presto / tardi	ah-**dehs**-soh / **prehs**-toh / **tar**-dee
today / tomorrow	oggi / domani	oh-jee / doh-**mah**-nee

For more user-friendly Italian phrases, check out *Rick Steves' Italian Phrase Book and Dictionary* or *Rick Steves' French, Italian & German Phrase Book and Dictionary*.

Road Scholar Feedback for ROME 2003

We're all in the same travelers' school of hard knocks. Your feedback helps us improve this guidebook for future travelers. Please fill this out (or use the online version at www.ricksteves.com/feedback), attach more info or any tips/favorite discoveries if you like, and send it to us. As thanks for your help, we'll send you our quarterly travel newsletter free for one year. Thanks! Rick

Of the recommended accommodations/restaurants used, which was:

Best _____

     Why? _____

Worst _____

     Why? _____

Of the sights/experiences/destinations recommended by this book, which was:

Most overrated _____

     Why? _____

Most underrated _____

     Why? _____

Best ways to improve this book:

_____

_____

I'd like a free newsletter subscription:

_____ Yes _____ No _____ Already on list

_____
Name

_____
Address

_____
City, State, Zip

_____
E-mail Address

Please send to: ETBD, Box 2009, Edmonds, WA 98020

Faxing Your Hotel Reservation

Use this handy form for your fax or find it online at
www.ricksteves.com/reservation. Photocopy and fax away.

One-Page Fax

To: _____ @ _____
         hotel   fax

From: _____ @ _____
          name   fax

Today's date: ____ / ____ / ____
                 day   month   year

Dear Hotel _____,

Please make this reservation for me:

Name: _____

Total # of people: _____   # of rooms: _____   # of nights: _____

Arriving: ____ / ____ / ____ My time of arrival (24-hr clock): _____
             day   month   year   (I will telephone if I will be late)

Departing: ____ / ____ / ____
              day   month   year

Room(s): Single___ Double___ Twin___ Triple___ Quad___

With: Toilet___ Shower___ Bath___ Sink only___

Special needs: View___ Quiet___ Cheapest___ Ground Floor___

Credit card: Visa___ MasterCard___ American Express___

Card #: _____

Expiration date:_____

Name on card: _____

You may charge me for the first night as a deposit. Please fax, e-mail, or
mail me confirmation of my reservation, along with the type of room
reserved, the price, and whether the price includes breakfast. Please also
inform me of your cancellation policy. Thank you.

_____
Signature

_____
Name

_____
Address

_____
City   *State*   *Zip Code*   *Country*

_____
E-mail Address

INDEX

accommodations: *see* sleeping
airfares: 4
airports: 273–274; information
    at, 20
Altar of Peace: 38, 269
amusement park: 263
ancient Rome: 17, 27–31;
    eating, 255–256, 257; guided
    tours, 25, 26; history,
    275–277; map, 59; sleeping,
    237–240; walking tours,
    58–105; Via Appia, 47–50
Antaquario Palatino Museum:
    83
Antoninus, Temple of: 70–71
Apollo Belvedere: 141–142, 147
Appian Way: 47–50
Ara Pacis: 38, 269
archaeological museums:
    Antaquario Palatino Museum,
    83; Etruscan Museum, 37–38;
    Museo Archeologico
    (Naples), 212, 213–215;
    Museum of Roman
    Civilization, 50–51; Museum
    of the Bath, 35–36, 100,
    104–105; National Museum
    of Rome, 35, 106–119; Ostia
    Museum, 205; Palazzo
    Nuovo, 32, 120, 121–123;
    Vatican Museum, 138–147
archaeological sites: Appian
    Way, 47–50; Ara Pacis, 38,
    269; Castel Sant' Angelo,
    40–41, 262; Colosseum, 30,
    58–62; in Ostia Antica,

201–206; Palatine Hill, 31,
    77–85; Pantheon, 33, 90–92;
    Pompeii, 223–227; Porta
    Ostiense, 46; Pyramid of
    Gaius Cestius, 46; Roman
    Forum, 30, 64–76; in Tivoli,
    207–208; Trajan's Column,
    Forum, and Market, 31,
    86–89; walking tours,
    58–105. *See also* ancient
    Rome; baths
Arch of Constantine: 30, 62–63
Arch of Septimius Severus: 74
Arch of Titus: 67–68
art museums: Borghese Gallery,
    37, 127–129; Doria Pamphilj
    Gallery, 34–35; general tips
    and hours, 3, 19, 28–29, 268;
    Montemartini Museum, 44;
    Octagonal Hall, 35, 100,
    103–104; Palazzo dei
    Conservatori, 32, 124–125;
    Vatican Museum, 40,
    137–138, 262. *See also*
    archaeological museums
ATMs: 6
Augustus: 38, 67, 70, 119,
    204, 276; House of, 84;
    Mausoleum of, 269; statue of,
    109–110

banks: 6, 21. *See also* money
bars and cafés: 245–246, 259,
    268; Capitol Hill, 126;
    Pantheon, 55–56
Basilica Aemilia: 71

Basilica of Constantine: 68, 190
baths (*terme*): of Caracalla, 19,
    44–45, 103; of Diocletian,
    35–36, 100–105; in Ostia
    Antica, 202, 204–205; in
    Pompeii, 224–225
Belvedere Torso: 143–144
Bernini, Gian Lorenzo: 35, 41,
    97, 125; biographical sketch,
    131; Borghese Gallery, 130–
    135; Four Rivers Fountain:
    54; St. Peter's Basilica,
    174–176; St. Peter's Square,
    165–169; *St. Teresa in Ecstasy*,
    36–37; tomb of: 193
bones, in Cappuccin Crypt: 38,
    262
Borghese Gallery: 28, 37, 127–
    129; map, 128; tour, 129–136
boutiques: 264
buses: 22–24, 207, 271; tours, 26
business hours: 5, 6, 264

cafés: *See* bars and cafés
Caligula: 111, 119, 167; Palace
    of, 71–72, 84
Campidoglio: See Capitol Hill
Campo de' Fiori: 43, 52–53,
    267; eating, 53, 252, 254;
    market, 52, 266; sleeping, 238
Canova, Antonio: 129–130
Capitol Hill: 31–33, 65, 120
Capitol Hill Museums: 32,
    120–121; map, 121; tour,
    121–126
Capitol Hill Square: 32, 120,
    122
Cappella Sansevero (Naples):
    219–220
Cappuccin Crypt: 38, 262
Caracalla: 117; Baths of, 19,
    44–45, 103
Caravaggio: 35, 38, 125, 268;
    Borghese Gallery, 134; San
    Luigi dei Francesi, 33, 92–94;
    Vatican Museum, 162–163
car travel: 10, 274

Castel Sant' Angelo: 40–41, 262
catacombs: 48–50, 262
Catherine, Saint: 98, 196–197
children: 2, 261–263; museum,
    262
Christianity (Catholic Church):
    42, 75, 118–119, 165, 275,
    278; Arch of Constantine, 30,
    62–63; catacombs, 48–50,
    262; Pilgrim's tour, 185–198.
    See also churches and cathe-
    drals; Jesus Christ; Vatican
    City; and specific saints
churches and cathedrals:
    Cappella Sansevero (Naples),
    219–220; general tips and
    hours, 29; Gesu Church, 33,
    94–97; Gesu Nuovo (Naples),
    218; Pilgrim's tour, 185–198;
    Saint Agnes: 54; St. Peter-
    in-Chains, 27–28, 181, 257;
    St. Peter's Basilica, 39–40,
    164–180; San Clemente,
    195–198; San Giovanni in
    Laterano, 44, 186–190; San
    Ignazio, 33, 98–99, 262; San
    Luigi dei Francesi, 33, 92–94;
    San Paolo Fuori le Mura, 44,
    185; Santa Chiara (Naples),
    218–219; Santa Maria degli
    Angeli, 35, 100–103; Santa
    Maria della Immaculata
    Concezione, 38; Santa Maria
    della Vittoria, 36–37; Santa
    Maria del Popolo, 268; Santa
    Maria in Cosmedin, 262;
    Santa Maria in Trastevere,
    42; Santa Maria Maggiore,
    190–194; Santa Maria sopra
    Minerva, 33, 97–98; Santa
    Prassede, 194–195; Santa
    Susanna, 37
Ciampino Airport: 274
Circus Maximus: 82–83
climate: 5, 285
Colosseum: 30, 58–62; eating,
    257; sleeping, 237–238

Column of Phocas: 75–76
Constantine: 48–49, 103, 118, 122, 144, 165, 277; Arch of, 30, 62–63; Basilica of, 68, 190; Room (Vatican Museum), 149–150; statues of, 124, 187
Cryptoporticus Tunnel: 84
cuisine: 248–251. *See also* eating
culture shock: 14–15
Curia (Senate House): 73, 187, 224
currency exchange: 5, 6, 230

da Vinci, Leonardo: 151, 162
da Vinci Airport: 266, 273–274
day trips: 2, 199–227
department stores: 264
Diocletian: 103; Baths of, 35–36, 100–105
Discus Thrower: 116–117
Domitian: 54, 79, 114
Domus Aurea: 28–30
Doria Pamphilj Gallery: 34–35
Dying Gaul: 122

eating: 2, 244–260; budgeting for, 4; Campo de' Fiori, 53, 252, 254; with children, 261; between Colosseum and St. Peter-in-Chains, 257; cuisine, 248–251; maps, 253, 258; near Pantheon, 255–256; near Piazza Venezia, 256–257; near Santa Maria Maggiore, 259–260; near Spanish Steps, 256; tipping, 14, 245; Trastevere: 252; near Trevi Fountain, 257; near Vatican City, 260; near Via Firenze and Via Nazionale, 257, 259. *see also* gelato
Egyptian art and obelisks: 56, 97, 139–141, 166–167, 268
e-mail: 13–14, 229
embassies: 22, 43
emergencies: 22, 281
Etruscans: 83, 125, 144–146,

214–215; Museum: 37–38
E.U.R.: 23, 45, 50–52
exchanging money: 5, 6, 230
Explora (children's museum): 262

Farnese Collection (Naples): 214–215
Farnese Gardens: 84, 85
fashion boutiques: 264
Faustina, Temple of: 70–71
feedback: 15; form for: 287
festivals: 284
Fiumicino Airport: 266, 273–274
flea markets: 266
Florence: 10; train travel, 273
food: cuisine, 248–251; seasonal produce, 249; shopping for, 255, 257, 260, 271. *See also* eating; gelato; markets
Foro Romano: *see* Roman Forum
fountains: 31, 35, 54, 56–57, 105; drinking from, 22

Gaius Cestius, Pyramid of: 46
Galleria Borghese: *See* Borghese Gallery
Galleria Doria Pamphilj: 34–35
gardens: *See* parks and gardens
gelato: 220–221, 252, 257, 263; Pantheon, 55, 56, 256
Gesu Church: 33, 94–97
Gesu Nuovo (Naples): 218
Gianicolo Hill Viewpoint: 42–43
Giotto di Bondone: 187
Greeks, ancient: 60, 70, 106, 111–113, 141–144, 227
guidebooks, recommended: 8–9

Hadrian: 41, 55, 91, 115; Castel Sant' Angelo, 40–41, 262; Villa of (Tivoli), 208
history: 2, 275–279
holidays: 284

Holy Stairs: 187, 189–190
hospitals: 22
hostels: 242–243
hotels: 228–230. *See also* sleeping
hours: 5, 6, 19, 264
House of Livia and Augustus: 84
House of the Vestal Virgins:
   72–73

Ignatius, Saint: 94, 96, 98–99
Il Gesu Church: *see* Gesu
   Church
Imperial Palace: 77–82, 83–84,
   114
information sources: 7–8, 20–21
Internet access: 13–14, 229
itineraries: 18–20

Jesus Christ: 192; Holy Stairs:
   187, 189–190
Julius Caesar: 34, 52, 67, 69,
   119, 146, 276; portrait head,
   108–109; Temple of, 70, 71
Julius II, Pope: 150, 153; tomb
   of, 181, 182–183

Keats, John: 47, 57

language: basic survival phrases,
   286; menu terms, 247
Laocoön: 142–143
Last Judgment (Michelangelo):
   157–160
Livia: 110–111; House of: 84
Loggia Stati Mattei Museum: 82
Luna Park: 263

Mammertine Prison: 31, 184
Marcus Aurelius: 32, 46, 56,
   122
markets: 89, 248, 264–266;
   Naples, 221; Via Andrea
   Doria, 138, 260, 265
metric system: 281, 285
Metro (subway): 10, 22–23, 207
Michelangelo Buonarroti: 43,
   91, 102, 143–144, 169;

Capitol Hill, 32, 122, 125; St.
   Peter-in-Chains, 181–183;
   St. Peter's Basilica, 172–173,
   178–179; Santa Maria sopra
   Minerva, 33, 97–98; Sistine
   Chapel, 40, 137, 151–152,
   153–160
money: 6, 119; budgeting, 4–5;
   exchanging, 5, 6, 230
Montemartini Museum: 44
Monte Testaccio: 47, 267
Moses (Michelangelo): 181–182,
   183
Mouth of Truth: 262
Musei Vaticani: *see* Vatican
   Museum
Museo Archeologico (Naples):
   212, 213–215
Museo Capitolini: 32, 120–121;
   map, 121; tour, 121–126
Museo della Civilta Romana:
   50–51
Museo Nazionale Etrusco:
   37–38
Museo Nazionale Romano
   Terme di Diocleziano:
   35–36, 100, 104–105
Museum of Roman
   Civilization: 50–51
Museum of the Bath: 35–36,
   100, 104–105
museums: for children, 262;
   general tips and hours, 3,
   19, 28–29, 268. *See also*
   archaeological museums;
   art museums
music: 267. see also opera
Mussolini, Benito: 32–33, 50,
   168

Naples: 209–221; maps: 211, 216
Naples Archaeological
   Museum: 212, 213–215
National Museum of Rome: 35,
   106; tour: 106–119
neighborhoods: 17; sightseeing
   by, 27–51. *See also specific*

neighborhoods
Nero: 29–30, 83, 113, 119, 165;
    Golden House, 28–30
nightlife: 267–270
Night Walk across Rome:
    52–57, 263

Octagonal Hall: 35, 100,
    103–104
Old St. Peter's: 165, 174
opera: 267; in Naples: 217
Ostia Antica: 199–206

Palace of the Civilization of
    Labor: 50
Palace of Tiberius and Caligula:
    71–72, 84
Palatine Hill: 31, 65, 77; map,
    78; sleeping, 237–238; tour,
    77–85
Palazzo dei Conservatori: 32,
    120, 124–125
Palazzo Nuovo: 32, 120,
    121–123
Pantheon: 33, 55, 90; churches
    near, 33–34, 92–99; eating,
    255–256; gelato, 55, 56, 256;
    sleeping, 238–240; tour,
    90–92
parks and gardens: 42–43, 44,
    207–208; Farnese Gardens,
    84, 85; Villa Borghese, 37,
    127, 128, 262, 274
Paul, Saint: 31, 44, 184, 185, 189
Peter, Saint: 31, 42, 165,
    173–174, 177, 189; chains,
    183–184
Phocas, Column of: 75–76
Piazza Capranica: 56
Piazza Colonna: 56
Piazza della Repubblica: 100,
    102, 105
Piazza di Spagna: 57. *See also*
    Spanish Steps
Piazza Farnese: 43, 254
Piazza Navona: 54–55, 131,
    267; eating, 55, 254, 263;

sleeping: 240
Piazza Popolo: 268
Piazza Venezia: 32–33; eating,
    256–257; sleeping, 240–241
picnicking: 248. *See also* markets
Pietà (Michelangelo): 178–179
Pilgrim's Rome, tour: 185–198
Pisa, train travel: 263
pizzerias (pizza): 247–248; in
    Naples: 221. *See also* eating
police: 21–22
Pompeii: 221–227, 263;
    map: 222
Ponte Sant' Angelo: 41
Ponte Sisto: 43, 252
pope, seeing the: 167
Porta Ostiense: 46
Porta Portese flea market: 266
post offices: 13; Vatican City,
    166
Protestant Cemetery: 47
Pyramid of Gaius Cestius: 46

Raphael: 35, 147, 150, 161–162,
    268; Borghese Gallery,
    135–136; Rooms (Vatican
    Museum), 40, 148–149,
    150–152; tomb of, 92
Remus: 69, 85, 110, 125, 275
Renaissance: 42, 146, 172–173,
    278; Borghese Gallery, 37,
    127–129; Vatican Museum,
    148–162. *See also* artists
reservations, hotel: 230;
    form: 288
restaurants: 244–245. *See also*
    eating
Roman Forum: 30, 64, 88: 65;
    tour: 64–76
Romans, ancient: 66–67, 75,
    177, 200–201, 275–277:
    See also ancient Rome;
    archaeological museums;
    archaeological sites
Romulus: 69, 85, 110, 125, 275
Rostrum (Rostri): 69, 74
Sacred Area: 34

safety tips: 6, 21–22, 27, 212
Saint Agnes church: 54
St. John Lateran: 44, 186–190
St. Paul's Outside the Walls: 44, 185
St. Peter-in-Chains: 27–28, 181, 257; eating, 257; tour, 181–184
St. Peter's Basilica: 39–40, 164–165; map, 170; tour, 169–180
St. Peter's Square: 165–169, 179
St. Teresa in Ecstasy (Bernini): 36–37
San Callisto, Catacombs of: 49–50
San Clemente church: 195–198
San Giovanni in Laterano: 44, 186–190
San Ignazio church: 33, 98–99, 262
San Luigi dei Francesi: 33, 92–94
San Paolo Fuori le Mura: 44, 185
San Pietro in Vincoli: 27–28, 181, 257; tour, 181–184
San Sebastian, Catacombs of: 50
Santa Chiara (Naples): 218–219
Santa Maria degli Angeli: 35, 100–103
Santa Maria della Immaculata Concezione: 38
Santa Maria della Vittoria: 36–37
Santa Maria del Popolo: 268
Santa Maria in Cosmedin: 262
Santa Maria in Trastevere: 42
Santa Maria Maggiore: 190–194; eating: 259–260; sleeping: 234–236
Santa Maria sopra Minerva: 33, 97–98
Santa Prassede church: 194–195
Santa Susanna church: 37
Scala Santa: 187, 189–190

School of Athens (Raphael): 151–152
Senate House (Curia): 73, 187, 224
Septimius Severus: 117; Arch of, 74
shopping: 17, 264–266; budgeting for, 5; VAT refunds, 6, 265
sightseeing: 2, 27–51; budgeting for, 4–5; general tips and hours, 3–4, 19, 28–29; itineraries, 18–20. *See also* tours; walking tours; *and specific sights*
Sistine Chapel: 40, 137, 153–160, 168
Sixtus V: 185; tomb of: 193
sleeping: 2, 228–243; budgeting for, 4; near Campo de' Fiori, 238; near Colosseum, 237–238; hostels and dorms, 235–236, 242–243; maps, 232, 239; northeast of Train Station, 236; near the Pantheon, 238–240; near Piazza Venezia, 240–241; reservations, 230; reservations form, 288; sleep code, 231; near Spanish Steps: 240; in Trastevere, 241; near Vatican City, 241–242; on Via Firenze, 231, 233–234; between Via Nazionale and Basilica Santa Maria Maggiore, 234–236
Spanish Quarter (Naples): 215, 217
Spanish Steps: 57, 267, 270; eating, 256; shopping, 17, 264; sleeping, 240
special events: 284
Stadium: 81
subway: 10, 22–23, 207

Tabularium: 32, 123–124
tavola calda: 247–248. *See also* eating

taxes: VAT refunds, 6, 265
taxis: 24–25, 274; Naples, 210, 212; tipping, 14
telephones: 10–13, 280–283
temperatures: 5, 285
Temple of Antoninus and Faustina: 70–71
Temple of Cybele: 85
Temple of Julius Caesar: 70, 71
Temple of Jupiter: 189
Temple of Mithras: 197–198
Temple of Saturn: 75
Temple of Vesta: 72
Termini station: 23, 271, 273; information, 20; sightseeing, 35–37; sleeping northeast of, 236
Testaccio: 45–47; map, 45; market, 265–266; nightlife, 267
theft alerts: 6, 21–22, 27, 212
Tiberius: 111, 119; Palace of, 71–72, 84
tipping: 14, 245
Titian (Tiziano Vecello): 35, 136
Titus, Arch of: 67–68
Tivoli: 207–208
Tomb of the Unknown Soldier: 33
tourist information: 7–8, 20–21
tours: 2, 10, 25–26; Pilgrim's Rome, 185–198; tips for tackling, 3–4. *See also* walking tours
train travel: 10, 271–273; budgeting for, 4; Naples, 210–212; Ostia Antica, 199; Pompeii, 210–212, 227. *See also* Termini station
Trajan: 86, 115; Column, 31, 86–87; Forum, 31, 87–88; Market, 31, 88–89
transportation: 10, 22–25, 271–274; budgeting for, 4.
Trastevere: 17, 42–43; eating, 252; map, 43; sleeping, 241

travel agencies: 10
Trevi Fountain: 35, 56–57, 263

Vatican City: 17, 38–41, 166–167; eating, 260; guided tours, 25, 166–167; hours, 19, 137; maps, 39, 167; pope, seeing the, 167; post office, 166; sleeping, 241–242; tours, 137–180; Web site, 8. *See also* St. Peter's Basilica; Sistine Chapel
Vatican Museum: 40, 137–138, 262; tour: 138–163
VAT refunds: 6, 265
Venice: 10; train travel: 273
Vestal Virgins: 72, 85, 114; House of: 72–73
Via Andrea Doria: 138, 260, 265
Via Appia Antica: 47–50
Via Condotti: 57, 264, 270
Via del Corso: 17, 27, 32, 268–270; map, 269
Via Firenze: eating, 257, 259; sleeping, 231, 233–234
Via Nazionale: 20, 105; eating, 257, 259; sleeping, 234–236
Via Sacra: 64, 65, 66, 68, 69
Via Toledo (Naples): 215, 217
Victor Emmanuel II: 92; Monument: 33, 270
Villa Borghese: 37, 127, 128, 262, 274
Villa d'Este (Tivoli): 207–208
Villa Giulia Museum: 37–38

walking tours: at night, 52–57; organized, 25–26; tips for tackling, 3–4
water, drinking: 22, 29
weather: 5, 285
Web sites: 7–8
wine: 246, 251; bars, 245, 254, 255–256, 259–260

zoo: 262

FREE-SPIRITED TOURS FROM
Rick Steves

Great Guides
Big Buses
Small Groups
No Grumps

Best of Europe ■ Village Europe ■ Eastern Europe ■ Turkey ■ Italy ■ Village Italy ■ Britain
Spain/Portugal ■ Ireland ■ Heart of France ■ South of France ■ Village France ■ Scandinavia
Germany/Austria/Switzerland ■ London ■ Paris ■ Rome ■ Venice ■ Florence ■ Prague

Looking for a one, two, or three-week tour that's run in the Rick Steves style? Check out Rick Steves' educational, experiential tours of Europe.

Rick's tours include much more in the "sticker price" than mainstream tours. Here's what you'll get with a Europe or regional Rick Steves tour ...

- **Group size:** Your tour group will be no larger than 26.

- **Guides:** You'll have two guides traveling and dining with you on your fully guided Rick Steves tour.

- **Bus:** You'll travel in a full-size bus, with plenty of empty seats for you to spread out and read, snooze, enjoy the passing scenery, get away from your spouse, or whatever.

- **Sightseeing:** Your tour price includes all group sightseeing. There are no hidden extra charges.

- **Hotels:** You'll stay in Rick's favorite small, characteristic, locally-run hotels in the center of each city, within walking distance of the sights you came to see.

- **Price and insurance:** Your tour price is guaranteed for 2003. Single travelers do not pay an extra supplement (we have them room with other singles). ETBD includes prorated tour cancellation/ interruption protection coverage at no extra cost.

- **Tips and kickbacks:** All guide and driver tips are included in your tour price. Because your driver and guides are paid salaries by ETBD, they can focus on giving you the best European travel experience possible.

Interested? Call (425) 771-8303 or visit www.ricksteves.com for a free copy of Rick Steves' 2003 Tours booklet!

Rick Steves' Europe Through the Back Door
130 Fourth Avenue North, PO Box 2009, Edmonds, WA 98020 USA
Phone: (425) 771-8303 ■ Fax: (425) 771-0833 ■ www.ricksteves.com

FREE TRAVEL GOODIES FROM

Rick Steves

EUROPEAN TRAVEL NEWSLETTER

My *Europe Through the Back Door* travel company will help you travel better *because* you're on a budget—not in spite of it. To see how, ask for my 64-page *travel newsletter* packed full of savvy travel tips, readers' discoveries, and your best bets for railpasses, guidebooks, videos, travel accessories and free-spirited tours.

2003 GUIDE TO EUROPEAN RAILPASSES

With hundreds of railpasses to choose from in 2003, finding the right pass for your trip has never been more confusing. To cut through the complexity, visit www.ricksteves.com for my online *2003 Guide to European Railpasses*. Once you've narrowed down your choices, we give you unbeatable prices, including important extras with every Eurailpass, **free:** my 90-minute *Travel Skills Special* video or DVD and your choice of one of my 24 guidebooks.

RICK STEVES' 2003 TOURS

We offer 20 different one, two, and three-week tours (200 departures in 2003) for those who want to experience Europe in Rick Steves' Back Door style, but without the transportation and hotel hassles. If a tour with a small group, modest family-run hotels, lots of exercise, great guides, and no tips or hidden charges sounds like your idea of fun, ask for my 48-page 2003 Tours booklet.

YEAR-ROUND GUIDEBOOK UPDATES

Even though the information in my guidebooks is the freshest around, things do change in Europe between book printings. I've set aside a special section at my website (www.ricksteves.com/update) listing *up-to-the-minute changes* for every Rick Steves guidebook.

*Visit **www.ricksteves.com** to get your...*

- ☑ **FREE EUROPEAN TRAVEL NEWSLETTER**
- ☑ **FREE 2003 GUIDE TO EUROPEAN RAILPASSES**
- ☑ **FREE RICK STEVES' 2003 TOURS BOOKLET**

Rick Steves' Europe Through the Back Door

130 Fourth Avenue North, PO Box 2009, Edmonds, WA 98020 USA
Phone: (425) 771-8303 ■ Fax: (425) 771-0833 ■ www.ricksteves.com

Free, fresh travel tips, all year long.

Visit **www.ricksteves.com**
to get Rick's free
64-page newsletter... and more!